BROKERS OF EMPIRE,
BROKERS OF EMPIRE

BROKERS OF FAITH, BROKERS OF EMPIRE

Armenians and the Politics of Reform in the Ottoman Empire

RICHARD E. ANTARAMIAN

STANFORD UNIVERSITY PRESS
STANFORD, CALIFORNIA

Stanford University Press
Stanford, California

©2020 by the Board of Trustees of the Leland Stanford Junior University. All rights reserved.

No part of this book may be reproduced or transmitted in any form or by any means, electronic or mechanical, including photocopying and recording, or in any information storage or retrieval system without the prior written permission of Stanford University Press.

Printed in the United States of America on acid-free, archival-quality paper

Library of Congress Cataloging-in-Publication Data

Names: Antaramian, Richard E., author.

Title: Brokers of faith, brokers of empire : Armenians and the politics of reform in the Ottoman Empire / Richard E. Antaramian.

Description: Stanford, California : Stanford University Press, 2020. | Includes bibliographical references and index.

Identifiers: LCCN 2019046787 (print) | LCCN 2019046788 (ebook) | ISBN 9781503611627 (cloth) | ISBN 9781503612952 (paperback) | ISBN 9781503612969 (ebook)

Subjects: LCSH: Armenian Church—Political activity—Turkey—History—19th century. | Clergy—Political activity—Turkey—History—19th century. | Armenians—Turkey—Politics and government—19th century. | Turkey—History—Tanzimat, 1839-1876. | Turkey—Politics and government—1829-1878. | Turkey—History—Ottoman Empire, 1288-1918.

Classification: LCC DR565 .A58 2020 (print) | LCC DR565 (ebook) | DDC 956/.015—dc23

LC record available at https://lccn.loc.gov/2019046787

LC ebook record available at https://lccn.loc.gov/2019046788

Cover design: Rob Ehle

Cover photo: Armenian Patriarch of Jerusalem, Harootiun Vehabedian, ca. 1900–1910. Library of Congress.

Typeset by Newgen in 10/14 Minion Regular

CONTENTS

	Acknowledgments	vii
	Note on Transliteration	ix
	Introduction	1
1	The Constitution	21
2	Nodal Governance and the Ottoman Diocese	49
3	Peripheralization	68
4	Ottomanism	100
5	A Catastrophic Success	128
	Conclusion	159
	Notes	171
	Bibliography	191
	Index	205

ACKNOWLEDGMENTS

This book relies on a wide variety of materials stored in archives and libraries in Salt Lake City, London, Paris, Vienna, Istanbul, and Yerevan, among others to reconstruct Ottoman Armenian communal life in the nineteenth century. These sources include administrative documents, personal correspondence, diplomatic dispatches, petitions, chronicles, pamphlets, newspapers, and assembly records. Research trips to consult, digitize, or otherwise acquire these materials were supported by a Fulbright Hays fellowship, the Armenian Studies Program at the University of Michigan, the Rackham Graduate School at the University of Michigan, and the Center for Religion and Civic Culture at the University of Southern California.

I have incurred a number of debts, personal and professional, in the course of writing this book, which I am happy to acknowledge here. My most significant intellectual debts belong to my mentors. Gerard Libaridian's support and encouragement over the last several years have known no limit. His example as a teacher and thinker is the one I try most to emulate. Müge Göçek's mark on this project is indelible. Always generous with her time, our many cross-disciplinary conversations over the years have shaped my thinking about Ottoman society more than I will likely ever realize. Ronald Suny, whose bold rethinking of Armenian history still inspires, shared his wisdom throughout the development of this project. Juan Cole remains a friend and confidant.

My thanks are due to a number of people who reviewed parts of the manuscript in its different stages. These include Sabri Ateş, Frank Castiglione, Jason Glenn, Paul Lerner, Devi Mays, Umut Özsü, Brett Sheehan, Josh White, and Murat Yıldız. Christine Philliou and İpek Yosmaoğlu read an early version of the manuscript in its entirety and flew to Los Angeles to provide me with invaluable feedback. Though my stubbornness sometimes kept me from heeding their advice, the final product has benefited immensely from their suggestions. Errors of judgment, fact, or argumentation are of course mine alone.

For their moral support and friendship over the years, I thank Boris Adjemian, Frank Castiglione, Vazken Davitian, Dzovinar Derderian, Christian Garbis, Carl Holtman, Asbed Kotchikian, Devi Mays, Josh White, Murat Yıldız, and Julien Zarifian. In Los Angeles, I have benefited from the support and camaraderie of Marjorie Becker, Bill Deverell, Josh Goldstein, Wolf Grüner, Kyung Moon Hwang, Maya Maskarinec, Lindsay O'Neill, Ben Uchiyama, and especially Ketaki Pant, Edgardo Perez-Morales, Jason Glenn, Paul Lerner, and Brett Sheehan.

My family's support cannot be overstated. Edward and Terry Antaramian, my parents, have taken special interest in the project from its beginning. My father's passion for family history opened a door to Ottoman Anatolia that will never be closed. Oleg and Larisa Ambartsumyan, my in-laws, have provided assistance at every stage of this journey.

Finally, Liliya Ambartsumyan, my love and my wife, has lived with this project since its inception more than a decade ago. Our sons, Raffi and Michael, joined her along the way. Their unconditional love, support, and patience have buoyed me at every turn. This book would not have been possible without their innumerable sacrifices. For these reasons and more, this book belongs to them.

NOTE ON TRANSLITERATION

I have followed a simplified system of transliteration for Armenian. Where appropriate, I have preferred the common rendering of Armenian names that have appeared in English; the reader will thus find Midhat Pasha's adviser referred to as Krikor Odian rather than Grigor Otean.

Ottoman Armenians used the Julian Calendar. I have not converted those dates. Gregorian dates are, however, listed alongside Hicri dates where appropriate.

All translations, unless otherwise noted, are mine.

BROKERS OF FAITH, BROKERS OF EMPIRE

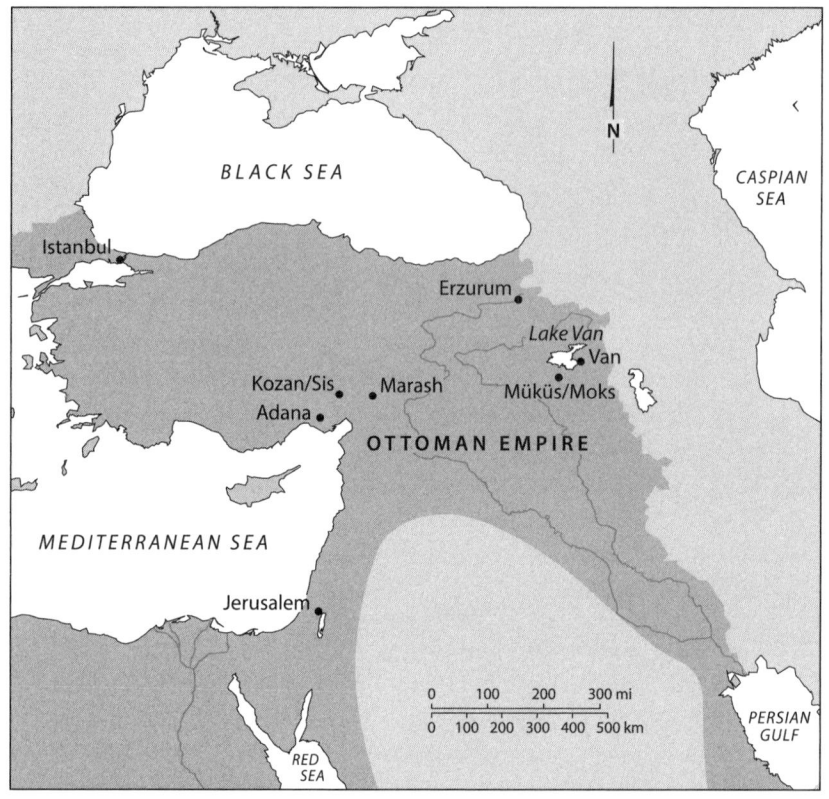

Important sites of social and political contention in the Ottoman Armenian community
Note: The darker portions on the map indicate the borders of the Ottoman Empire until 1878.

INTRODUCTION

MKRTICH DIKRANIAN KNEW CONTROVERSY WELL. As an Armenian bishop from Diyarbakir, a largely Kurdish region in southeastern Anatolia, Dikranian found that trouble had made a habit of tracking him down. Despite these challenges, he had made a name for himself as an author and activist, most notably in the arena of education. His efforts in that field, which had begun in the 1840s, had won him the support of Armenian liberals in the Ottoman capital, Istanbul, who then used their influence with both the Armenian Church and the Ottoman imperial government to advance his career. With their patronage, Dikranian enjoyed appointments to a number of desirable positions in both the capital and the provinces. Those same efforts, however, had also earned Dikranian enemies among the provincial Armenian elite and their allies in the clergy, as unanticipated scrutiny accompanied his newfound notoriety. Opponents of reform slandered Dikranian in letters sent to Armenian Church authorities in the 1860s and 1870s. The most prominent Ottoman Armenian satirist of the nineteenth century mercilessly mocked Dikranian as a superstitious provincial buffoon who performed "miracles" for the ignorant.[1] Dikranian, the scribe explained, would instruct the faithful to apply holy water he had blessed to fix any problem, be it an upset stomach, a broken window, or even a room that had flooded after a downpour.

These modest forays that Dikranian had made in the field of education attracted such attention because they were loaded with political meaning. Dikranian's efforts were fully enmeshed in the nineteenth-century Ottoman reform program known as the Tanzimat, which commenced in 1839 when Sultan Abdülmecid (r. 1839–1861) issued the Edict of Gülhane. Like their imperial counterparts elsewhere, the Ottomans responded to the upheavals ushered in during the Age of Revolutions through a series of policies that recalibrated the relationship between state and subject.[2] These policies included the introduction of institutions and initiatives such as the redrawing of administrative boundaries; secular courts; laws on nationality; the privatization of land; and, perhaps most significant, the expansion of a rationalized bureaucracy through which Ottoman sovereignty would be exercised. Most notably, the Gülhane edict announced the end of discrimination against non-Muslims in public life. This wholesale reorganization of the empire constituted a reinterpretation of the politics of difference in Ottoman imperial governance and society and thus extended to the empire's non-Muslim communities.

As a Muslim empire, the Ottomans employed markers of religious difference to organize and legitimize their rule. Non-Muslim clergymen were tasked with securing the loyalty of their flocks to the Ottomans and ensuring that their communities observed certain discriminatory practices, including a prohibition on access to instruments of coercion, sartorial restrictions, and the remittance of special taxes to the imperial treasury. In exchange, non-Muslim communities enjoyed the right to administer their own internal affairs, practice their religion without interference from the government, and enjoy the protection of life and property by the state. Such arrangements encouraged the integration of non-Muslim religious communities—namely, the Orthodox Christians, Apostolic Armenians, and a variety of urban Jewish groups—into the imperial body politic on unequal bases. They also afforded the clergy particular incentive to guard the status quo. And they wielded the instruments to do so. Regulation of communal affairs meant that clergymen produced bureaucratic documents (such as baptismal records) and approved the transfer of wealth (by blessing marriages and inheritance) in accordance with religious prescription. Clergymen also had access to state coercion. For example, a rabbi could appeal to the government to enforce Jewish dietary laws, while an Armenian priest might use a local jail to enforce the Lenten fast or persecute Protestants. The extension of imperial reform into the administration of the non-Muslim communities introduced new constraints on the clergy. Scholars have read the subsequent rise of lay elites in communal administration as secularization and, in keeping with the modernization paradigm, connected reform to the formation of national identities.[3] The clergy, who had attracted the attention of eighteenth- and nineteenth-century European observers, thus disappear from Ottoman historiography, where they instead give way to a motley assortment of bankers; bureaucrats; and, most telling, revolutionaries and intellectuals who charted routes out of empire. The substitution of nationality for religion proved incompatible with the imperial ethos.

Historians working against this line of thought have demonstrated that the formation of ethnic or national identities in the nineteenth century frequently accommodated imperial belonging.[4] Religion did not, however, disappear from the Ottoman political landscape; in fact, I argue the opposite was true during the reform period. Clergymen, as a result, found themselves at the fore of Ottoman politics. Satire was thus not the only distraction with which Mkrtich Dikranian had to contend. In 1874, for example, rival clergymen accused him of conducting illegal ordinations.[5] The substantiation of these charges likely would have resulted in the defrocking of Dikranian as an Armenian priest. Dikranian's opponents among the clergy probably had more immediate goals. First, targeting Dikranian's position as a clergyman would impede his ability to conduct reform. Second, the controversy—as demonstrated by how the records of these accusations were archived—threatened to trigger international discord that could rock the tenuous stability of Armenian Church institutions in the Ottoman Empire. In making such charges, Dikranian's conservative adversaries were not simply reacting to changes in nineteenth-century Armenian society; they were trying to preserve a specific iteration of Ottoman imperial governance.

Brokers of Faith, Brokers of Empire seeks to capture how the Armenian community of the Ottoman Empire and its institutions participated in imperial governance during the reform period in the nineteenth century. In so doing, it reframes nineteenth-century Ottoman history by narrating imperial reform from the vantage point of Armenian experiences. The ecclesiastical reorganization of the Armenian Apostolic Church during this period had far-reaching consequences that extended beyond the parochial borders of the Armenian community. Although the Armenian clergy received their license from the imperial state—and this was quite literally the case for those holding high office in the Church's administration—the relationship of the clergy to imperial politics and society did not run exclusively along a state-subject axis. Just as the politics of empire extended beyond the state, so, too, did the role of the Armenian clergy. They used the privileged position afforded to them by the politics of religious difference to forge relations with other powerful actors in imperial society at local, regional, and imperial levels. In so doing, the clergy embedded the institutions of the Armenian Church in dense and layered webs of connections that structured Ottoman society as a contiguous empire, brokering the relationships that made the movement of capital and the exercise of Ottoman sovereignty throughout its sprawling intercontinental domains possible. Any effort to tug at the ecclesiastical organization of the Armenian Church or otherwise place constraints on its clergy—projects in which Dikranian and other clergymen were clearly invested—thus constituted an effort to reorganize Ottoman imperialism itself.

The book argues that the ecclesiastical reorganization of the Armenian Church in the Ottoman Empire was therefore key to the centralization of the imperial state in the nineteenth century. Centralization, I contend, is better understood as the state's efforts to establish itself as the sole institution for exercising imperial sovereignty. The introduction of the so-called *millet* system in the nineteenth century contributed to this effort by rearranging intercommunal networks that had structured imperial society prior to the onset of reform. Here, I benefit from Karen Barkey's use of social capital theory to explain Ottoman imperialism.[6] Barkey's path-breaking book *Empire of Difference* describes how social capital was accrued by those able to position themselves as brokers between differentiated networks in an imperial society.[7] The decision to forge a connection—and thus construct or expand a network—was theirs to make. The state in this setting was not the only player and thus had to share sovereignty with a variety of partners in imperial politics. The Armenian Church was one such partner. This book therefore uses network analysis and the social capital metaphor to locate Armenians and their religious institutions in larger structures of Ottoman power and identify how the connections they forged helped make imperial society. Doing so takes us away from the vantage point of the state and its dominant sociological element, the Sunni Turks, and to the margins of imperial society to understand how Ottoman power was constituted.

As partners of the state, Armenians used their religious institutions to contribute to a horizontal version of Ottoman imperial governance. The connections fostered through the Armenian Church, which crisscrossed the empire, brought together a whole host of actors, including provincial Muslim notables, the imperial government, tax collectors, merchants, bankers, and of course the Armenian clergy, to share in the benefits of empire and thereby suture an imperial polity. These relationships come into view only during the reform period. Each effort by Armenian reformers to censure, remove, or otherwise punish a clergyman shed more light on how the Armenian community was, in fact, integrated into Ottoman imperial society. This book therefore uses the paper trail—composed in Armenian languages and produced by Armenian institutions—generated by the conflict between two different visions of Armenian communal participation in Ottoman governance to rethink the dynamics of imperial politics. In the course of corresponding with one another, petitioning the Patriarchate of Constantinople, or simply recording their observations, Armenian priests implicitly described a complex imperial polity and their place in it. This is because clergymen ultimately found themselves caught between different poles in a contentious politics in which multiple powerful actors had a stake. I follow the evidence these clergymen have left us to identify those connections and how they integrated the Armenian community into imperial society. The stakes were high. Opponents of reform thus came for Dikranian's career; other clergymen would pay more dearly for trying to reform their community.

Historians' approaches to the reform period have fallen broadly into two strains. One has emphasized the methods used by the state to extend its authority beyond the capital and into the provinces. The other has paid closer attention to the state's efforts to combat what many regard as nascent nationalism among the empire's non-Muslim communities by reintegrating them into the imperial body politic. These processes did not, however, unfold in isolation from each other. Armenians bidding to reorganize their own communities and to place constraints on the clergy were actively engaged in unmaking the connections that supported a version of imperial governance that was horizontal and networked. In so doing, Armenian reformers partnered with the state in its efforts to produce a top-down polity that was legible to the imperial center. The fact that they did so provides us an opportunity to build upon recent critiques on paradigms central to the writing of Ottoman historiography—namely, the *millet* system and the center-periphery binary.

CENTER AND PERIPHERY

The center-periphery binary has exerted a strong influence over the fields of Ottoman and Middle Eastern studies for several decades.[8] It has understandably left a particularly significant imprint on the study of the reform period. The central government's bid to expand its authority in the nineteenth century brought it to loggerheads with provincial notables across Anatolia, the Balkans, and the Levant who regarded such developments as an encroachment upon their prerogatives. Such encroachments provoked a response that, scholarship on the topic has held, facilitated the formation of national identities. This analytical paradigm, which is familiar to historians of empire, migrated into Ottoman historiography from positivist sociology in the 1960s. The modernization assumptions implicit in the center-periphery paradigm found fertile soil in fields still finding their footing in the North American academy. Only in the past two decades have scholars, particularly those studying the Ottoman Levant, begun to interrogate the causal link between imperial reform and nationalism.[9]

The enduring influence of the paradigm presents an obstacle to the integration of Armenian experiences into Ottoman historiography. In this historical literature, the juxtaposition of a periphery differentiated by language, culture, or ethnicity against the imperial center ultimately normalizes the preeminence of the state and its sociological majority, the Sunni Turks. Both of these elements enjoy prevalence as the constant variable in a series of analyses organized geographically (e.g., the juxtaposition of Damascus, Beirut, or Baghdad each against Istanbul). Moreover, the reification of political tension to that between Muslim notables in the periphery and the government in Istanbul precludes appreciating the ecumenical constitution of imperial politics. Much as is the case with studies of the imperial center, non-Muslim elites, cleaved from their communities and their politics, incoherently dot the social landscape of the periphery as merchants, moneylenders, priests, or victims.

The center-periphery framework fails to explain how Armenian reformers such as Dikranian articulated their agendas in the context of imperial reform in the 1860s and 1870s. Understanding how Armenians engaged imperial governance requires breaking down the center-periphery binary as an enduring feature of Ottoman history and recognizing the contingency of each as a category that gained salience only in the nineteenth century. Armenian reformers enthusiastically embraced the challenge of reorganizing their communities precisely because it embedded them in imperial policies that produced center and periphery both discursively and structurally. In place of the various metaphors derived from center-periphery analysis to explain Ottoman imperialism, such as spoke-and-hub-without-the-wheel, I instead propose that the empire be viewed as a tapestry.

The tapestry model sees empire as a dense cluster of layered, overlapping, and differentiated networks through which imperial sovereignty was exercised. Their collective organization was messy and uneven, and they oftentimes facilitated the forging of relationships that the imperial center later found intolerable. For the most part, however, the interaction of these various threads provided actors all across the empire a set of shared interests that invested each in the political enterprise of empire; their interaction also ensured that the benefits of these relationships ultimately flowed upward to the ruling class. The stability of the ensuing political formation owed a debt to the brokerage of the Armenian community. The Armenian community was a networked space woven into this tapestry through religious institutions; clergymen and ecclesiastics thus rested at the intersection of relationships that helped stitch the empire together but did so in a manner that drew imperial society toward Istanbul. The two perspectives I employ in this book—the tapestry and the networked communal space—allow me to observe Armenian communal politics as a connected phenomenon that interacted simultaneously with the state and a multitude of other actors across the empire.

Armenian communal reform pursued two objectives: support the state's efforts to dismantle the networks that had propped up horizontal connections that had made one order of things, and then use the Armenian institutions newly freed from those webs of relationships to weave together a new system of governance in which state institutions alone exercised sovereignty. Reform advocates such as Dikranian saw this as a direct pathway into the politics of state that would unburden the great bulk of Armenians, who were overwhelmingly engaged in subsistence-level agriculture, from the informal power structures that exacted heavy tolls on them. Lay Armenians likewise interpreted reform of the community's administration as a pathway to state power and began organizing around clergymen with whom they shared political agendas. Because Armenian religious institutions and the clergy who led them functioned as nodes through which the community was woven into imperial governance, ecclesiastics became a site of intense contention; these were the knots that had to be cut.

In other words, Armenian engagement with imperial governance as explored in this book runs counter to many of the long-standing assumptions about Ottoman non-Muslims during the long nineteenth century. Reform did not secularize but rather politicized religion and Armenian Church offices in a manner they had never been previously in Ottoman governance. Instead of nationalization, Istanbul and the legitimacy afforded by the imperial center assumed a significance in communal politics that it had not enjoyed in prior centuries. Communal reorganization very clearly directed all Ottoman Armenian politics toward the Sublime Porte, an orientation that arguably persisted until the end of the Allied occupation of the Istanbul following World War I. Armenians viewed themselves as partners of the government in reform. In the course of restructuring governance, however, Armenian reformers helped irreversibly change the meaning of difference in the Ottoman Empire and how it could be deployed to make claims. An Ottoman Empire that no longer needed the Armenian community to forge network structures that pulled the polity toward Istanbul had little incentive to hold up its end of the partnership.

NON-MUSLIM COMMUNITIES IN OTTOMAN HISTORY

Empires enforce regimes of difference to ensure a system of inequality that benefits the ruling class; the benefits of any imperial enterprise ultimately flow back to the center.[10] For the Ottomans, religion was a primary marker of difference. Exploring non-Muslim engagement with imperial governance is thus essential to any comprehensive analysis of Ottoman history. As has been well documented, the Ottomans' masterful management of diversity fueled the empire's rapid transformation from a tiny *beylik* in the Bithynian marches to a global power. Early aggrandizement at Byzantine expense, for example, owed much to the fact that Christian strongmen such as Köse Mihal had allied with the nomads' charismatic leader, thus becoming *osmanlı* themselves. Postconquest Ottoman administrations in the late medieval and early modern periods tended to have a laissez-faire quality to them, where the imperial authorities usually preferred to co-opt indigenous elites and exploit their local knowledge rather than impose more costly and potentially consequential forms of direct rule. Accommodation (*istimalet*) deterred opposition and oriented conquered communities' politics and economies toward the nascent imperial center.

The Ottomans' flexibility in governance extended to religious practice in what has typically been described as a *millet* system. Consonant with Muslim political practice, the empire's non-Muslim religious communities, or *millet*s, received guarantees of life, property, and freedom of religious practice in exchange for loyalty and subjection to certain discriminatory practices, including sartorial restrictions, exclusion from the military, and the payment of extraordinary taxes to the imperial treasury. Early scholarship on Ottoman non-Muslims held that the empire instituted this system following the conquest of Constantinople by Sultan Mehmed II in 1453 that finally extinguished the smoldering embers of what was once the Byzantine Empire.[11] The sultan supposedly invested authority over the growing empire's Christian population in Gennadios, a Greek Orthodox bishop, shortly after the Ottomans had established themselves in the city. Cognizant of the doctrinal differences separating Christian churches, Mehmed II later called his friend Hovakim, an Armenian bishop in Bursa, to the imperial capital to preside over the Armenians as Gennadios did the Greek Orthodox. Eventually, each of the three principal non-Muslim communities—the Greek Orthodox, the Armenian Apostolic, and the Jewish—had an ethnarch based in the capital who governed his community on behalf of the government. The Ottomans thus incorporated, much as they did local elites elsewhere, the indigenous religious institutions that they encountered by giving the clergy a stake in imperial governance. The clergy so empowered had that much more incentive to stamp out heretical movements that might be used to mobilize social discontent, as had been the case in the Muslim community.

There is much to question here. While the clergy did establish an important role in Ottoman governance, scholars have devoted considerable energy to dismantling the *millet* system paradigm. The best-known salvo in this deconstruction was Benjamin Braude's 1982 chapter "Foundation Myths of the *Millet* System" in the two-volume collection *Christians and Jews in the Ottoman Empire*.[12] Braude's chapter describes how many of the documents used to establish the timelessness of the *millet* system were, in fact, forgeries made by clergymen in the early nineteenth century to establish precedent for the prerogatives they hoped to claim as the empire experimented with reform. The deconstruction of the *millet* system paradigm subsequently opened different pathways for exploring non-Muslim historical agency in Ottoman imperial society. Scholars, particularly those interested in gender, social, or cultural histories for the early modern period, have turned to sources such as court records to demonstrate the porosity of communal boundaries.[13] Although organized by religion, non-Muslim communities in the Ottoman Empire were neither parochial nor undifferentiated. They were also not stable political or social formations.

The ease with which historical actors transgressed communal boundaries has called into question not only the *millet* system paradigm but also whether we can speak of *millet*s in Ottoman history. Scholars have scoured a number of archives to find documents that demonstrate the contingency of church prerogatives in imperial governance across time and space. By and large, the rights and responsibilities of non-Muslim communities were determined on an ad hoc basis and were generally the result of negotiation between a clergyman and the government. To this end, scholars have tracked how the terms used by the Ottoman authorities for non-Muslim communities changed over time. Only in the nineteenth century did the term "*millet*" begin to gain salience as an increasingly discernible category in the lexicon of Ottoman law and politics.[14] This development built upon the growing ecclesiastical authority that the Armenian and Greek Orthodox patriarchs began wielding in the eighteenth century; that expansion of authority in turn laid the institutional framework of what could become a *millet* system in the nineteenth century. It was within the parameters of this framework that patriarchs, non-Muslim elites, and representatives of the imperial government would negotiate the rights and responsibilities of each party throughout the reform period.

Scholarship focusing on the nineteenth century has, however, preferred to treat *millet*s as stable and fixed communities that seamlessly underwent processes of nationalization and secularization in the course of the reform program. Despite critical reconsiderations of the violence that gripped Orthodox Christian communities in both Greece and the Slavic-speaking regions of the Balkans, as well as the failure to present any evidence that demonstrates Ottoman Armenians' desire to create an independent state, Carter Findley, a preeminent scholar of the field's mainstream, declared with confidence that

> while reinforcing Ottoman solidarity and creating conditions for specific communities to flourish were philosophically reconcilable, under Ottoman conditions *communal reforms could not be carried out without reinforcing separatism and thus undermining Ottomanism*. Inasmuch as the religious differences basic to *millet* reform seldom matched the ethnic differences basic to modern nationalism, variable and unpredictable consequences ensued, as the Greek Orthodox and Armenian cases illustrate. Among Ottoman religious minorities only to the Jews were ideas of nationalism or separatism foreign in this period.[15]

The enduring resilience of modernization theory underpins the assumption, as described above, that *millet* yields nation. Why has the depiction of a contingent, fluid community made by scholars of the early modern period failed to disrupt the national teleology that holds such sway among historians of the nineteenth century? The failure to reconcile these approaches has, in the words of one scholar, rendered the first half of the nineteenth century a dead space.[16] One explanation rests in the étatist inclinations of Ottoman historiography. The historical literature that demonstrates the contingency of community has done so through the prism of state documents. Highlighting how churches coaxed concessions out of the state in the course of their negotiations is useful to an extent but tells only a sliver of the story, as this entails juxtaposing a non-Muslim community such as the Armenians against the state in order to afford the former any meaning.[17] The relationship between the two so reified precludes understanding how internal communal politics were, in fact, part of a broader imperial political contention on which the state was only one (albeit by far the most significant) claimant. Reading non-Muslim politics along a state-subject axis alone reduces the complexity of those communities' historical experiences to only one facet of how they navigated empire. Like much of Ottoman historiography, the integration of non-Muslim historical experiences into the narrative hinges on displacing the centrality of the state.

Imperial sovereignty is layered and shared.[18] States were not hegemonic actors but instead had to negotiate with a variety of forces in imperial society to inscribe legitimacy in the subjects over whom they claimed dominion. Imperial governance, as Christine Philliou argued, extends beyond the state and instead encapsulates a series of relationships, networks, and cultures that are committed to preserving an order of things.[19] These are crucial starting points for displacing the centrality of the state in our thinking about Ottoman history generally and the relationship of non-Muslim communities to imperial governance in particular. Rather than interrogate how the state used non-Muslim communities to facilitate imperial rule over non-Muslim subjects, we may more productively ask how communities helped establish and perpetuate a social and political order.

Non-Muslim communities were key to brokering and maintaining relationships between more powerful forces in Ottoman imperial society. They employed a number of techniques to play such a role. Although there remains debate about the prerogatives and responsibilities of churches and clergymen, non-Muslim communities did retain the right to administer their own religious affairs. These affairs included more than just weekly liturgical services or the confession of faith. Baptisms, marriages, and funerals were ceremonies loaded with cultural meaning that could ascribe religious sanction to significant economic exchanges and the social bonds they sometimes forged. Although scholars may parse the language used by the imperial government to delineate the relationship of the church to the state, clergymen on the ground policed interactions that were of consequence beyond the community. As such, clergymen were well positioned to make alliances with other actors who wielded power.

The non-Muslim churches' role in tax collection reinforced that position. As Tom Papademetriou showed in the Greek Orthodox case, the church was originally a tax farm.[20] The Ottomans, as the Byzantines before them, recognized the efficiency that ecclesiastical structures could furnish for the purposes of tax collection. Clergymen's stake in the movement of goods and cash thus provided them that much more incentive to forge alliances with those power brokers. Locally, this tended to take the form of relationships with Muslim notables, their clients, and the provincial government officials who had to navigate such networks. The ecclesiastical organization of the churches also attracted the investment of the wealthy and influential among their flock. These connections aided the relative stability enjoyed by the empire throughout much of the eighteenth century, particularly in the decades following the Patrona Halil uprising. In both the Armenian and Greek Orthodox cases, the rapid expansion of patriarchal authority and the influence of non-Muslim elites in imperial governance during the eighteenth century were interrelated developments.[21]

These non-Muslim elites—Armenian *amira*s, a class of Istanbul-based bankers and bureaucrats, and Greek Orthodox Phanariots, (mostly) Greek notables who served as Danubian governors and government translators—played significant roles in brokering relations between the groups vying for power at the top of the Ottoman Empire. Although most clearly tied to the imperial government, Phanariot households benefited from relationships with provincial notables, tax collectors, Janissaries, and the Greek Orthodox Church—an institution on which they brought their incredible wealth and prestige to bear. Armenian *amira*s meanwhile used their financial capital to underwrite much of the empire's tax collection system, thus placing themselves between provincial notables, the imperial government, the clergy, and the Armenian peasantry. For the *amira*s especially, the clergy and the church were ideal instruments for building intercommunal relationships that could protect investments and ensure that the benefits of empire—in this case, profits from tax farming—flowed upward and into the coffers of provincial notables, the state, and the Armenian elite. The empire-wide community was thus fully integrated into imperial politics and society.

CUTTING THE THREADS OF EMPIRE: ARMENIANS AND THE TANZIMAT

The Armenian Church and its institutions were thus key to facilitating a horizontal networked world of Ottoman governance in which major claimants on politics shared power. As I argue in subsequent chapters, the community was a communal space woven into the fabric of imperial society by a series of network connections that were threaded through the institutions of the Church. The overlap of imperial subjectivity and the universality of spiritual belonging organized the Ottoman Armenian community into a space that spanned the empire.[22] The brokering of relationships by clergymen and their lay allies among merchants and bankers with the imperial government and provincial Muslim power brokers through this space made the Armenian community crucial to the fashioning of empire. Clergymen and Armenian ecclesiastics added another layer of complexity to this networking world—a world that would have to be unmade for the state to pursue its centralization policies in the nineteenth century. The transformation of the Armenian community was seminal for the reorganization of the empire. The Tanzimat we see from this perspective did not lay out a path to inclusion but instead exacerbated structural inequalities by reinforcing regimes of difference while eliminating the advantages—most notably mechanisms for making claims on imperial politics and society—they once provided. Centralization meant, above all, state control.

To better appreciate how Armenians enriched that complexity, we return to the archival folder in which the accusations against Dikranian are stored. Nestled next to those rest a similar set of accusations against another prominent reformer, Bishop Eremia Tevkants.[23] Like Dikranian, Tevkants had provincial roots. In this case, the background of the accuser—Timoteos Saprichian—betrays his political motivations. Saprichian, a published author and clergyman, was a member of the St. James Order at the Armenian Patriarchate of Jerusalem. In the 1870s, he found himself in a remote corner of eastern Anatolia; this did not, however, diminish the fraternal loyalties he felt toward his companions at home in Jerusalem. Communal reform during the Tanzimat period legislated the near-total subordination of Armenian Church institutions to the Patriarchate of Constantinople, stipulations that threatened both the autonomy and prestige that Jerusalem had enjoyed in ecclesiastical matters. By striking at Tevkants, Saprichian—like Dikranian's accusers—hoped to slow the reform program by provoking an ecclesiastical controversy. Saprichian also provided an example of how high-ranking clergymen circulated throughout the empire. Nineteenth-century reformers who had hoped to make the community's administration more legible tried in vain to restrict this type of mobility.

The authority of the Patriarchate of Constantinople in Armenian ecclesiastical and religious matters was always contested. Exacerbating its claims to authority was the presence of three other major Armenian Church seats in the Ottoman Empire—the Patriarchate of Jerusalem, the Catholicosate of Cilicia, and the Catholicosate of Aghtamar. These seats, like other major monasteries, enjoyed the right to ordain priests and, in the case of the catholicosates, the right to consecrate bishops. Once ordained, these priests could serve any Armenian community anywhere. Those clergymen ordained by church institutions of some stature enjoyed a cachet unavailable to others; the more significant the ordaining institution, the greater the wealth it controlled, the more access it had to the wealthy (and connected) patrons, and the more likely it was to profit from pilgrimage. These priests were thus initiated into not only the orthodoxies of the Armenian Church but also the high-stakes political games in which the Church was embedded. They were therefore ideal candidates for positions across the empire. To their new appointments they brought not only their social, political, and religious know-how but also the connections that their ordaining institution could furnish. From these positions to which they were appointed, they in turn forged new connections with both local power brokers and local clergy.

These other major church seats, as well as a handful of prosperous monasteries across Anatolia, thus constituted nodes in a network setting that integrated the communal space into a series of vertical and horizontal relationships. As such, the community played that much more of an important role in brokering between rival claimants on imperial politics by facilitating the distribution of empire's spoils to the groups with which they were connected. In the pre-Tanzimat period, this was not only tolerated but rather encouraged so long as the connections forged weighed imperial society toward the capital. The institutions of the Armenian community thus facilitated horizontal connections that helped provide some network stability throughout imperial society but, through the gradual expansion of the Patriarchate of Constantinople and the movement of *amira* financial capital, pulled those connections toward the Sublime Porte and the Sultanate. Although not all roads led to Istanbul, the Armenian community helped ensure that, even though they may have encountered detours along the way, most eventually did.

Istanbul had tolerated such an arrangement to a point. The Tanzimat's policies that aimed to extend the influence of the state into as many spheres of social and political life as possible changed that. Ottoman losses to Egyptian forces, which had been recurrent throughout the 1830s before culminating in the disastrous Battle of Nezib in 1839, conveyed the urgency for massive reorganizations of state and society to guard against further territorial losses. These included the expansion of the bureaucracy, the institution of local councils, the privatization of land via the Ottoman Land Code of 1858, a series of laws that redrew provincial boundaries and ordered their administrations, and the Ottoman Nationality Law of 1869. The reform program has thus been read as a foray of sorts in, if not liberal democracy, at least some form of participatory government. All policy initiatives evinced the spirit of Ottomanism, or the formation of a supranational Ottoman identity that was to transcend parochial communal boundaries. A transition of sorts from subjects to citizens was to take place. Subjects would gain nationality, they could purchase land to integrate into the economy, more clear lines of authority would connect citizen to state without the needless intercession of religious authorities, and secular courts would help to abolish markers of difference that had precluded the establishment of a horizontal comradeship across the empire. Provincial notables and other conservatives, whose prerogatives were threatened by the new arrangements, resisted change and bid to reject the reform programs.

These reform policies are better understood less as efforts to create a participatory society than as the state's desire to establish a monopoly on sovereignty and exercise greater control over its subjects. The Tanzimat, like the reform initiatives of the decades that preceded it, were restorationist.[24] The Armenian community's piece of imperial sovereignty, which it possessed because of confessional difference, was shared not only with the imperial government but also with the other claimants on imperial politics. The Ottoman state had been trying since at least the second half of the eighteenth century to remove those other claimants from the political arena. Their primary targets were a number of provincial notables, particularly in the Balkans, and the Janissaries. Assaults on Balkan notables fomented the Greek Revolution of 1821, which culminated in not only Greek independence but also the removal of Phanariot households from imperial governance. Without the mediating role of the Phanariots to mitigate tensions between the government and the Janissaries, the writing was on the wall for the latter: in 1826 the Ottoman state oversaw the massacre of Janissaries and their near-total removal from imperial politics. Fewer claimants on imperial politics entailed the greater centralization of power in the imperial government, which then developed new methods for filling the void left by these departures. Individuals, including many Armenians, filtered into the expanding bureaucracy to help the state exercise its growing authority over its subjects.

Tearing apart the networked world of governance to replace it with a newly reorganized and centralized imperial polity thus meant reconceiving how difference could be deployed to make claims on imperial politics. Reforming non-Muslim communities and then offering them pathways to inclusion was less about incorporating Christians into the imperial body politic—evidenced by the fact the reform efforts did little to address the structural gaps produced by centuries of enforced inequality—than it was liquidating their claim to shared sovereignty by undermining the meaning of the marker of difference that had justified such a claim in the first place. The Armenian community's investment of its share of sovereignty in networks had afforded its leadership prestige and wealth and the community a certain amount of protection against the most outrageous abuses in exchange for legal and structural discrimination. The promise of equality and equal access to justice and property negated that claim and thus delegitimized the Armenian role in the networking world that had helped other actors in imperial society develop power-sharing arrangements with the central government. The Armenian community thus had to be transformed from a communal space into a *millet* that collaborated with the imperial state for the latter to create top-down governance.

Reform was not something that only Armenians from Istanbul, particularly those influenced by European thinking, pursued.[25] Many Armenians of provincial or lower-class backgrounds—including Dikranian and Tevkants—embraced the reform program and tried to shape it. For decades, they had seen how the higher-ranking members of the clergy and Armenian elite had used the institutions of the community to further their own interests at the expense of the guildsmen, labor migrants, and peasantry. The benefits of empire, for provincial Muslim notable and Armenian elite alike, were predicated on the extraction of resources from the vast majority of the Armenian population who bore the brunt of unequal rule. Although they may not have understood the extent to which their community was integrated into imperial and regional networks, Armenian reformers recognized the potential of allying the community with the state and its coercive apparatus against the groups in society that had exploited the flock. Armenian reformers, led by clergymen connected to the guilds, set about wresting control from the elite and the old clerical establishment. They believed that participation in the project of state centralization entitled them to the share of imperial sovereignty that the community claimed. They failed, however, to understand that participation in the reordering entailed relinquishing that claim by severing the connections that had given it meaning as part of the previous iteration of governance.

RELIGION AND THE TRANSFORMATION OF IMPERIAL GOVERNANCE

This book traces how Armenians navigated the reordering of Ottoman imperial governance in the nineteenth century. This reordering, which commenced in earnest under Sultan Selim III (r. 1789–1807) entailed nothing less than a wholesale transformation of the politics of difference in the Ottoman Empire. The introduction of the *millet* system in the nineteenth century thus contributed to this effort by segregating religion—in this case, non-Muslim religious institutions—from the economic, political, and social relationships that had anchored non-Muslim communities in imperial governance. This had the effect of "thinning out" a thick political culture that had consisted of differentiated networks that provided Armenians (and other nondominant groups) multiple points of interaction with other forces in imperial society.

Rather than provide non-Muslims with greater autonomy over their own internal affairs, the *millet* system rendered communities legible before the state, subjected them to greater surveillance, and placed severe constraints on their ability to participate in imperial governance. As has been noted in the case of the 1835 selection of the first official *hahambaşı*, the Ottoman Jewish community leader, the impetus for the creation of the office came from the government rather than the community.[26] A similar observation may be made of the Armenian community, where regulations ultimately placed the clergy under the watchful eye of the government. To become the primary instrument in people's daily lives for adjudicating grievances or disputes, the state had not only to usurp the role of the clergy as intermediary but also to divest non-Muslim religious institutions from imperial society in general.

The thinning out of governance through centralization did not just liquidate the community's claim to a share of imperial sovereignty, it therefore also removed the clergy's ability to accrue social capital by brokering across networks. Their location at the intersection of multiple communities—as well as the state—differentiated them from their flock. Old order clergymen therefore activated every tool at their disposal to disrupt the introduction of reform. The explosiveness of fraternal tension and ecclesiastical politics resulted in deaths, imprisonments, and acts of intimidation, and it very nearly created a schism that had nothing to do with doctrine or belief. These strong reactions against the reform program authored by old order clergymen provide us with a unique prism for understanding how the structural transformations of imperial governance in the nineteenth century produced a politics that eliminated any meaningful space for non-Muslim communities to participate.

This book uses that contention among clergymen to reconstruct how the Armenian community's partnership with the imperial government changed over time. The first chapter sets the stage by introducing the Armenian National Constitution, which was initially ratified in 1860, and offers a revisionist account of the tensions that produced it. The Constitution legislated a new empire-wide Ottoman Armenian diocese that saw itself as a partner of the imperial government. The historical literature on the Constitution, however, typically presents it as the product of class tensions among Armenians in the imperial capital of Istanbul. While tensions certainly informed communal politics, the struggle between lower-class Armenians and the elite requires contextualization if we are to understand the stakes over which they battled. That political contention was, I argue, bound up in the overlapping and interconnected processes of elite formation, the sharpening of Armenian ecclesiastical jurisdiction, and the centralization of the state. It was for these reasons that the collective elements of the Armenian community—its flock, its Church, its elites—constituted an empire-wide space that was a suitable partner for the imperial state as it bid to exercise its sovereignty throughout the empire. The communal reforms deepened this partnership, leading Armenians to believe that they were not only centralizing the state but also making a multivocal Tanzimat. The Constitution and the written texts it produced thus belong to the corpus of materials that constituted the Tanzimat.

The Constitution therefore politicized the ecclesiastical organization of the Armenian Church. Chapter 2 looks at how the effort to introduce the diocese was confronted by an "on the ground" Armenian Church that was organized as nodes in a networked setting. These nodes depended on the support of well-to-do Armenians from all across the empire, who invested their financial capital in the Church to protect their investments in long-distance trade and tax collection. Conservative clergymen, who had benefited from this nodal organization of governance, deployed all the formal and informal components of Church culture—including ecclesiastics, canon, charity, and the formation of "families" within monasteries—to strike back at the government-backed reformers.

Chapters 1 and 2 thus lay out how the Armenian Church and its clergy found themselves split between two visions of imperial governance: one top-down, the other horizontal. Chapter 3 analyzes how the conflict between those two would commence the process of removing Armenians from imperial governance. As noted above, historians have argued that the *millet* system came to be only in the nineteenth century. The arduous task that the reformers set out to accomplish through the introduction of the Constitution and earlier pieces of legislation—namely, extricating the community's religious institutions from networks—may therefore be understood as the transformation of the communal space into a *millet*. Here I offer a subtle but important corrective to the scholarship on the *millet* system: the *millet* system did not create but rather displaced a legally plural order and attempted to replace it with a legally centric one. Those who had benefited from legal pluralism—clergymen invested in networked governance—used multiple tools to preserve the legal order that had given them wide authority to police others' action. The networking strategies they deployed, however, ultimately peripheralized Armenians in imperial governance by reducing the points of contact the community had with other forces in society.

The fourth chapter builds upon the trajectory set out in the preceding chapters by looking at the career of Mkrtich Khrimian to offer a reconceptualization of Ottomanism. Mainstream scholarship, as the preceding Carter Findley quote demonstrates, regards Ottomanism as a failure. I offer a reconceptualization in response. Khrimian, a native of Van, was probably the most important Ottoman Armenian clergyman of the nineteenth century. He, like Dikranian and others, saw the centralizing policies of the reform program as a solution to provincial Armenian problems, which included regular exploitation committed by local Muslim power brokers and their allies among the Armenian clergy. Khrimian therefore gained the support of Armenian bureaucrats at the Sublime Porte and set about taking control of communal institutions away from clergymen embedded in networks. In the course of doing so, he integrated his local knowledge of Van and its culture into an Armenian cultural toolbox and thus developed an Ottomanist repertoire of action. Deploying this Ottomanist repertoire allowed Khrimian to do what the reformers in the capital had hoped: pair the Armenian Church institutions on the ground with the government in its centralizing efforts. In the course of doing so, he and the reformers made Istanbul the starting point for any Armenian political discourse originating in the provinces. They cast themselves as vanguards of the reform program, tasked with using their religion to build state and society.

In the end, the Armenian community's experiment with reform was too successful; in the course of embracing Tanzimat policies, they were, in certain respects, more committed to state policy than the state itself. Chapter 5 follows the last two decades of Khrimian's life in the Ottoman public, which commenced with the pomp and excitement surrounding his election as Patriarch of Constantinople—the highest position in the Ottoman Armenian religious hierarchy—and concluded with internal exile to Jerusalem. Khrimian took the community's partnership with the government seriously. Because personal experience had demonstrated the interconnectedness of Ottoman governance, he fully believed that the reform program empowered the Armenian community itself to make claims on imperial politics. The success of Armenian reform, coupled with the networking strategies of reactionary clergymen, had effectively liquidated any role for the Armenians in governance and therefore eliminated points of communication between the community and other political forces in imperial society. The state not only turned an increasingly deaf ear to Armenians' exhortations on imperial politics and provincial life, it also came to view them as subversive. On the eve of his exile, Khrimian effectively abandoned the projects to which he had devoted decades of work and activism and instead turned control of communal institutions back over to the very individuals he had spent decades trying to remove from power.

Reform had, however, shredded the networked world that furnished those reactionary clergymen with place of privilege in imperial governance; simply returning them to power would not restore the old order of things. No longer needing to work through a series of intermediaries to express its sovereignty, the Ottoman state now enjoyed an increasingly free hand with which to address challenges to the nascent status quo. Armenian clamoring for the seat at the table that they had been promised was one such challenge. Khrimian was removed from Ottoman public life in 1885 for making such a challenge. Other clergymen who dared to raise their heads would suffer fates worse than that.

1 THE CONSTITUTION

CELEBRATIONS BROKE OUT AMONG ARMENIAN communities in the Ottoman Empire in May 1882.[1] Public merrymaking was not unheard of among Ottoman Armenians, though it was typically reserved for religious holidays such as Easter. These particular celebrations, however, marked something much different: the twenty-second anniversary of the Armenian National Constitution. Much had happened in the intervening two decades that had elapsed between the celebrations and the original ratification of the Constitution by the Ottoman government in 1860. Fallout from the Russo-Turkish War of 1877–78 had left Armenians across the empire, particularly those in their homeland, in an increasingly precarious position. The pomp with which Ottoman Armenians greeted this anniversary of the Constitution conveyed a desire to rekindle the euphoria they had once associated with the document. Why, though, had the Constitution been received with such pomp by provincial Armenians? What stake did they have in its introduction, and why were they invested in its application? What exactly was the Constitution, and what did it do? Finding answers to these questions requires crafting a revisionist account of the Constitution, the political and social tension that generated it, and the context in which it unfolded. Doing so entails revisiting how Armenians and their institutions participated in imperial governance and how not only the Constitution but also prior instances of reform changed the contours of that participation.

The Constitution was, of course, tied to the 1856 Imperial Reform Edict by which the Ottomans, as a concession to their French and British allies in the Crimean War, agreed to permit the empire's non-Muslim communities to reorganize their own internal administration. As such, it has been tempting to frame the post-1856 charters granted to each community as experiments in European modalities—namely, nationalization and secularization. The introductory paragraphs to the Armenian Constitution, for example, appropriate French political language on rights and responsibilities. And, as others are quick to highlight, many of the Constitution's authors had traveled to France to study.[2] Yet we would be remiss to reduce this history to Eurocentric analysis by prioritizing either European influences or the intervention of European governments in negotiating non-Muslim prerogatives.[3] The vast remainder of the document, however, devotes substantial space to ecclesiastical administration, the oversight of clergymen, and how Armenian Church offices should interact with the imperial government. And if we look past 1856, we see that the Constitution is better understood as the culmination of an ecclesiastical restructuring that had consistently increased the authority of the Armenian Patriarchate of Constantinople since the middle of the eighteenth century.

The sharpening of ecclesiastical hierarchies and their points of interaction with the imperial government were central to the reordering of governance ushered in by successive Ottoman reform programs. Although these particular reforms were carried out in the institutions of the non-Muslim communities, they had consequences that extended to the rest of Ottoman imperial society. Armenians, particularly those in the provinces, therefore understood initiatives such as the Constitution as opportunities for them to transform Ottoman imperial governance. Although these regulations set forth what the organization of the community should look like, they omit any articulation of what precisely they aimed to reorganize. Non-Muslim communities as such interacted with multiple groups in Ottoman imperial society, of which the state was only one; the Armenian Church subsequently found itself enmeshed in an imperial order that was complex and brokered along horizontal and vertical axes. This chapter therefore advances the argument that, in the context of Ottoman imperial governance, the Armenian community be framed as a networked communal space. Observing communal dynamics from this vantage point allows us to see how Armenian institutions played a key role in forging together one iteration of imperial society. Such an order of things vaulted numerous Armenian actors—namely, the high-ranking clergy and a communal elite that possessed both financial and technical expertise—to the top of imperial society; the combination of their financial capital and administration of a far-flung ecclesiastical institution placed them between multiple groups with interests in the Ottoman imperial project. Most important, it made the community an attractive partner of the imperial state itself.

This chapter devotes most of its attention to understanding how the partnership between the Armenian community and the imperial government changed within the context of the reform period in the nineteenth century. The principal change was the transformation of the community from a space into a *millet*. The government's attempt to centralize the state, as we see in these chapters, necessitated distancing itself from the Armenian financial capital that underwrote much of a system of governance where networking was paramount for ensuring tax collection policies continually produced benefits for major claimants on imperial politics. The Armenian elite owed much of their success to strategic investments they had made in the Armenian Church, which provided them with significant influence over an institution that regulated the social and cultural aspects of the empire-wide Armenian community but also access to the myriad groups in imperial society with which the Church interacted. Cleaving elites from the administration of the Church meant placing the institution's ecclesiastical structures in service of a different vision for imperial governance, thereby changing the partnership between the community and the imperial state. This ultimately entailed the more thorough integration of the Armenian Church—not only its institutions but also its canon, laws, and traditions—into the apparatus of the official state.

The more complete integration of the Church into the state apparatus deepened the politicization of Armenian ecclesiastics. Armenians on either side of this nascent political divide—those committed to governance by informal networks and those in favor of standardizing practice to eliminate abuses—saw control of Church institutions as pathways to participation in governance. For the elite, this meant preserving the role of Armenian ecclesiastics in networks; for the reformers, moving the community into the state meant an opportunity to contribute to the making of new governing institutions and the writing of Ottoman law. For them, the Tanzimat—like other charters in Ottoman history—was an open text, multivocal, contested, and subject to negotiation; legal documents Armenians themselves produced—including the Constitution, the materials it generated, and their reflection of Armenian experiences—belonged to the corpus of texts that constituted Ottoman law. The elite had helped make an Ottoman politics where connections mattered; the reformers bid to make one where their community institutions worked as part of the imperial bureaucracy. The integration of an institution such as the Armenian Church, loaded with (at that point) a 1,600-year ecclesiastical tradition rife with contradictions and inconsistencies, into the apparatus of a state bureaucracy focused on centralizing power was, of course, fraught with difficulties. This ensured that Ottoman Armenian politics remain confessionalized rather than secularized.

TANZIMAT: REVISITING AN OPEN TEXT

The Tanzimat is inarguably a watershed not only for the history of the Ottomans but also for the histories of the Balkans and the Middle East. In many respects, the reorganization of government that it introduced laid the institutional groundwork for future nation-states in those regions. Tanzimat policies aimed to transform most every major facet of Ottoman imperial governance. Major reforms, many of which cut to the heart of imperial politics, served to marginalize factions that had wielded immense influence to that point. The abolition of tax farming, for example, targeted not only non-Muslim bankers, or *sarrafs*, whose capital underwrote many state initiatives, but also groups such as the ulema, who had amassed fortunes through exploitation of the tax system. The marginalization of these groups paved the way for the expansion of a professional bureaucracy under the aegis of the Ottoman Prime Ministry, or Sublime Porte, which theoretically introduced institutional and legal uniformity throughout the empire and thereby centralized the state's administration. Although the centralization of the state was a primary feature of the Tanzimat period, scholars have warned against overemphasizing the state. Decentering the state from our analysis requires taking a more expansive view of the Tanzimat.

For historians of the Ottoman Empire, the Tanzimat immediately conjures two dates: 1839 and 1856.[4] The original Tanzimat decree, the *Hatt-ı Şerif* of Gülhane, which was issued by Sultan Abdülmecid I in November 1839, abolished tax farming and ended discrimination against non-Muslims before the law. The 1856 *Islâhat Fermânı* (Reform Edict) built upon these earlier initiatives, particularly as they pertained to non-Muslims. Neither of these dates or edicts should be regarded as a rupture, however. The process of reform was fluid as policies were articulated in response to political challenges from all over the empire. Selim III (r. 1789–1807) took the first major steps toward transforming Ottoman imperial governance. He is best known for introducing the New Order troops (*Nizâm-ı Cedîd*) in 1797 as a response to Janissary shortcomings during the Russo-Turkish War of 1787–92. Of course this angered the Janissaries, who in addition to their military service had come to constitute a distinct social and political class that contended for influence with the Palace, Porte, and the ulema. The Janissaries claimed their revenge during another war with Russia by organizing a coup in Istanbul in 1807; they murdered Selim the following year in 1808 by order of his cousin and successor, Mustafa IV.

In the midst of this turmoil, Bayraktar Mustafa Pasha, a Muslim notable from Vidin, left the front lines to march on the capital in a bid to put down the uprising. Even though he failed to save Selim, he did depose Mustafa and installed Mahmud II in his place. As reward for his service, Bayraktar Mustafa Pasha was made Grand Vizier. He also oversaw the institution of the Deed of Agreement (*Sened-i İttıfak*) in 1808, which helped to regulate relations between the Sublime Porte and provincial notables. The diminishing influence of groups such as the Janissaries—whose number had been reduced greatly when Bayraktar Mustafa Pasha attacked them in Istanbul—left provincial notables with fewer resources to challenge the authority of the Sublime Porte. Reactionaries' ability to challenge Porte-sponsored reform was mitigated even further when Mahmud II—whose would-be executioners were actually in the room when Bayraktar Mustafa Pasha's men saved him—claimed his revenge on the Janissaries when he oversaw the bloody massacre of the corps in 1826.

The waning of antireform forces facilitated the eventual proclamation of the Tanzimat, which Abdülmecid did shortly after his enthronement in 1839. That the declaration was read by the Grand Vizier, Mustafa Reşid Pasha, who had probably authored the text, signals the extent to which the Sublime Porte now directed imperial policy. Significant reform policies punctuated the following decades of Ottoman history, including the 1856 Reform Edict, the 1864 Provincial Law that aimed to make imperial administration more legible, the 1869 Nationality Law, and of course the 1876 Ottoman Constitution. Educational reforms, which aimed to prepare bureaucrats for government service, produced thinkers such as the Young Ottomans, whose work would have political and cultural consequences for Ottoman society.[5]

The common denominator for each of these developments is the agency of the central state—namely, the Sublime Porte. The Tanzimat is thus viewed as a part of the progressive unfolding of developments that witness the state experimenting with solutions that it could apply to different parts of the empire. This vantage point has encouraged historians to write top-down narratives that treat the Tanzimat as an authoritative text. Such a view has been exacerbated by other intertwined trends in Ottoman historiography. First, early scholarship on the period gave undue weight to European influence on the authorship of the Tanzimat edicts and the content of reform policies.[6] Modernization theory and positivism thus fueled the scholarly agenda at an early point in the field's development.[7] Historians have made forceful rejections of these approaches. Modernization theory has, however, managed to survive through the center-periphery paradigm. Mapping the history of the policies that constituted the Tanzimat onto the center-periphery binary has made it possible to juxtapose a periphery, marked by geographic (and sometimes also ethnic or confessional) difference from the imperial center, against an order of things claiming to be normative. The agency of those marked by difference thus remains a secondary concern, as those actors are granted little more than the opportunity to negotiate that which was promulgated from above.

In response, scholars have argued that the Tanzimat and the content of its reform policies had pronounced roots in an Ottoman political culture.[8] In addition, they have shown that culture and politics "on the ground" in the provinces could influence the elaboration of reform policies at least as much as bureaucrats in the imperial capital did. Still, I would contend that our approach to the Tanzimat relies on narrow assumptions about what constituted Ottoman politics. The institutions and individuals that made up non-Muslim communities were thoroughly enmeshed in Ottoman governance and played important roles in each of the major events just described. The Tanzimat was therefore produced, made, and remade through dialogical engagement in the context of a contentious Ottoman politics.[9] Rather than authoritative, the Tanzimat was an open text, the corpus of which was multilingual, multilocal, and multiconfessional. The Tanzimat grew from roots that were Muslim, non-Muslim, imperial, and provincial. Armenian engagement with the Tanzimat was not about passively awaiting whatever dictates may emanate from above, pluralizing them, or instrumentalizing new forms of imperial rule to settle scores inside the community. Armenian engagement was about employing difference to make claims on Ottoman politics and society. Their primary vehicle for doing so was the nominal head of the Armenian Church in the Ottoman Empire, the Patriarchate of Constantinople.

PARTNERS OF THE EMPIRE

To trace the contours of Armenian engagement with and contribution to the Tanzimat, we must first make an effort to understand how Armenians and their institutions participated in imperial governance. Though they did increase the scope of lay participation in communal administration, the charters granted to the non-Muslim communities following the 1856 Reform Edict did not secularize the non-Muslim communities. In the Orthodox case, the Greek Patriarch of Constantinople in fact assumed executive powers it had not previously enjoyed.[10] For the Armenians, the expanding role of the clergy and the Armenian Church in imperial governance overlapped with not only long-term reform projects (which predated the Tanzimat) but also efforts by the imperial state to centralize its administration. The struggles of the community's nominal head, the Armenian Patriarchate of Constantinople, to extend it authority over its flock and other seats in the church hierarchy provide us with insight on the community's role in imperial politics and the stakes over which the introduction of the Armenian Constitution would be fought.

Broadly speaking, the experience of the Armenian Apostolic Church in the Ottoman Empire during the eighteenth and nineteenth centuries mirrors that of the Greek Orthodox Church, a process that Molly Greene has described as a transformation "from patriarch to patriarchate."[11] As others have noted, the authority of the Ecumenical Patriarch of Constantinople was largely tethered to that of the central state.[12] The same argument could be made in the case of the Armenian Patriarch of Constantinople; in fact, the growing authority of the Patriarchate over adherents of the Armenian Apostolic faith across the empire was consonant with efforts made by the central government in Istanbul to expand its own authority. The position was supposedly created by order of Sultan Mehmet II in 1461 when he called his friend Hovakim, the Armenian bishop of Bursa, to the recently conquered capital and invested him with ecclesiastical authority over the nascent empire's Armenian subjects. This narrative does not withstand scrutiny.[13] The earliest evidence of an Armenian clergyman calling himself Patriarch of Constantinople dates only to 1543. More important, the Armenian community of Erzurum successfully petitioned the state for independence from the Patriarch's jurisdiction in 1608. It was not until the seventeenth century and especially the eighteenth century that the Patriarchate began adding dioceses to its ecclesiastical jurisdiction. In 1726, the supreme head of the Armenian Church—the Catholicos of Etchmiadzin—formally recognized the Patriarch of Constantinople as his deputy before the Ottoman government. In the nineteenth century, Etchmiadzin finally transferred authority over all Ottoman Armenian churches and dioceses to the Patriarch. Later that century, Etchmiadzin also ceased sending nuncios to the Ottoman Empire to collect alms, delegating that authority to the Patriarch of Constantinople, who was then responsible for ensuring the transfer of those alms to the Catholicosate. In other words, from this point forward Etchmiadzin ceded its right to interfere in the affairs of the Armenian Church in the Ottoman Empire without first working through Constantinople.

Actors on the ground, who may have previously used connections to Etchmiadzin to challenge Constantinople, thus lost some leverage when bidding to challenge the ecclesiastical authority of the Patriarchate of Constantinople. Those who continued to oppose the expanding authority of the patriarch would still have to do so on ecclesiastical grounds and consequently find themselves challenging the very makeup of Ottoman political and social structures. The authority of the patriarchate was simply not connected to the central state; in part because of processes of confessionalization that had unfolded in the eighteenth century, imperial politics had made the non-Muslim religious institutions partners of the empire. The strengthening of Ottoman non-Muslim communities, much as had been the case in the Habsburg and Russian Empires examples, provided more clearly defined lines of authority—clearly predicated on difference—between ruler and ruled. Both the Habsburgs and the Russians—through the consolidation of rabbinates and partial revival of Jewish civic law in the former, and the institutions of the Orenburg Muslim Spiritual Assembly in the latter—introduced efforts that aimed to integrate subject communities' religious institutions into the imperial administration.[14] The Ottoman case arguably goes further. Because of how far-flung these communities were, particularly in the case of the Greek Orthodox and the Armenians, their ecclesiastical hierarchies could be used not only to facilitate Ottoman rule over the empire's indigenous non-Muslim subjects but also to project Ottoman authority into the provinces.

Whether measured socially, politically, or geographically, the distance between Istanbul—home to both the central state and the patriarchate—was immense. Both the government and the patriarchate were therefore compelled to rely on a different set of intermediaries to help bridge these divides and underwrite their policies. Each institution thus turned to a wealthy and influential group of Armenians called the *amira*s to do precisely that.

CLASS CONFLICT AND IMPERIAL REFORM

The introduction of the *amira*s into our story affords us the opportunity to question a central tenet of the historical literature on the Armenian Constitution—namely, its emphasis on the role of class tensions within the

Armenian community of Istanbul.[15] Certainly, as discussed below, class tension was an important dynamic in Armenian communal politics, particularly outside the capital. Many of the clergymen who would come to the fore as leading champions of reform and the Constitution hailed from families of artisans and guildsmen. And, as we see, manifestations of those tensions in the capital would, in fact, spur some of the institutional reshuffling connected to the Constitution and the Tanzimat. Yet I believe that a discussion of the *amira*s that places them in an imperial context offers an opportunity for revisiting not only the stakes over which Armenian community politics were fought but also the very idea of what a non-Muslim *millet* was in the nexus of Ottoman imperial governance.

How the term *amira* gained meaning in Armenian is not wholly clear. Although it undoubtedly owes its origin to the word *amir* or *emir*, the term for "commander" in Arabic and Ottoman Turkish, respectively, *amira* in Armenian usage had no connection to the military realm.[16] Nor did those who claimed the title *amira* dare to do so outside the confines of the Armenian community. In an Ottoman context, they would have had to content themselves with titles and honorifics such as *bey*, *efendi*, or *pasha*. Their appearance as a discreet class in the imperial capital dates to at least the middle of the eighteenth century. Most *amira*s, if not all, had roots in Akn (Eğin, or present-day Kemaliye near Erzincan), an Armenian town in eastern Anatolia. They seem to have initially made their fortunes through long-distance trade.[17] Upon arrival in Istanbul they used the capital they had accrued to enter one of two realms: banking (*sarrafs*) or government service as technocratic bureaucrats (e.g., director of the imperial mint or as overseers of gunpowder production).

The technocrats among the *amira*s provided the community another point of access to upper echelons of the imperial government. However, it was the bankers who connected them to a wider number of constituencies in imperial governance. Bankers provided the capital that made the *iltizam* system of tax farming, and by extension the functioning of the government, possible. This privileged location in Ottoman society thus allowed the *amira*s to extend their influence over the Patriarchate of Constantinople. The *amira*s found themselves more or less positioned to buy and sell patriarchs as they pleased. Even strong-willed patriarchs, such as Krikor Basmajian (r. 1764–1773) or the politically deft, such as Hagop Nalian (r. 1741–1749, 1752–1764) struggled to repel *amira* influence.[18] *Amira*s could thus use the growing authority of the patriarchate as a mechanism by which they could project their own influence onto the empire-wide Ottoman Armenian community. They did this in large part by having themselves appointed (ostensibly by the patriarch) as trustees, or *mütevelli*, of most Armenian Church properties in the Ottoman Empire.[19] Church properties were not only parish churches but also monasteries (which sometimes also operated as prelacies) and any properties they had come to possess, such as mines or farms. Trustee oversight of church properties meant that the *amira*s controlled the finances of most all Armenian communal institutions.

Across the empire, but most notably in the capital, artisan guilds (*esnaf*) began challenging *amira* command of the community. The most explosive public manifestation of the tension between these two groups was the controversy surrounding funding plans for an Armenian school located in the Üsküdar district of Istanbul.[20] The original plans for the school, which opened in 1838, had been designed by *amira*s, the imperial architects Garabed Amira Balian and Hovhannes Amira Serverian. The school was intended to educate Armenian boys from all social backgrounds. The sons of well-to-do families were to be charged a higher tuition, and the *amira*s pledged to sponsor the education of boys from less affluent families. Moreover, the Patriarchate of Jerusalem had pledged to make an annual payment of 120,000 kuruş to help offset the cost of the school's day-to-day operations. The school was compelled to close in 1841, however, after the *amira*s persuaded the Patriarchate of Jerusalem to cease providing the support it had promised. The imperial government quickly took possession of the building and converted it into a military hospital.

The closing of the school demonstrated the resurgence and resiliency of *amira* influence in both the community and imperial society. The abolition of tax farming in the 1839 Tanzimat decree initially portended trouble for the *amira*s, particularly the bankers among them. Tax farming had provided them not only a windfall but also the opportunity to forge connections with other powerful actors in Ottoman governance. The partial reinstatement of the practice in the 1840s, however, signaled the temporary return of the *amira*s to community leadership. The school's closure was only one in a series of *amira* victories. In 1841, they deposed Patriarch Stepanos Aghavni Zakarian—who had overseen the construction of the school—and replaced him with their own candidate, Asdvadzadur II. Less than one year later, they organized the Anatolia and Rumelia Company, which collected taxes at Ottoman ports on behalf of the imperial treasury; this was a clear signal to their coreligionists that *amira* relations with the imperial government had been restored.[21]

As was the case with any non-Muslim elites, the *amiras*' privileged relationship with the government was contingent, in part, on their ability to maintain tranquility within their own community. Introduction of the Üsküdar school had presented guildsmen and other nonelite Armenians the promise of social mobility by offering their children the opportunity to acquire the skills necessary to participate in a reorganized imperial society. The guildsmen thus did not take the closure of the school in stride; they organized a series of anti-*amira* demonstrations that were joined by labor migrants—many of whom hailed from the eastern provinces and worked as porters near the Grand Bazaar—with whom they shared a working space. These anti-*amira* actions thus threatened to disrupt one of the capital's most important commercial centers. The guildsmen also submitted petitions to the government that used the language of the Tanzimat to denounce the *amira*s. Eventually, the government intervened. Although the authorities did arrest some guildsmen, the tumult had demonstrated the ineffectiveness of *amira* communal leadership. The government thus pressured the *amira*s to grant some concessions to the guildsmen through the institution of changes in the community administration. These changes included the installation of Matteos Chukhajian, a "well-known partisan for the people" against *amira* influence, as Patriarch of Constantinople in 1844.[22]

PATRIARCH TO PATRIARCHATE

The *amira*s would eventually engineer Chukhajian's removal from office. Yet the levers they ultimately had to pull to do so would demonstrate not only how much their influence had waned but also the extent to which Chukhajian's four-year reign had transformed the administration of the patriarchate. Chukhajian's efforts would, in large part, complete the transformation of the patriarch into a patriarchate that could legitimately claim ecclesiastical authority over all institutions of the Armenian Apostolic Church throughout the Ottoman Empire. This reorganization of the community would lay the institutional groundwork for the eventual introduction of the Armenian Constitution a decade and a half later.

Chukhajian understood that the Patriarchate of Constantinople, particularly from the eighteenth century forward, drew its legitimacy and importance as a political institution in Ottoman governance from three sources: the ecclesiastical hierarchy of the Armenian Apostolic Church, recourse to the coercive force of the Sublime Porte and the imperial government, and the brokerage furnished by *amira* financial and political capital. Ultimately, of course, the community was defined in confessional terms; the ecclesiastical was bundled together with the political and social. Chukhajian, who wished to excise the role of *amira* capital as a broker in these relations, could bid to do so by turning to the confessional and ecclesiastical. He thus looked to the Catholicosate of all Armenians in Etchmiadzin for support.

Constantinople's claim to ecclesiastical authority over Ottoman Armenian religious institutions was tenuous. Most other major seats of the Armenian Church traced their history back to Armenian kingdoms and, as a result, had fashioned arrangements that ensured a functional hierarchy that could preserve the Church's unity. That the Patriarchate of Constantinople had been created by the Sunni Muslim Ottomans cast doubt on these arrangements. As stated earlier, Etchmiadzin had only recognized Constantinople as its deputy to the Ottoman government in 1726. Yet the significance of this recognition seems to have waned over the years, and relations between Constantinople and Etchmiadzin fell into disrepair. In response to the Russo-Turkish War of 1828–29, the Patriarchate had actually ceased remembering the name of the Catholicos during the liturgy.[23] The failure to do so was an affront to the hierarchy of the Church, and could have been interpreted as either an act of rebellion by Constantinople or a declaration of independence from the Mother See. Chukhajian thus set about repairing that relationship as part of his effort to wrest control from the *amira*s. Within two months of his enthronement, Chukhajian issued an encyclical to the churches under his authority that mandated they remember the name of the Catholicos of All Armenians during the liturgy.[24] He then submitted a formal letter of submission to the Catholicos whereby he pledged his fealty to the Church and its laws. The Catholicos, in turn, conferred Chukhajian with the Order of St. Anna and reaffirmed Etchmiadzin's recognition of Constantinople as its representative before the Ottoman government.

The importance of this reaffirmation must not be understated. With recognition as Etchmiadzin's deputy in hand, the Patriarchate now acted with ecclesiastical and spiritual legitimacy when extending its authority over other Church seats in the Ottoman Empire. The Catholicosate of Cilicia, for example, would now find itself in violation of Etchmiadzin's dictates should it bid to challenge the authority of Constantinople. Constantinople could, in turn, pair that legitimacy with the coercion offered by the Sublime Porte to partner with the imperial state in reshaping imperial governance and, in the process, pursue its own institution building without needing to rely on the mediating role of the *amira*s. In 1847, Chukhajian oversaw the introduction of two new institutions into the administration of the patriarchate—the Supreme Council (*geragoyn zhoghov*) and the Spiritual Council (*hogevor zhoghov*).[25] Only clergymen sat on the latter council, which bore the responsibility of adjudicating questions of religion. The former, however, consisted of twenty laymen, the spots to be divided equally between the *amira*s and the guildsmen. In other words, Chukhajian had secured a formal stake in the management of communal affairs for the guilds.

The introduction of councils came on the heels of other victories scored by Chukhajian. These victories emphasized the extent to which he as patriarch and the patriarchate as an institution had freed themselves from a dependency on the mediation of the *amira*s with the imperial government. In 1845, for example, Chukhajian managed to ingratiate himself to the imperial government when attempted to assuage interconfessional animosity between the empire's non-Muslim communities.[26] This acrimony had been stoked in large part by the politics of each community's elite and their corresponding connections to contending political factions in the upper echelons of Ottoman society.[27] These tensions had, in fact, erupted in occasional episodes of violence. These efforts endeared Chukhajian to some in the government, whom he later approached to request the reopening of the school in Üsküdar. The Sublime Porte subsequently returned the building to the Armenian community, where instruction resumed in October 1845.[28]

The *amira*s had little to celebrate when they finally managed to depose Chukhajian in 1848. They did so by ensnaring him in a scandal. The *amira*s demanded he reveal the identity of Garabed Amira Balian, an imperial architect, who had made an anonymous donation to the patriarchate. Chukhajian's refusal to do so placed him at odds with the Supreme Council, which enjoyed jurisdiction over patriarchal finances. The Porte ultimately agreed with the *amira*s and demanded Chukhajian's resignation, which he did in September. His farewell address invoked early Christian martyrs.[29] Just as they had sacrificed for the faith, Chukhajian had given his tenure to reform. Even in defeat, however, Chukhajian had won. The Supreme Council that ultimately toppled him—as well as its successor under the Constitution, the Political Council—would be the engine of reform within the community over the next four decades.

MOVING BEYOND CLASS TENSION

To this point, I have largely built upon the consensus that class tension within the Armenian community was a primary catalyst for eventually bringing about the Constitution in particular, and reform in general, in the Ottoman Armenian community. This approach is understandably persuasive. In fact, many of the staunchest proponents of reform, particularly in the provinces, hailed from nonelite backgrounds and were oftentimes the sons of guildsmen. These men used the introduction of the Constitution in 1860 as an opportunity to pressure the local well-to-do, much as had been the case between the guilds and the *amira*s in the capital. Yet limiting the scope of this analysis to class tension among Armenians reinforces a national narrative that enjoys some autonomy from an imperial context.[30] Most work on the Constitution to this point has, after all, treated the subject as a key component of Armenian national identity formation. But taking a closer look at those who helped shepherd reform—both that over which Chukhajian presided in the 1840s and the Constitution itself—muddles this picture. Doing so encourages us to rethink the political stakes over which Armenian reform battles were fought and, more important, to revisit how a non-Muslim community functioned in imperial governance.

I do not mean to dismiss the importance of class tension. Not only were Chukhajian's anti-*amira* sentiments genuine, the pressure applied by the guilds did facilitate significant transformation in the community's administration, as we have seen. Yet Chukhajian's principal ally in the introduction of reform was Hagop Grjigian, a bureaucrat and moneylender who hailed from *amira* circles.[31] Grjigian won the friendship and confidence of the father of the Tanzimat, Reşid Pasha, whom he accompanied to London and Paris when the latter served as the Ottoman Empire's ambassador to England and France. Reşid Pasha later brought Grjigian to work in the Sublime Porte as an adviser and translator. It was ultimately Grjigian who persuaded Reşid Pasha to authorize the introduction of the Supreme and Spiritual Councils into the administration of the patriarchate in 1847. Only after Grjigian had done so was Chukhajian invited to the Porte to discuss these reforms with a protégé of Reşid Pasha, Ali Efendi. Thereafter, Chukhajian convened an assembly at the patriarchate, where he announced that reform had been introduced by imperial order.

Grjigian would not be the first or only pro-reform Armenian of *amira* background (or recipient of *amira* patronage) with deep ties to the Porte. In 1853, an auxiliary council on education was introduced into the administration of the patriarchate, which became a platform for a new cohort of Armenians connected to the Porte to pursue projects of reform. Members included Servichen Efendi (Serovpe Vichenian), the son of a banker; Nigoghos Balian, a son of the imperial architect who had made the initial plans for the Üsküdar school; and Krikor Efendi Odian, the future statesman who would collaborate with Midhat Pasha to write the 1876 Ottoman Constitution and hailed from a family that Balian patronage had ushered into public service. Along with others connected to the Porte, these Armenians would be the primary authors and stewards of the Armenian Constitution.

Class did constitute a significant divide in the community, as made clear by its social and cultural manifestations. *Amira*s were multilingual, traveled abroad for their education, lived in palatial estates along the Bosporus, and interacted with government ministers and sultans. Guildsmen, meanwhile, possessed crude epistolary skills, toiled in bazaars where they mingled with some of the most impoverished of their coreligionists daily. Yet the apparent transgression of that boundary by successive cohorts of Armenians compels us to rethink the political stakes of the community's internal contention. Control of community institutions was not, as others have argued, simply a consolation prize for prosperous Armenians who were otherwise unable to express their prestige politically.[32] Rather, the recurrent interventions by the Porte in internal Armenian affairs—at the behest of these well-to-do Armenian and ostensibly on behalf of the guildsmen—conveys that the opposite was true.

MILLET AS NETWORKED AND COMMUNAL SPACE

I contend that the totality of things Armenian in the Ottoman Empire—the Church, its institutions, its adherents, and their wealth and capital—is best understood as a networked communal space. Reconceptualizing the community as such makes it possible to understand why Armenian political contention was so explosive; the stakes of reform, such as the Constitution; and how Armenians contributed to endowing the Tanzimat with meaning. It also explains why non-Armenian forces, such as the Sublime Porte or the various provincial powerbrokers—namely, Türkmen *derebey*s and Kurdish tribal leaders, as discussed in Chapters 3 and 4—became partisans in the conflicts over Armenian reform that was ostensibly internal to the community. Before examining the consequences of this for how we understand Ottoman history, I will explain what made the Armenians of the Ottoman Empire a space, communal, and networked.

The overlap of these three components made the community a dynamic feature of Ottoman society and an important player in imperial governance.

Membership in a religious community in the Ottoman context must not be reduced to the simple confession of faith, though this was important. A religion's claim to spiritual authority over adherents is universal. In Ottoman governance, this universalism mapped onto the boundaries of the empire to produce a legal category. Although the meaning of this category could be contested, given contingencies of time and place, religion ultimately inscribed the subjectivity of its adherents as both Ottoman subjects and, in the case examined here, Armenians. This universalism also provided members of the Armenian Apostolic Church a road map, dotted by familiar signposts, for navigating Ottoman politics and society. Yet these signposts—the holy sacraments, the Church calendar, holidays, Sunday liturgy, a parish church as a physical place, the clergy and its hierarchy, among others—also helped in part to homogenize Armenians' experiences as an imperial and subject community.

The pressure exerted by these influences was varied and uneven, but did produce a "religion-space" that was culturally, socially, and politically Armenian. Armenians occupied this space wherever they found themselves in the Ottoman Empire and could leave it only through conversion or emigration. Spatial history challenges the hegemony of center-periphery analysis by highlighting the porosity of borders.[33] Because of its internal heterogeneity and porous borders, the communal space merged into other similar spaces in its imperial setting. The religious community as a space was, as noted, defined in part by the limits of the Ottoman polity. To enforce markers of difference and police communal boundaries, the Ottoman state shared imperial sovereignty with non-Muslim religious institutions. Familiar signposts, such as the clergy, churches, or monasteries, did not simply organize Armenian action for engaging with Ottoman governance. As conduits for the transmission of Ottoman power, institutions of the Armenian Church structured the Armenian communal space and helped shape the terms of its interaction with other forces in imperial society. This investment of sovereignty in the Armenian Church made its institutions nodes around which power, prestige, and wealth would accumulate, and thus act as a primary point of contact between the Armenian community and others in Ottoman society. The charge to enforce regimes of difference invested the Armenian Church in the status quo and encouraged its clergy to build interconfessional alliances in both local and regional contexts. As examples in the following chapters will illustrate, more intrepid clergymen skillfully exploited the location of Church institutions in this setting to build relationships with other notable power brokers and institutions at local and imperial levels.

Churches, monasteries, and other Armenian religious institutions thus acted as an adhesive by which the Armenian community could connect itself with other formations in Ottoman society. The ability to forge interconfessional relationships that integrated religious institutions into local society located the Armenian community in network structures of power. Tension internal to the community thus portended the possibility for reorganizing those networks responsible for structuring imperial governance and society. Not only Armenians, therefore, had a vested interest in Armenian politics. Yet the networked features of the Armenian community did not simply manifest locally. Armenian ecclesiastics and the peripatetic careers of some clergymen produced another set of networks that traversed the empire-wide community. The clustering of networked power around Armenian religious institutions thus had outlets to numerous sites throughout the empire. Armenian networks possessed the ability to disseminate various forms of capital, power, and control. The communal space did not simply embed Armenians in imperial society, but also enjoyed the potential to help suture multilayered sites of imperial power.

NETWORKED COMMUNAL SPACE AND IMPERIAL GOVERNANCE

The late Hagop Barsoumian has done the most to advance our thinking on the *amiras* and the roles they played in Ottoman imperial governance and society. While his work argues that the *amiras* constituted a discrete class in Istanbul, he does not explain how the two groups he identifies among their ranks—bankers and bureaucrats—ever cultivated a set of shared interests that they collectively defended as a social class. Thinking of the *millet* not only as a series of arrangements through which the Ottomans ruled over non-Muslims but also as a networked space that was key to the fashioning of imperial politics brings the *amiras*' interests vis-à-vis community institutions into sharper focus.

Ottoman imperial governance underwent a paradigm shift in the eighteenth century as the state began efforts to centralize its administration. In particular, it endeavored to pioneer new strategies for extending Istanbul's authority over powerful regional actors in the provinces. One such strategy was a growing emphasis on confessional markers of difference. In particular, it was during this period that official Islam came to occupy an increasingly central role in imperial governance as the empire transitioned to a limited monarchy.[34] This emphasis on confessional markers placed subjects into more easily identifiable categories for administrative purposes. As Molly Greene pointed out, this "confessionalization" of imperial governance was also part of the state's efforts to identify new partners.[35] As such, the Ecumenical Patriarch of Constantinople owed its transformation from "patriarch to patriarchate" to its partnership with the imperial government. Much like in the Armenian case, the Istanbul-based Ecumenical Patriarchate witnessed an increase in its ecclesiastical authority over the course of the eighteenth and nineteenth centuries.

In the Armenian case, this period witnessed not only the expansion of the authority enjoyed by the Armenian Patriarchate of Constantinople but also the rise of the *amira*s as moneylenders and bureaucrats. These developments were not mutually exclusive. Armenian clergymen, scattered as they were throughout the empire in villages, cities, and remote monasteries, were positioned to forge relations with powerful actors near them. The ecclesiastical hierarchy of the Church, which theoretically governed these clergymen, promised to be a powerful tool in the hands of a variety of actors. For the central state, as discussed in the Greek Orthodox case, it could be used to police communal boundaries as part of an effort to place imperial subjects into more clearly defined categories. Yet the imperial state also stood to benefit from monitoring these clergymen, who had likely forged alliances with some of the very power brokers whom the government wished to influence. Finally, as financiers of the state and its tax-collecting regime, Armenian moneylenders stood to benefit from access to clergymen throughout the empire who not only could report on their business partners' activities but also might participate in the work of collecting those taxes.

In other words, the patriarchate, both the banker *amira*s and the technocrats (state employees who wished to preserve their relations with high-ranking government officials), and the imperial state were all allied in the project of state centralization. It was not just the Patriarchate of Constantinople that had been a partner of the central state; as a networked space, the entire empire-wide Armenian community was also a partner. Beginning in the second half of the eighteenth century and continuing into the nineteenth, the banker *amira*s were the near-exclusive financiers of both the Porte and the Palace. Even outside the capital, Armenian capital was deployed on the side of the central state and its partisans. Manuk Bey Mirzaian's relationship with Bayraktar Mustafa Pasha, who jostled with Janissary-affiliated notables for influence in the Balkans, is perhaps the best-known example of this. In fact, Armenians expressed contempt for the Porte's enemies—namely, the Janissaries—in the rare instances they permitted themselves to comment on non-Armenian actors in Ottoman politics.[36]

The contours of an "*amira* politics" that extended beyond the confines of either the community or the imperial capital thus become increasingly clear. The Armenian community brokered numerous relationships—economic, religious, social, and cultural—that influenced the ebb and flow of governance between the capital and the provinces. This positioned the clergy and the *amiras* to partner with the Sublime Porte in a mutually beneficial iteration of governance that tugged the threads of empire toward the capital. Banker and technocrat *amira* alike were therefore both invested in their support of the government (against other claimants on imperial politics) and the preservation of Armenian Church institutions as a broker. Unsurprisingly, the government therefore took a heavy hand against the community's leadership when it failed to handle a series of ecclesiastical challenges instigated by high-profile conversions to Catholicism. The departure of elite Armenians from the Apostolic fold threatened to slice the number of connections the community marshaled and thereby weaken its role in imperial governance.[37] This, in turn, weakened the government.

Amira politics was imperial insomuch as it sought to ensure that the benefits of empire flowed to the top. The *amiras* and the clergy ultimately helped the state manage a networked imperial society. To aid that effort, it was the *amiras*—with the backing of the government—that took steps not only to expand patriarchal authority, but also codify the community's ecclesiastical organization through a series of statutes introduced between 1824 and 1830.[38] The role of the Armenian Church and its hierarchy in imperial governance, however, would shift as the Sublime Porte reformulated its centralization policies from management toward, in the words of anthropologist James Scott, gridding and legibility. The ensuing tension in the Armenian community produced by this shift did not simply reverberate along class divisions; it also brought to the fore two contending visions of imperial governance. One bid to preserve the networking world of governance to which *amira* politics belonged, which had strengthened the Patriarchate of Constantinople as part of an effort to bring together Armenian clergymen, merchants, and bankers together with Muslim landlords, governors, and tax collectors in a complex system of power sharing arrangements. The other vision aimed to deepen the community's partnership with the state through a rigorous ecclesiastical reorganization. The internal contention of the Armenian community, which regularly found expression ecclesiastically, was not simply integrated into an imperial framework; it was itself an articulation of imperial politics. The various regulatory charters, statutes, or constitutions that Armenians produced ostensibly for their own internal consumption were Armenian contributions to Ottoman law.

INTRODUCING A CONSTITUTION

The transformations of imperial governance during the nineteenth century ushered in a recalibration of political alliances in both the Armenian community and the empire at large. Although pressure from the Istanbul-based guilds had compelled the community and the Sublime Porte to authorize the introduction of new councils into the *millet* administration prior to 1856, no guildsmen enter the record as leaders of reform. That role was instead played by their new allies, Porte-employed Armenians hailing from *amira* families, who used the new councils as a platform for pioneering reform. These Armenian statesmen, whom others have wrongly considered Armenian equivalents of the Young Ottomans, were well placed to tackle the various obstacles—social, political, and ecclesiastical—to reform that would be erected by their opponents.[39]

The 1856 Reform Edict was not a watershed for the Armenians. Communal reform and the attendant reordering of political alliances was already afoot. The edict did reenergize reform efforts, however, and provided a new impetus for drawing up community regulations. Armenians began drafting more comprehensive regulations for the community shortly after the edict's announcement. *Amira*s, such as members of the *bartçubaşı* Dadian family, used their influence with the government to prevent the implementation of these early drafts.[40] Pressure mounted on the community leadership to produce a new set of regulations. This led to the elevation of Servichen Efendi, a confidant of the prominent Tanzimat statesman Fuad Pasha, to the Supreme Council in 1858. Servichen was a well-known constitutionalist who convinced the Supreme Council in May 1859 to create a special Constitutional Committee that would evaluate the previous proposals. This committee, which included Krikor Odian, ultimately authored the Constitution.[41]

The reigning Patriarch of Constantinople, Kevork Kerestejian, was an arch conservative who abhorred any effort to constrain the clergy's prerogatives. Sensing the direction being charted by the Sublime Porte and its employees on the Supreme Council, Kerestejian tendered his resignation on April 21, 1860. He was replaced by Bishop Sarkis Kuyumjian, who approved the Constitution and submitted it to the Porte for ratification a little more than a month after

Kerestejian's resignation. On May 24, an assembly of clergymen convened at the patriarchate, where they declared that the Constitution did not violate the laws of the Armenian Church. The Supreme Council subsequently endorsed the document, at which point the Constitution became the law governing the *millet*.

THE CONSTITUTION

Although the Constitution's primary authors hailed from Istanbul and the *amira* class, the text they drafted reflected many of the concerns of their non-elite allies from the provinces. Despite the wide cultural gap, Armenians from the provinces—particularly clergymen—and the well-to-do of the imperial capital were somewhat familiar with each other.[42] Those among the prosperous who embraced the Ottoman state's centralization policies most tightly forged relationships with provincial reformers, especially ones investing their efforts in education. The authors of the Constitution were probably well aware of capital's circulation through the networked space of the community and how it negatively impacted the vast majority of provincial Armenians.

Because of the condensation of power around Armenian Church institutions, provincial Armenians stood—in theory—to benefit from some regulation of the clergy. Provincial Armenians had bemoaned clergymen's abuses for some time but lacked any real mechanism to seek redress. Ordination to the holy orders and the culture of monasteries provided the clergy a great deal of autonomy over their own affairs and set them even further apart from their flock; of course this only widened the gap between provincial Armenians and the local government. In this regard, the interests of most provincial Armenians coincided with those of the reformers and their goal of centralizing the state. The ecclesiastical reorganization of the Church promised to benefit both parties.

Laymen have participated in the administration of the Armenian Church since its founding in the early fourth century. Nineteenth-century Armenians had to grapple with the question of deciding which laymen would participate. In earlier decades, the *amira*s had deployed a number of strategies for precluding the involvement of others to ensure that they would be the primary beneficiaries of the Armenian community's share of sovereignty. The Constitution produced a National Administration that comprised a Religious Council, a Political Council, and a National Assembly that would seat Armenian representatives from all over the Ottoman Empire.[43] The National Assembly bore the responsibility of electing the Patriarchate of Constantinople. Only Ottoman Armenians who had been consecrated bishop by the Catholicos of Etchmiadzin would be eligible for the position of patriarch. The National Administration was reproduced at the provincial level; the lone difference was the establishment of a Provincial Assembly in place of the National Assembly.[44] The Provincial Assembly, elected by popular vote, in turn selected both its own representatives to the National Assembly and, more important, a prelate. The prelate would then be subordinate to the Patriarchate of Constantinople and be charged with representing the community—which now enjoyed a check on him and his position—to the local government. Because authority flowed from the Sublime Porte and the Patriarchate, local actors could also appeal to the imperial capital if a prelate or other well-entrenched clergyman failed to conform to constitutional standards. Pro-reform Armenians all over the empire, but especially in Van and Erzurum, seized this opportunity in a bid to wrest control of community institutions from well-connected clergymen and monasteries, which suggests that provincial reformers' experiences were reflected in the language of the Constitution.

In theory, the Constitution removed the intermediary role played by *amira*s and their capital and replaced it with formal lines of authority that furnished individual Armenians with greater access to the official government. This portended the transformation of the communal space into a *millet* that was a gridded political community. For the reformers, this change made the *millet* a partner in the Tanzimat and the programs of centralization. By providing the community control over its own institutions and linking them to offices of the official government, clergymen and other actors such as bankers and merchants would have fewer opportunities to participate in informal networks of power. As such, Muslim opponents of centralization would also find themselves with fewer options to resist the policies of the Sublime Porte. This is how the Constitution and the reformers would attempt to change Ottoman society.

Resting at the heart of this reform and the redistribution of imperial sovereignty was the creation of a more clearly defined Ottoman Armenian diocese wherein the Patriarchate of Constantinople oversaw a number of prelacies.[45] In other words, the Sublime Porte and its Armenian employees were using the ecclesiastical organization of the Armenian Church to reform the empire and project central authority. Secularization was therefore not a feature of the reform program. Religion did not retreat from the public sphere, but instead became a highly contested site of politics. Opponents of reform who sought to preserve the networking society in which they were embedded would make resort to ecclesiastical challenges to disrupt the reform program. The Patriarchate of Jerusalem and its St. James Monastery would be the first to challenge the legitimacy of the Constitution along these lines.

IMPERIAL REFORM AND ECCLESIASTICAL FAULT LINES

The National Assembly officially opened on August 25, 1860, three months after the Constitution was introduced as the law governing the community. The assembly's first several sessions were rocky. Reformers expended a great deal of energy explaining procedural minutiae to the newly elected members. Some representatives graced the assembly with self-laudatory speeches. It was not until the November 4 session when the first real item of business, the St. James Monastery at the Patriarchate of Jerusalem and the debt it had accrued, appeared on the assembly's agenda.[46] Jerusalem's resistance to Constantinople's centralization efforts would provide other opponents of reform a framework for disrupting the implementation of the Constitution.

As guardian of the Holy Places, the Patriarchate of Jerusalem occupied a place in the Armenian Church and its administration. Pilgrimage to the Holy Land, facilitated in large measure by the presence of Armenian institutions, was a religious act that could connote both spiritual and social standing. For the laity, many upper-class Armenians bore the title *mahdesi*, or some derivation thereof—a corruption of the Arabic term *muqaddasah*. For the clergy, membership in the Brotherhood of St. James carried a cachet that other orders did not. Priests who had entered the clergy at Jerusalem did tend to possess an erudition that their counterparts elsewhere lacked, were more likely to host and interact with both pilgrims and dignitaries from all over the world, and likely traveled with some regularity. Moreover, donations from wealthy patrons all over the Ottoman Empire meant that Armenian clergymen from Jerusalem were charged with overseeing and operating the daily activities of a large enterprise. Despite these holdings, which included significant amounts of real estate in Istanbul, the Patriarchate of Jerusalem had accrued significant debt. Ibrahim Pasha's assaults on the Levant in the 1830s had disrupted Jerusalem's administration, led to the loss of properties in the holy city, and resulted in St. James falling behind on its tax obligations. The monastery's financial problems threatened to compound these problems by not only endangering the presence of the Armenian Church in Jerusalem but also portending the possible forfeiture of Church properties throughout the empire.

The mismanagement of finances was the justification the Porte-employed reformers needed to intervene in the internal administration of the Patriarchate of Jerusalem and the Order of St. James. The unexpected death of Hovhannes Movsesian on December 23, 1860, provided the reformers an opportunity. During his decade-long reign as Patriarch of Jerusalem, Movsesian had thumbed his nose at Constantinople by refusing an order to pay down Jerusalem's debts and twice ignoring calls to report to the capital.[47] The vacancy resulting from Movsesian's death afforded the reformers the chance to place an individual of their own choosing on the patriarchal throne. Claiming that they needed to stabilize Jerusalem's situation in advance of Easter, when pilgrimage numbers would be at their highest, the reformers rushed to appoint a locum tenens patriarch. At the behest of the Political Council—comprised almost entirely of Porte-employed or Porte-affiliated Armenian reformers—the National Administration introduced a set of regulations that would require Jerusalem to receive Constantinople's consent before selling any of its properties. These regulations did not stop at real estate. Ominously for Jerusalem, they gave Constantinople the right to select Jerusalem's patriarch and to administer its finances.

The members of the Order of St. James had no desire in supporting Constantinople's assaults on their autonomy. In open defiance of Constantinople, they immediately elected their own patriarch—an election the National Administration swiftly nullified. They also fired off missives to Constantinople to express their objections to the regulations and the program of centralization. Their arguments took two tacks. One sought to reduce the program of reform to "illumination" and learning.[48] Jerusalem contributed to Armenian letters through its monastery, which produced some of the most learned Armenian clergymen in the Ottoman Empire, and its press. In other words, there was no reason for Constantinople to extend the reform program to Jerusalem. More important, however, Jerusalem sought to dissociate itself from other antireform actors who had earned reputations for abusing their positions.

The second tack was more effective. In particular, Jerusalem invoked the Anathema of Karapet II (Catholicos of All Armenians, r. 1726–1729), which stipulated that whoever held the position of Patriarch of Jerusalem be a member of the Order of St. James. Although recourse to "illumination" was abstract, the invocation of an anathema struck at Constantinople's claim to ecclesiastical authority. Moreover, it rallied conservative clergymen who resented the curbs placed by the Constitution on their prerogatives and encouraged them to bog down the work of the National Administration. Caught flatfooted by ecclesiastical and canonical technicalities, the Porte-affiliate members of the Political Council watched helplessly as emboldened clergy attempted to reinterpret all aspects of community politics as questions of religion, and therefore subordinate to the jurisdiction of the priests sitting on the Religious Council. Then, on August 2, 1861, a hastily organized and unofficial meeting of bishops issued its opinion that ruled against Constantinople's decision to install its own candidate as Patriarch of Jerusalem.[49] The bishops added that a Patriarch of Jerusalem need not be a bishop but must be a member of the Order of St. James.

Sarkis, the Patriarch of Constantinople, found the bishops' argumentation persuasive and sided with them. His decision to do so left members of the Political Council, who had worked to elevate Sarkis to his post, feeling betrayed. By endorsing the bishops' arguments, Sarkis had opted to restore a feature of Church governance that had facilitated the networking world that conservatives sought to preserve. The elements that composed the bishops' main stipulation—that a non-bishop from Jerusalem could become Patriarch without Constantinople's consent—ensured that monastery politics, which were connected to forces beyond the community, would dictate the administration of Jerusalem and that Constantinople would have no viable check over whatever course of action St. James might charter. The whole aim of the Constitution was thus undermined. Disoriented by this turn of events, Servichen, one of the leading reformers, forged an impromptu alliance with the former Patriarch of Constantinople, Kevork Kerestejian, who had resigned in protest of the Constitution one year earlier. Kerestejian had, in fact, ingratiated himself to the reformers by initially taking their side in the Jerusalem controversy. In return, the reformers tabbed Kerestejian as the next Patriarch of Jerusalem.

Although Servichen likely thought the alliance had substance, Kerestejian exploited the partnership to further undermine the Constitution. Together they convened an emergency session of the National Assembly on August 5, 1861, three days after the bishops' meeting.[50] Announcements for the emergency session included the proviso that "the honor of the Constitution and the National Administration" was at stake. During this emergency session, the National Assembly declared the bishops' meeting an illegal gathering, ruled its judgment null, and accused Patriarch Sarkis of violating the Constitution. The next day, the members of the Political Council traveled to the Sublime Porte to have an audience with Prime Minister Ali Pasha.[51] Servichen and the Armenian reformers likely believed that their allies at the Porte would help them dethrone Sarkis. Little did the reformers realize that Kerestejian, who later endorsed the August 2 meeting of the bishops, had already won. By exploiting the Jerusalem controversy to bring conflict between the conservative members of the clergy and the reformers out into the open, he had publicly embarrassed the latter and demonstrated the shortcomings of the Constitution. On August 6, 1861, Patriarch Sarkis was called to the Porte. Rather than demand his resignation, the government simply informed him of its decision to suspend the Constitution.

CONCLUSION: REDISTRIBUTING POWER IN THE COMMUNAL SPACE

The government did not withdraw the Constitution because it formed a state within a state, as some might argue; had this been the case, the Sublime Porte would have never authorized the reinstitution of a revised Constitution that afforded the Patriarchate of Constantinople even more regulatory power. The Armenian reformers remained in contact with their allies in the Sublime Porte, which organized a commission to draft a new constitution in January 1862.[52] The following month, the Porte reconvened the suspended National Assembly to select members to add to the commission, who subsequently participated in revising the Constitution.[53] A draft was ultimately submitted in February 1862.

The draft, which became law in March 1863, included a letter to the Porte from the commission members dated February 18, 1862.[54] This letter is a useful primer for understanding the differences between the 1860 and 1863 versions of the Armenian Constitution. The letter pleads for a simplification of the processes and institutions produced by the Constitution, highlighting in particular the need to give a clearer definition to the National Assembly, its role, and its membership. It also suggested the need to expand the role of the Political Council to preempt controversies such as that exacerbated by the meeting of bishops on August 2, 1861. Finally, it reemphasized the sources of legitimacy on which the National Administration and the Patriarchate of Constantinople rested—namely, maintaining the *millet*'s loyalty to the state, remaining just toward "the nation," and not finding itself in opposition to the Catholicosate of Etchmiadzin.[55]

The new Constitution consisted of 99 articles, a significant decrease from the 150 that had been in the original. This reduction masks the expansion of central prerogatives in the regulation of communal affairs. Most obvious among these is a new section (Articles 17–22) dedicated to the Patriarchate of Jerusalem that walked the tightrope of respecting the Anathema of Karapet II while granting Constantinople the right to select the Patriarch of Jerusalem. Yet it also accounts for the implications of the challenge posed by Jerusalem.

As part of the effort to expand the authority of the Political Council, the new Constitution placed a number of newly created subcouncils under its jurisdiction, including councils on education; courts; finances; and, most important, monasteries. Although Jerusalem was a patriarchate, it was first and foremost a monastery with its own order. The internal politics of this order ultimately insulated it from central authority, as its rival factions could connect to non-Armenian political forces to further embed these institutions in imperial society. The wealth and prestige of Jerusalem was exceptional, but all major monasteries—particularly those recognized as the seats of prelacies by the Statutes of 1824, 1826, and 1830—were similarly embedded in local and imperial networks of power. In this respect, the challenge authored by Jerusalem against the Constitution in 1860–61 threatened to provide other monasteries a template to follow. The 1863 Constitution preempted this possibility by providing the Porte-affiliated members of the Political Council the right not only to interfere in monastery finances but also to select monastery abbots. In other words, authority over all community institutions passed into the hands of the Armenian employees of the Porte in the Political Council.

This redistribution of power from the network-embedded monasteries to the Patriarchate of Constantinople and the Political Council found its most clear expression in Article 95 of the Constitution. Article 95, which outlined the provincial administration of the *millet*, forbade a monastery abbot from serving as prelate. Because it cut the final threads that connected monasteries to both local power brokers and *amira* support, Article 95 made it possible to transform the *millet* into a gridded community in which peripheries (provincial prelacies) were subordinate to a center (the Patriarchate of Constantinople), one in which a peasant theoretically enjoyed a clear line of communication to a governor (via a provincial prelate) or a Grand Vizier (via the patriarch).

These intertwined components of the provincial administration as delineated by the Armenian Constitution—the removal of monasteries from local networks of power and the pairing of ecclesiastical bodies with the imperial bureaucracy—placed Armenian reformers on the frontlines of the state's centralization. Reorganization of the Armenian community did not simply help to extend the bureaucracy into the provinces; by removing communal institutions from networks of power, Armenian reformers also undercut the ability of potential opponents of state centralization—such as provincial notables—to activate relationships that could facilitate a rejection of the reform program. In this respect, the introduction of the Armenian Constitution captures how the role of a non-Muslim community in imperial governance changed in accordance with the state's agenda. While once seminal to the fashioning of a networking society in which different claimants on the empire's politics shared sovereignty, the transformation of the Armenian communal space into a proper *millet* now bolstered the state's efforts to isolate each of those groups. Communal divisions subsequently deepened not along the lines of national mobilization or Ottoman loyalty, but instead along two contending visions of Ottoman governance.

The partnership between the state and the community so reconfigured integrated Armenian Church canon into the corpus of texts that comprised the Tanzimat reforms. In such a setting, the question of who enjoyed the right to ordain a priest or consecrate the Holy Chrism remained consequential. It also meant that actors who wished to disrupt the reform program could make recourse to the culture and tradition of the Armenian Church to do so. Sometimes, as the Jerusalem example demonstrated, an anathema could do the trick. More frequently, they would pull other levers.

2 NODAL GOVERNANCE AND THE OTTOMAN DIOCESE

AS THE ARTICLES OF THE REVISED CONSTITUTION show, the Armenian reformers had learned their lesson from the controversy instigated by Jerusalem's resort to Armenian Church canon and anathemas. For the 1863 version of their document, the reformers crafted language that would preempt future attempts by conservatives to mount challenges that exploited the more chaotic elements of Armenian ecclesiastics and its feudal antecedents. It was precisely the diffuse character of the administration of the Armenian Church in the Ottoman Empire that had allowed major church seats and monasteries to establish deep roots in imperial society and governance. Bishop Esayi Talastsi, the Patriarch of Jerusalem, bid to preserve precisely that order of things when the reformers called him to the imperial capital in 1865. Those deep roots had contributed to the Armenian community's role as a partner in governance that participated in the exercise of Ottoman imperial sovereignty. I argue that the order of what Esayi and other conservatives defended was a phenomenon called *networked nodal governance*.

An example from the other side of the empire brings into relief the stakes over which Jerusalem and the reformers battled. The Armenians of Khanjalis, a small village near the town of Başkale that was tucked into the Ottoman-Qajar frontier, had suffered dispossession at the hands of local Muslim notables. The Timurzade clan, a powerful family that exerted tremendous influence between Van and the border, had exploited the 1858 Ottoman Land Code to claim ownership of the village's land, after which they evicted the native Armenian population and settled members of an allied Kurdish tribe in their stead.

The plight of Khanjalis comes to us from a report composed by Bishop Eremia Tevkants in the course of his travels to the Armenian communities of the eastern provinces in the early 1870s.[1] Tevkants had been deputized by the Patriarchate of Constantinople to compile information on Armenians, survey their condition, and enforce the implementation of the Constitution. While his report expresses nothing short of contempt for the Timurzades, he devotes more attention to the clergy responsible for shepherding the community at Khanjalis. The monastery that enjoyed jurisdiction over Khanjalis, Holy Apostles, was an anomaly in the Armenian Church administration of the Ottoman Empire. The abbot of this monastery was appointed not by the Patriarch of Constantinople, as was typical, but by the Catholicos of Etchmiadzin in the Russian Empire. The internal politics of the clergy were thus directed toward the Catholicosate rather than the Patriarchate and all the connections to imperial governance it could offer. Holy Apostles Monastery constituted a jurisdictional black hole that was not just disconnected from the Patriarchate of Constantinople (and, through it, the Sublime Porte) but also the empire-wide communal space that vaulted clergymen to positions of prestige and through which Armenians made claims on imperial politics.

Their seemingly divergent experiences aside, both Khanjalis and Jerusalem illustrate a dynamic key for understanding how Armenians and their institutions were woven into the tapestry of Ottoman imperial society and participated in its governance: employing difference to make claims was contingent on inclusion in the empire-wide communal space. Armenian Church centers of any size, through their links with the Patriarchate of Constantinople, were nodes in a networked setting. The Patriarchate connected them to both the Sublime Porte and *amira* financial capital; monasteries themselves, in turn, produced clergymen who served local communities, forged connections with non-Armenian power brokers, and facilitated the movement of different forms of capital across the empire. Khanjalis possessed no point of access to that world. Jerusalem's renown and wealth, meanwhile, afforded it a place of privilege and influence and a large degree of autonomy in such an order of things. The effort to transform the communal space into a *millet* through the construction of an Ottoman Armenian diocese encountered two significant obstacles. One, as discussed in Chapter 1, entailed using the ecclesiastical supremacy of the Catholicosate of Etchmiadzin—the highest seat in the Armenian Church—

to resolve contests over jurisdiction that could be mobilized to undermine imperial reform. The more entrenched challenge was to sever the connections between clergymen, the Armenian elite, and provincial power brokers that anchored the community in horizontal networks. Doing so would remove Armenian Church institutions as nodes of empire and thereby limit (if not eliminate entirely) the extralegal prerogatives enjoyed by clergymen, particularly those attached to powerful monasteries.

Nodal governance, I argue, brought together at least four groups through Armenian Church institutions to produce network connections that contributed to the structuring of imperial society and the exercise of imperial sovereignty: provincial power brokers (viz., notables), Armenian clergymen, Armenian *amira*s (primarily in the capital, but also merchants and moneylenders all across the empire), and the imperial state. In particular, Armenian *amira*s underwrote the activities of the Armenian Church and the imperial government.[2] *Amira* capital thus brokered the partnership in governance between the Patriarchate of Constantinople and the Sublime Porte. As actors on the ground, clergymen's role in policing and enforcing regimes of difference positioned them to broker connections between closed networks, which they did by operating at the interstices of the Armenian community, Muslim notables, and government officials. As brokers between communities, the clergy accrued social capital that they then deployed to strengthen their positions in imperial society. Removing Armenian institutions from these relationships to make them part of a clearly defined diocese thus required more than simply resolving Church canon or tradition (though the Jerusalem example demonstrated how these could be used to disrupt reform) but instead entailed cutting the tightly wound knots that had tied the community into systems of governance and woven the financial capital of Armenians, the clergy, and the flock they shepherded into the tapestry of imperial society.

This chapter therefore looks at not only how the culture and practice of clergymen and monasteries contributed to the making of networked governance but also how the structural resilience of these networks could derail reform efforts during the Tanzimat period. Armenian financial capital was a crucial component of networked governance and locating Armenian Church institutions as nodes in it. While the temporary abolition of tax farming in 1839 threatened to remove the *amira*s from imperial politics, their investments in the Armenian Church made it possible for them to perpetuate their influence. As I show in this book, monasteries were particularly fundamental to this.

Monasteries did not simply produce clergymen that tended to the religious needs of the community subordinate to them; over time they also accumulated shops, mines, and other properties gifted to them by wealthy patrons, giving the clergy an additional economic stake in the status quo. Although many of the clergymen produced by those monasteries remained local, either by continuing to reside in the monastery itself or only serving the community subject to its immediate jurisdiction, the more entrepreneurial were provided opportunities to forge empire-wide fraternal links with other monasteries. Clergymen circulated throughout the empire to collect donations, teach, learn, and preach. It was not unheard of for one celibate clergyman to enjoy affiliation with multiple monasteries in different parts of the empire.

Church seats such as Cilicia, Aghtamar, and Jerusalem, and individual monasteries across the empire, together with their myriad local networks and economic interests, therefore did not exist solely in tension with the Patriarchate of Constantinople; they were connected to and reinforced one another as nodes that operated at the intersection of numerous types of interactions, including religious, economic, and political. The nodal structuring of the communal space through religious institutions made the Armenian community an ideal partner for the imperial government when it was content to share sovereignty. Those same features, coupled with the ecclesiastical inconsistencies of a feudal institution such as the Armenian Apostolic Church, would in turn become a significant obstacle to centralization during the reform period.

MONASTERIES AND CAPILLARY POWER

The appearance of Armenian *amira*s as prominent players in imperial governance and society in the middle of the eighteenth century owes much to their shrewdness in trade and investment.[3] Their ability to forge a long-lasting partnership with the government—they were the near-exclusive financiers of the both the Porte and the Palace in the decades straddling the turn of the nineteenth century—was fundamentally connected to the strategic investments they had made in the Armenian Church. As the religious institution of a non-Muslim community, the Armenian Church enjoyed a share of imperial sovereignty and the right to make claims on the empire's politics. Although this alone would have made the church an attractive investment opportunity, its ecclesiastical organization provided those who could exert pressure over it access to an empire-wide system of monasteries and other church offices from which they could then project their influence (as well as that of their ally, the imperial state) throughout the empire. *Amira* investment thus made monasteries and other church offices nodes in a networked world of imperial governance.

The primary instrument by which the *amira*s integrated their capital into the institutions of the Armenian Church, thus allowing them to reap the benefits of the community's share of imperial sovereignty, was the position of *mütevelli*, or trustee. Armenian religious institutions in the Ottoman Empire were, like their Muslim counterparts, considered *vakıf*, or pious foundations.[4] Pious foundations typically relied on endowments, usually in the form of real estate, to fund their operations. As is well documented in the Muslim case, they were also subject to vicious financial abuses by the wealthy, who sometimes operated pious foundations as early modern tax havens.[5] While Armenian pious foundations were likely no different in this regard, the position of trustee—a layman responsible for managing the institution's finances—had more far-reaching consequences for understanding how the Armenian Church was integrated into Ottoman structures of power.

Trustees, like monastery abbots, were appointed by the Patriarch of Constantinople, whose selection, in turn, had earlier been ratified by the imperial government. Patriarchs were not autonomous, however; they were indebted to the *amira*s who had worked with the Sublime Porte to have them elevated to the position in the first place. Unsurprising, *amira*s quickly had themselves appointed as trustees of all Armenian pious foundations throughout the Ottoman Empire. In so doing, they controlled not only the finances of a monastery but also its leadership. Clergymen on the ground therefore had incentive to lead their communities in a manner that was palatable to the Istanbul-based elite; this positioned the clergy to forge connections with other groups in society, particularly with respect to collaboration in the collection of taxes.

Provincial clergymen thus developed a dependence on the *amira*s and the Patriarchate that encouraged even the most entrepreneurial men of the cloth to acquiesce to Constantinople more often than not. The example of Kaspar Agha Hamamjian, the trustee of the Lim Monastery on Lake Van in the 1850s, sheds light on why this was the case.[6] On multiple occasions, the monastery's abbot, Hagop Topuzian, wrote Hamamjian to implore his assistance with respect to Lim's stake in a mine that had been gifted by a patron. Topuzian decided to seek Hamamjian's intervention only after local authorities had failed to bring him redress. Notably, Topuzian asked that Hamamjian take the issue to the Patriarch, in the hopes that the latter would then compose a *takrir* for delivery to the Sublime Porte. In other words, the trustee did not simply manage the monastery's finances or hold sway over the selection of its abbot; the holder of the position also controlled the monastery's access to the Patriarchate and, by extension, the imperial government.

Moreover, the example of Lim demonstrates how the position of trustee helped foster an empire-wide network of wealthy Armenians. Following the work of Barsoumian and others, scholars have framed the Armenian wealthy as a discrete class in Istanbul loath to share power with their coreligionists. Doing so has masked the roles played by provincial Armenian elite in the context of an empire-wide community. Although Hamamjian resided in the capital by the time of his appointment as trustee, he was actually a native of Van, a major provincial town near Lim. He engaged primarily in trade and had moved his offices to Istanbul sometime earlier. Investment in Lim thus afforded Hamamjian the opportunity to maintain the relationships he had forged in and around Van despite having relocated to the other side of the empire. Hamamjian's ability to win appointment as trustee shows that the Istanbul-based *amiras* had embraced him as one of the community's elite. Important to note, Hamamjian's movement in such social circles does not appear to be a post-1839 development where *amiras*, wounded as they were by the abolition of tax farming, may have been less inclined to exclude provincials from their world. Lim's trustee in the early nineteenth century was in fact an Armenian in the Balkans.[7]

Ottoman power in this networked setting was capillary and the institutions of the Armenian Church a conduit for its transmission. The sharpening of the Church's ecclesiastical organization and the expansion of the Patriarchate's authority in the eighteenth century made connections between different Church offices more robust, thus producing a stronger framework for forging relationships both within and across communal boundaries. The Armenian elites' strategic investments in both the Patriarchate of Constantinople and the empire-wide system of monasteries allowed them to grow their capital—both financial and social—and integrate into the ecclesiastical structures of the Armenian Church such that they effectively marshaled the community's share of imperial sovereignty for themselves.

MAKING A DIOCESE

The Armenian Church of the late eighteenth and early nineteenth centuries, commanded as it was by an empire-wide network of lay elites and high-ranking clergymen, was a partner of the imperial state in governance. The communal space produced by the interaction of ecclesiastics, markers of difference, financial capital, and state coercion facilitated the construction of networks that brought together clergymen, merchants, state officials, and provincial notables, among others. The state thus had a vested interest in the efficacy of the Armenian communal space and its ecclesiastical underpinnings. When the spread of Catholicism among *amira*s threatened the integrity of the community, as discussed earlier, the state pushed the Armenian elites to negotiate a peace among themselves. The state reacted harshly to the breakdown of negotiations, leading to the temporary exile of several prominent Armenians in government service.[8] Recognizing the seminal role of Armenian Church institutions to the propagation of Ottoman power is thus a crucial starting point for understanding how the Armenian Constitution was designed to transform imperial governance.

The initial effort by the government to eliminate tax farming in 1839 delivered a body blow to the Armenian elite and their ability to participate in nodal governance. The Constitution's construction of an Ottoman Armenian diocese, which aimed to deliver the coup de grâce, captures the transformation of the community's partnership with the state. Article 46 of the 1863 version of the Constitution placed the administration of monastery finances under the authority of the Patriarchate's Political Council, the membership of which was overwhelmingly Armenian employees of the Sublime Porte. Without explicitly saying so, Ottoman bureaucrats eliminated the position of trustee and subordinated monasteries to a centralized jurisdiction.

Centralization was the hallmark of the diocese legislated by the Constitution, which transformed the community from a networked space to a top-down gridded system that paired Church institutions that no longer had to negotiate the brokerage of the Armenian elite (see Figures 1 and 2). Smaller ecclesiastical administrative units (*vichak*s) were combined into larger prelacies headed by prelates (or primates), who were indirectly elected by the flock that they shepherded. Prelacies, in turn, were subordinate to the Patriarchate of Constantinople, which they could petition without having to appeal to a trustee first. In many respects, the diocese elaborated by the Constitution was designed to mimic the relationship between the Sublime Porte and the provincial administration, a point that provincial Armenian reformers would later attempt to refine.

The Constitution put forth other articles that placed constraints on monasteries and aimed to curb access to the clergy, its internal politics, and the ability of either to connect with anything beyond the limits of the community.[9] Still, the Patriarchate of Constantinople, under which this diocese was organized,

```
┌─────────────────────────────┐                                    ┌─────────────────────────────┐
│ Catholicosate of Etchmiadzin│                                    │ Ottoman imperial government │
│ (supreme seat of the Armenian│                                   │ (Sublime Porte and Palace)  │
│ Church, located in Russian  │                                    └─────────────────────────────┘
│ Empire since 1828)          │                                                  ▲
└─────────────────────────────┘                                                  │
           │     ▲                                                               │
           │     │ Etchmiadzin deputizes Constantinople as representative        │
           │     │ to the Sublime Porte; recognizes Constantinople as            │
           │     │ legitimate leader of Armenian Church in the Ottoman           │
           ▼     │ Empire                                                        │
                                                                                 │
                              Patriarchate represents community before the imperial government
                              (refers petitions); also carries out a number of bureaucratic functions
                              on behalf of state
                                                                                 │
┌─────────────────────────────┐                                                  │
│ Patriarchate of Constantinople ├──────────────────────────────────────────────┘
│ (National Administration of │
│ Patriarch + National Assembly)│
└─────────────────────────────┘
           ▲
           │ Prelacy elects National Assembly delegates;
           │ delegates elect Patriarchate;
           │ Patriarchate ratifies selection of prelate;
           ▼ prelate submits petitions to Patriarchate for referral to Porte
                                                          Prelate forwards community complaints to local governor
┌─────────────────────────────┐                                    ┌─────────────────────────────┐
│ Provincial prelacy          ├───────────────────────────────────▶│ Provincial government       │
└─────────────────────────────┘                                    └─────────────────────────────┘
           ▲
           ▼
┌─────────────────────────────┐
│ Provincial Armenian         │
│ community                   │
└─────────────────────────────┘
```

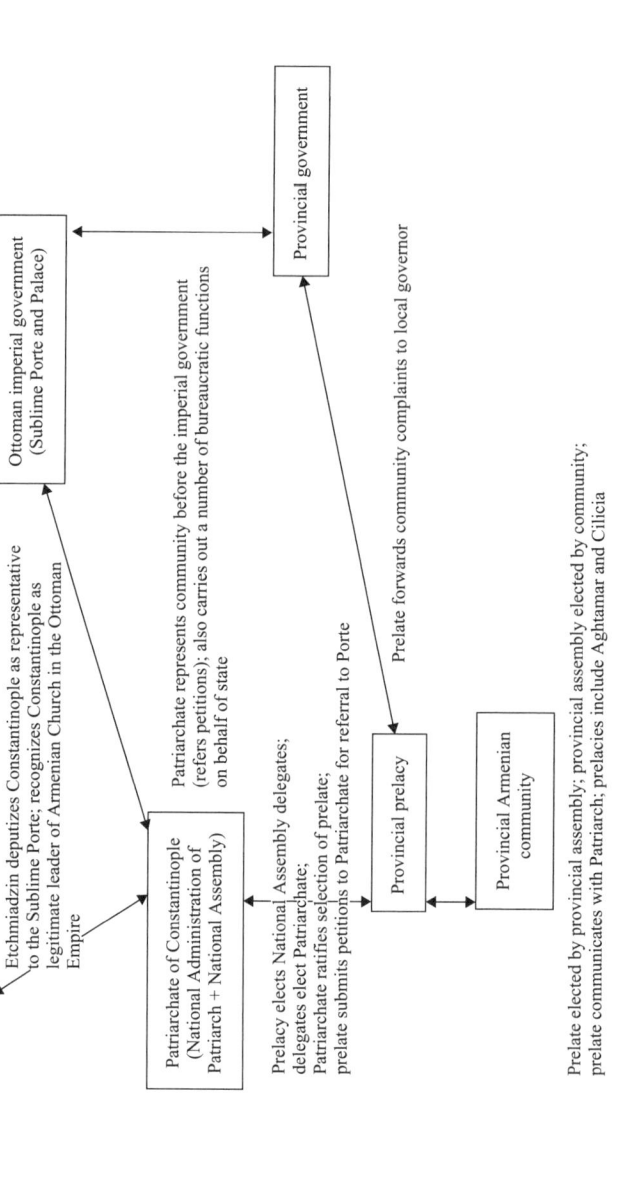

Prelate elected by provincial assembly; provincial assembly elected by community; prelate communicates with Patriarch; prelacies include Aghtamar and Cilicia

FIGURE 1. Organization of Ottoman Armenian community and its relationship to imperial government as dictated by the Armenian Constitution

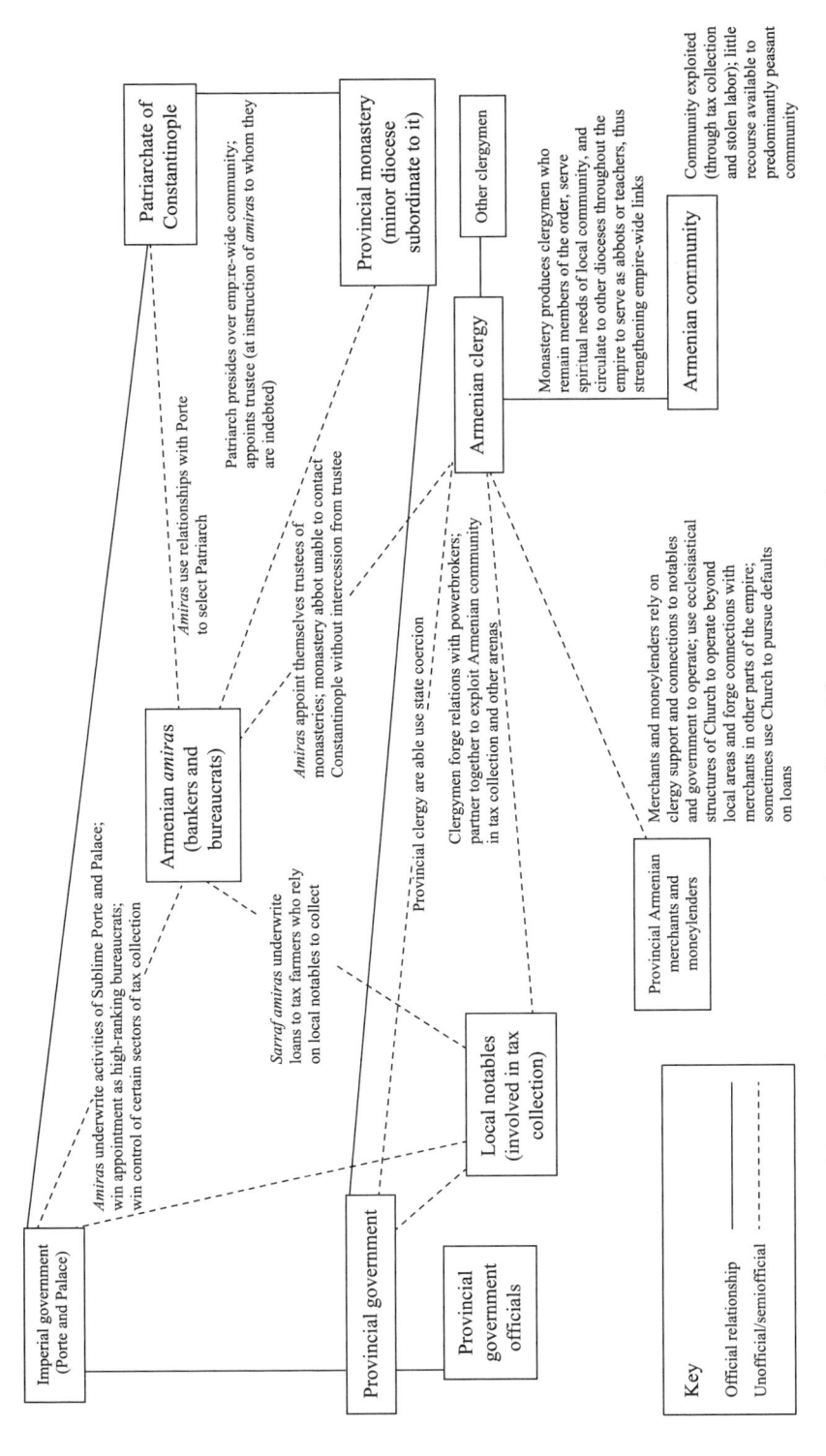

FIGURE 2. Organization of Ottoman Armenian community as part of imperial governance in practice

remained dependent on the legitimacy afforded it by the Catholicos of All Armenians in Etchmiadzin to extend its jurisdiction over Armenians in the Ottoman Empire. As a patriarchate created by the Ottomans, Constantinople lacked the right to consecrate bishops, bless the holy chrism, or perform other functions critical to the Armenian Church's confession of Christian faith. Armenian clergymen attached to the Patriarchate of Jerusalem, the Catholicosate of Aghtamar, or the Catholicosate of Cilicia enjoyed the ability to blend the high ecclesiastical politics that had disrupted the introduction of the Constitution in 1860 with on-the-ground monastery politics to form a potent repertoire of action that they deployed in their bid to preserve nodal governance.

OTTOMAN ECCLESIASTICS AND THE PRESERVATION OF NODAL GOVERNANCE

At its session on July 22, 1866, the Armenian National Assembly rejected claims staked to the thrones at Cilicia and Aghtamar.[10] In defiance of the Patriarchate of Constantinople, two local clergymen had navigated networks of power and its attendant connections with monastery politics to declare themselves catholicoi. This defiance, explored in more depth in Chapter 3, proved largely successful. In so doing, they bid to preserve the nodal organization of Ottoman governance and the role that the Armenian Church played in it. In turn, this helps explain the challenge posed by Jerusalem and why its rejection of Constantinople's authority compelled the Sublime Porte to withdraw the Constitution in 1861. As we saw with the case of Jerusalem in Chapter 1, these three seats enjoyed recourse to Church canon and tradition, which in turn allowed them to become bases of support for others to challenge the Patriarchate and its role in empire-wide reform. In response, Constantinople tried a heavy hand and in autumn of 1863 once again attempted to impose a patriarch on Jerusalem.[11] The failure to do so resulted in the postponement of talks with Jerusalem until February 1865, when Esayi, the Patriarch of Jerusalem, arrived in the capital to argue for the implementation of regulations at Jerusalem that the Order of St. James itself had prepared.

From the vantage point of Constantinople, Jerusalem was in no position to dictate terms. Mismanagement by the clergy at St. James had resulted Jerusalem accruing a massive debt that the rest of the community had to shoulder. The community had been compelled to liquidate numerous properties to meet its obligations. Dissension within the brotherhood had also led to the secession of Egypt from Jerusalem's jurisdiction, further exacerbating the debt. The reformers thus saw Esayi's presence before the National Assembly as an opportunity to impose its order on Jerusalem and complete its de facto transformation into a simple prelacy subordinate to the Patriarchate of Constantinople. Any illusions Esayi may have had about his role in the impending discussion were quickly dispelled when the National Assembly ruled he would not be permitted to speak.[12]

The subsequent discussion over regulations for Jerusalem therefore frames the larger issue at stake here—namely, what vision of imperial governance the community and its institutions would serve. The contours of this debate between the two Armenian patriarchates demonstrate how the politics and culture of a monastery functioned as cornerstones of the nodal organization of Ottoman imperial governance. The discussion in the National Assembly revolved around several issues but emphasized financial regulations, authority internal to the monastery, entrance to the clergy, and expulsion from the Order of the St. James. Taken as a whole, Constantinople tried using these to undo the formation of factions or cliques within the Order.

CLERGY FACTIONS

Rival factions within a monastery competed with one another over control of resources. Although it was a patriarchate with its own diocese, Jerusalem was also a monastery that had its own resident order that ordained clergymen. The Patriarch of Jerusalem thus served concurrently as the abbot of his own monastery and the prelate of his own diocese. In other words, clashes and squabbles between members of the Order of St. James could have ramifications not only for the flock immediately subordinate to Jerusalem but also the entire Ottoman Armenian community.

A Patriarch of Jerusalem who had successfully navigated the monastery's internal politics to ascend to his post was expected to use his position to reward his allies. Relationships of patronage dictated the distribution of power, resources, and prestige within the brotherhood. Constantinople used certain tools to take aim at these relationships, such as attempting to appoint its own treasurer to Jerusalem to help oversee finances.[13] Though in debt, its voluminous *vakfiye* records show that Jerusalem still owned substantial real estate throughout the empire.[14] Jerusalem remained wealthy and still possessed substantial means. These were overseen by the *lusarar*, which was the second most important position in any Armenian monastery. As its name suggests, the primary responsibility of a *lusarar* was to light the church's candles in preparation for services. Over time, the position grew in importance and began to resemble that of a sexton in the European tradition. By the nineteenth century, a *lusarar* could expect to oversee the daily activities of a monastery, tend to its upkeep, and distribute goods within the Order. In other words, a *lusarar* tended to be the right hand of the patriarch to whom he reported. In its regulations for Jerusalem, Constantinople undermined the personal authority of the Patriarch of Jerusalem by placing the office of *lusarar* under the jurisdiction of a newly created executive council within the Patriarchate. Moreover, Constantinople required that someone appointed to the position be at least forty-five years of age and have no fewer than fifteen years of experience as a clergyman at Jerusalem.[15] This condition further eroded the authority of the Patriarch by increasing the possibility that a *lusarar* be well-enough established within the monastery to withstand the inevitable pressure that partisans within the Order would apply.

Here, Constantinople implicitly invoked the aforementioned factions. It is telling that some reformers referred to these factions as "extended families" or "clans." Fictive kinship within the monastery was a useful instrument for organizing relationships of power. Clergymen typically considered the bishop who had ordained them a "spiritual father." Fictive agnatic lines not only made it possible to identify "brothers" but also allowed for the transmission of internecine politics across generations as clergymen produced genealogies that reinforced familial bonds. The National Assembly took aim at the construction of these factions by abolishing the practice of "child ecclesiastics" (*pokravor*). Clergymen could grow their families by bringing children or adolescents into the monastery, who in turn became the "sons" of their better established patron. Many of these children were either orphans or came from poverty. Membership in a religious brotherhood therefore offered these children the only sets of meaningful interpersonal relationships they would know and, as a result, ensured strong bonds of loyalty in the course of these intrabrotherhood conflicts.

Child ecclesiastics were thus socialized not only into the culture of the Church from an early age but also its politics. They saw how battles were fought and won for control of the monastery. They also learned how to interact with government officials and other notables in the landscape of Ottoman politics and society. Jerusalem was special in this regard, however, as its prestige made it a site for various types of circulation: capital in the form of donations of immovable property from all over the empire, a steady stream of pilgrims, and extended visits from priests and laymen alike wishing to study in the holy city. Clergymen socialized from a young age into the Church at Jerusalem were thus also positioned to forge connections with powerful actors across the empire.

This explains, at least in part, the career trajectory of Harutiun Vehabedian, one of the most powerful Armenian clergymen of the nineteenth century.

THE FUTURE PATRIARCH: HARUTIUN VEHABEDIAN, ECCLESIASTICAL NETWORKS, AND REJECTION OF THE TANZIMAT

The political culture of monasteries, particularly that at the Armenian Patriarchate of Jerusalem, was an embedded feature of Ottoman politics and society. Clergymen whose careers began in Jerusalem were uniquely positioned to participate in resistance against the imperial reform program. In the following sections, I review the careers of two such clergymen to demonstrate how they connected sites of power in a bid to preserve the nodal organization of governance and the Armenian Church.

The first, Harutiun Vehabedian, had entered the Order of St. James at Jerusalem as a child ecclesiastic. The details surrounding his early life are unclear. He was born in Egypt to a poor, presumably Coptic, family in 1812, 1819, or 1823.[16] A bishop named Giragos, who had traveled to Egypt as overseer of Jerusalem's properties there, "adopted" the boy and brought him to Jerusalem in 1834. He was subsequently baptized, given the name Apraham, and put to work in the monastery's press. Soon thereafter, he changed his name to Hovsep Giragosian to identify himself with his patron. In 1839, he was dispatched to the imperial capital to continue his education and oversee Bishop Giragos's interests there. Another member of Giragos's clan, Harutiun Sahatjian, accompanied him in these endeavors. The future bishop later enrolled at the Protestant seminary in Bebek, operated by the American missionaries. His American connections likely influenced his decision to travel to the United States to study medicine. He left the United States and returned to Istanbul in 1846, where the reigning Patriarch of Constantinople and future Catholicos of All Armenians, Matteos, made him a teacher of arithmetic and English.

Vehabedian's participation in the monastery politics of the St. James Order had thus placed him in influential circles in the imperial capital and enabled him to forge links with Matteos. The election of his "father," Giragos, to the patriarchal throne at Jerusalem in 1846 was a victory for the clan. Giragos called his "son" back to Jerusalem in 1847 before returning him to the capital, where he made arrangements for his ordination as a deacon in 1849. In Istanbul, he collaborated with a bishop named Hovhannes (r. 1850–1860), another member of the St. James Order, who succeeded Giragos as Patriarch of Jerusalem following the latter's death in 1850. As part of his bid to strengthen his faction against that of Giragos's predecessor, Zakaria (r. 1840–1846), the newly elected Patriarch of Jerusalem ordained Vehabedian a celibate priest. It was at this point that the newly ordained clergyman selected the name Harutiun Vehabedian. This name conveyed both power and ambition: his first name translates as "resurrection" and the surname "supreme leader," likely a nod to his association with the reigning patriarch.

In 1852, Vehabedian returned to the imperial capital. There, a new Patriarch of Constantinople, Hagopos Seropian (r. 1848–1856), placed him in charge of the patriarchal crosier. One year later, Seropian made Vehabedian a patriarchal vicar, and in 1857 he was appointed Prelate of Kharpert (Harput or Elazığ). Two years later, Patriarch of Constantinople Kevork Kerestejian (r. 1856–1860)—who, as discussed in Chapter 1, had exploited the controversy at Jerusalem to engineer the suspension of the Constitution by the Sublime Porte—appointed Vehabedian the Prelate of Karin (Erzurum). Vehabedian held this position from April 24, 1859, until 1880.

CONNECTED RESISTANCE: CLERGY AND CONTEMPORANEOUS REBELLION IN THE OTTOMAN ARMENIAN CHURCH

The relationship between Order of St. James networks (and their location in intramonastery feuds) and the Patriarchate of Constantinople is already clear. Vehabedian's mastery of them facilitated his rise to prelate of one of the two most important Armenian prelacies in eastern Anatolia. His relationship with Kerestejian also suggests that anti-Constitutionalist clergymen in the capital and the Patriarchate of Jerusalem had coordinated their actions. Yet it is his time in Erzurum that is most important for understanding how resistance to the reform program was connected as clergymen and their allied tried to preserve nodal governance.

First, Vehabedian vehemently objected to the introduction of reform in his prelacy. He refused to convene constitutionally mandated councils or hold elections. During his travels to eastern Anatolia in 1873, Bishop Eremia Tevkants admonished Vehabedian for failing to employ a dragoman to conduct official business with the government.[17] He abused his power not only to ingratiate himself to local notables—both Armenians and Muslims—but also to engage in usury. Per a report from the British consul, he had amassed a personal fortune of 15,000 liras, an exorbitant sum at a time when most families, particularly in the provinces, would have struggled to put together ten.[18] His failure to implement the Armenian Constitution drew the ire of reformers and the guilds alike. They actually succeeded in having Vehabedian temporarily removed a number of times in the 1860s.[19] In 1868, it was intervention by Governor İsmail Paşa and the Armenian well-to-do that helped to realize "the return of their intriguing bishop Harutioon."[20]

Vehabedian's tenure in Erzurum unfolded within a larger context. Beyond his connections to Constantinople and Jerusalem, Vehabedian's fingerprints may be found all over the other major episodes of antireform resistance in the second half of the nineteenth century. The Catholicos of Aghtamar, who is a subject of Chapter 3, organized the murder of his predecessor in 1864. In another example of intramonastery strife, Bishop Khachadur Shiroian and his allies had collaborated with Kurdish notables to kill Bedros Bülbül, the reigning catholicos, after he had agreed to the implementation of reform dictated by Constantinople. Working with various actors, Vehabedian helped to engineer Shiroian's eventual exoneration. The internal politics of Aghtamar were deeply connected to those of nearby Van, where an Armenian clergyman named Boghos Melikian fought his own decades-long rebellion against the reform program. As in Erzurum, reformers successfully removed Melikian a number of times in the 1860s and 1870s. On numerous occasions, however, Vehabedian used his influence at Constantinople—amplified by Jerusalem and its delegation there—to intervene on Melikian's behalf.[21]

The antireform charge originally led by the Patriarchate of Jerusalem did not operate in isolation. Clergymen inimical to the expansion of lay participation in the regulation of Armenian Church affairs—in other words, the ability of nonelites to stake claims on the community's share of Ottoman sovereignty and thereby reorder the connections that shaped imperial governance—activated network structures to preserve the networking Ottoman world. In the process, they linked Church sites—around which local networks of power that brought together Armenian and Muslim interests alike had collected—to forge a connected resistance.

EXPULSION AND CONNECTION

Jerusalem's location as a primary node in the nexus of connections that constituted the networked space of the community thus endowed resistance to the reform program. From the Patriarchate of Jerusalem, clergymen entered the holy orders and gained access to networks that linked them to other men of the cloth who were embedded in local structures of power across the empire. This context explains Constantinople's desire to break up the cabals of clergymen whose bonds facilitated nodal governance. In theory, the Constitution resolved these issues by delegating controls on clergymen to the Religious Council based at the Patriarchate of Constantinople. To retain its influence in empire-wide networks, the Patriarch of Jerusalem sought to establish a prerogative for itself: the right to control the fate of a clergyman expelled from the St. James Order.

Much like Vehabedian, members of the St. James Order served in high-ranking positions all across the empire. The right to control the fate of a clergyman who had been expelled from the order therefore made it possible for Jerusalem to extend its influence into other prelacies. This was untenable, of course, in the eyes of Constantinople. Likely, the reformers in the capital had the example of a few clergymen in mind. One in particular must have been Mkrtich Kefsizian, the future Catholicos of Cilicia.

Kefsizian was born to a poor family in the Cilician town of Marash in 1815.[22] He was not a child ecclesiastic, like Vehabedian, and had actually been married for a brief period. Following the untimely death of his wife, he chose to join the St. James Order at Jerusalem in 1845. As did Vehabedian, Kefsizian enjoyed the patronage of Bishop Giragos. It was at Giragos's behest that Bishop Davit of Erzurum, who had ordained Vehabedian as a deacon, made Kefsizian a celibate priest on May 1, 1849. That same year, Giragos appointed Kefsizian as chief dragoman for St. James. As chief dragoman, Kefsizian was not simply a translator but also a primary adviser to the Patriarch of Jerusalem and its deputy before the imperial government. Kefsizian learned very quickly how to exploit this opportunity to enrich himself.

Kefisizian therefore enjoyed at least two connections to Vehabedian in the form of their mutual patron, Giragos, and their ordination by the hand of Bishop Davit. Yet Kefsizian found himself at odds with Hovhannes, Vehabedian's other patron and Giragos's successor. As part of his effort to consolidate rule, Hovhannes systematically removed a number of priests from their positions at St. James. In the course of this reshuffling, Patriarch Hovhannes sent Kefsizian to Damascus in 1853 as an overseer of Jerusalem's holdings there. Not taking this demotion lightly, Kefsizian used his charisma as an orator to rally the Armenians in Damascus to his side. He called on them to join him in his rejection of Patriarch Hovhannes's rule and attempted to split Damascus from Jerusalem's jurisdiction. Hovhannes responded by ordering the governor to arrest to Kefsizian, who was eventually captured, imprisoned, and transferred to the St. James monastery. In 1856, Hovhannes delivered the final blow by expelling Kefsizian from the brotherhood.

Expulsion from Jerusalem did not mean defrocking from the Armenian clergy, and at a moment when Constantinople had yet to articulate its jurisdiction over clergymen who had been expelled from Jerusalem, Kefsizian managed to find a soft landing in the capital. There, he ingratiated himself to the well-to-do and later won appointment as Prelate of Ankara by order of the anti-reform Patriarch of Constantinople, Kevork Kerestejian. Two years later, Kefsizian traveled with Vehabedian to Etchmiadzin to be consecrated bishop. He returned to Ankara, where he had embedded himself in local power networks. His abuse of power, though, reached the point where he was compelled to flee in 1864. He made his retreat to Egypt where he stayed until making a return to his native Cilicia in 1871. Exploiting the upheavals that included the Sublime Porte's military intervention against the *derebey*s, Kefsizian used his charisma once more to convince the people there to elect him Catholicos of Cilicia. In this capacity, he continued his rebellion against Constantinople and the program of reform until his death.

CONCLUSION: BERATING A PATRIARCH

Although the clergy of Jerusalem (discussed throughout this chapter) and of Holy Apostles near Başkale (introduced at the chapter's start) rest at opposite ends of the spectrum in terms of the influence they could extend, their experiences are illustrative of the same overarching theme. The Armenian Apostolic community's ability to enjoy the share of sovereignty afforded to it by the organization of difference in the Ottoman Empire along confessional lines was contingent on whether its leaders and institutions could participate in the empire-wide networks that shaped imperial governance. These networks—which were commercial, financial, religious, and political in nature—ultimately orbited institutions of the Armenian Church, which became nodes in a network setting. As nodes connecting these various interests, the Church became a broker among sites that linked the community to local power brokers, the formal government, and Armenian financial and commercial capital. In this network setting, this meant that Church institutions accrued social capital—a social capital that was, in turn, exploited by the well-to-do through trusteeships. Jerusalem was uniquely positioned to benefit from this order of things, as the networked space of the community permitted its clergymen to reach high office all over the empire. In Başkale, however, disconnection from these networks meant disenfranchisement from Ottoman society.

The Patriarch of Jerusalem, Esayi, hoped to negotiate the preservation of this nodal organization of the community and its institutions when he went before the National Assembly in 1865. He and other clergymen across the empire were committed to retaining the roles and the prerogatives they had carved out for themselves in Ottoman governance. Doing so required contesting the construction of an Ottoman Armenian diocese, the Armenian National Constitution that had legislated it, and ultimately the Tanzimat program of which it was a part. As such, Esayi questioned the authority of the Patriarchate of Constantinople and its claim to jurisdiction over the Armenian community of the empire. When Nerses Varjabedian, a future Patriarch of Constantinople, explained that Jerusalem was in fact subordinate to Constantinople, Esayi wondered aloud if Constantinople could only make such a claim because the Ottomans had established it. Ultimately, this provoked a response from the speaker of the assembly, Abro Sahag Efendi, who made clear that

> only the Armenian Patriarchate [of Constantinople] may have direct relations with Etchmiadzin, which no other order or monastery may have. They must go through the Constantinople Patriarchate. When a monastery or order wishes to have direct relations [with Etchmiadzin], it is saying that it is independent of the Constantinople Patriarchate. The regulations show that the Jerusalem Brotherhood is dependent on the Constantinople Patriarchate, and only through [Constantinople] may it have contact with the Sublime Porte. Moreover, the [Ottoman] State has recognized the Religious Council here and has given it jurisdiction over [all] the Armenians of Turkey.[23]

Responses to Esayi's challenge did not end there. When Esayi tried to argue that, as a patriarchate, Jerusalem should enjoy a special status in the eyes of the National Administration, Servichen simply stated that "the Jerusalem Monastery is not to be viewed any differently from other monasteries." Offended, Esayi prepared to storm out of the session, much to the delight of conservatives in the National Assembly. However, he chose to remain and focus his criticism on the role of the laity in determining the relationship between two patriarchates. Esayi was of course making reference to the subordination of the religious seats, such as prelates and abbots, to the Political Council, which comprised lay members of the community, many of whom worked for the Sublime Porte. Varjabedian once more seized the opportunity to note that that the Church belonged to the people and that to deny them a role in making these decisions would amount to "acting like Catholics."[24] The invocation of confessional practice carried the day. The National Assembly passed the regulations and, after promising to work with Constantinople "for the pride and honor of the national church," Patriarch Esayi set off for Jerusalem.

Esayi's bid to preserve the nodal organization of the community—which had embedded its institutions in structures of power—failed. Instead, he and other clergymen were now faced with a Patriarchate of Constantinople that had instrumentalized the sources of the community's political legitimacy—the Ottoman state and the Catholicosate of All Armenians in Etchmiadzin—to make itself the primary node in the organization. This Ottoman Armenian version of "spoke and hub without the wheel" permitted the Patriarchate of Constantinople to broker between the community and the state and, in the process, expropriate the vast majority of the social capital that had accumulated in monasteries and other Church offices throughout the Ottoman Empire. Here, network analysis shows us that resolving tensions between center and periphery was not the paradigm of Ottoman governance; rather, it was a policy goal of the reform program in the latter half of the nineteenth century. The power of clergymen to connect Armenian financial capital, merchants, and local power brokers waned. Reformers saw Armenian participation in this project as part of a wider program of imperial reform; the loss of social capital in provincial areas would be offset by the creation of the diocese and its system of prelacies that would now represent the community. Instead, more communities would begin to resemble Başkale as the clergy continued to lose the extramural prerogatives it had cultivated in the networked world of governance. The creeping authority of the Patriarchate via the Constitution thus posed an existential threat to the very organization of social forces throughout Ottoman society. Clergymen who sought to carry out this reform consequently found themselves targets of violence.

3 PERIPHERALIZATION

A LONE VOICE OF PROTEST CASCADED through the chambers of the Armenian National Assembly. As the legislative body moved to conclude its discussion on the Jerusalem matter in March 1865, a conservative delegate once more interrogated Constantinople's claim to ecclesiastical supremacy over other notable seats of the Armenian Church in the Ottoman Empire. Bishop Nerses Varjabedian, a pro-reform clergyman who would later serve a consequential term on the patriarchal throne, parried the challenge by resorting to precedent. "With an order from the Patriarchate of Constantinople," he explained, "I can go to the dioceses in Sis [Cilicia] and carry out reforms, as has happened in the past. . . . I can enter Aghtamar's [Holy] See and, with an order from the Patriarchate of Constantinople, carry out any type of reform."[1]

Varjabedian's retort is significant for understanding the introduction of the *millet* system and its implications for non-Muslims. His invocation of the Catholicosates of Aghtamar and Cilicia—two seats that technically trumped Constantinople in the Armenian Church hierarchy—seemed to resolve the ecclesiastical controversy over Jerusalem, a mere patriarchate. Moreover, the assembled delegates would have implicitly understood Varjabedian's other reasons for lumping Jerusalem together with Aghtamar and Cilicia. Remnants from Armenia's feudal past, the catholicosates each had a long history of contesting ecclesiastical authority. In the context of the Ottoman Empire in the 1865, the catholicosates posed a more menacing challenge to Armenian reformers and their allies in the Sublime Porte. The catholicosates had, over the preceding centuries, integrated their own religious institutions and their culture into dense networks of local and regional power that allied them with Muslim notables: the *derebey*s with the clergy at Cilicia and Kurdish *emirs* with Aghtamar. Varjabedian did not simply invoke Armenian Church hierarchy; he painted Constantinople's ecclesiastical rivals as enemies of state.

During the nineteenth century, imperial states discursively produced peripheries or "orients" to justify the implementation of policies formulated by central authorities.[2] The fashioning of a *millet* system as part of the Tanzimat reforms was key to these processes because it provided the state another tool for extending a normative order and making society legible.[3] Centralization—with its attendant biases and stereotypes—entered into the Ottoman Armenian political lexicon as community reformers, hand in hand with high-ranking government officials, articulated both a normative order and peripheries that were deviant from that order. The *millet* system possessed the potential to "thin out" imperial governance by reifying complex sets of relationships and reducing them to a center-periphery binary. The Tanzimat and the *millet* system were inclined to produce peripheries because the ideology of Ottoman reform was legal centralism.[4]

Describing Ottoman reform as an exercise in centralization is hardly novel. Framing the *millet* system as an example of legal centralism, however, invokes the concept of legal pluralism and thus compels us to refine our theorizations of non-Muslim engagement with Ottoman imperial governance. Scholars have used legal pluralism, defined as the presence of more than one legal order in a social field, to describe non-Muslims' ability to petition different venues—generally the Islamic court or their own communal courts, over which clergymen presided—as a positive attribute of the imperial system. Forum shopping could, in some cases, provide non-Muslims a competitive advantage over the empire's Muslim subjects. Court-centric analysis, however, misconstrues what constituted legal regimes in the Ottoman Empire, how most non-Muslims experienced them, and how pluralism operated in the context of Ottoman imperialism. Typologies of difference mingled with one another in a social field to endow it with meaning. Cleaving confession of religion from that social field and analyzing it in isolation from other types of difference precludes making a proper accounting of how the implementation of the Tanzimat and the *millet* system impacted the provinces and transformed the scope of non-Muslims' engagement with and participation in Ottoman imperial governance.

The legal order targeted by the Tanzimat was a complex assortment of laws, traditions, customs, and religious canons that overlapped with one another to blend formal rules with informal prerogatives. Those perched at the top of various hierarchies, such as clergymen, landlords, and shaykhs, collaborated to produce networks that reinforced one another's position in local and regional structures of power. This chapter therefore takes Constantinople's contest with each Aghtamar and Cilicia to understand the ramifications for non-Muslims of extending reform into the provinces. Centralism articulated and inscribed peripheries discursively; structurally, it entailed rearranging networks that had afforded certain actors positions of privilege. Unmaking legal pluralism thus entailed not only articulating a periphery geographically but also disentangling the networks that had structured it. The disentanglement of these networks, which included severing the connections that clergymen had forged, resulted in the growing isolation of Armenians in imperial society.

The introduction of the legally centric Tanzimat and the *millet* system had negative consequences for the Ottoman Empire's Armenian community. To explore these implications, this chapter is organized into three sections. Part 1 describes an Ottoman legal pluralism that displaces the state and its courts as the primary components of a plural legal regime. Non-Muslims had to contend with multiple legal orders in a given social field. The luxury of forum shopping, however, was generally reserved for those of some means or who, at the very least, resided in more populous towns. Ottoman Armenians at the edges of the empire instead had to contend with multiple overlapping orders that were difficult to navigate. Part 2 looks at this plural legal order in practice. In particular, it highlights how two Armenian bishops—Khachadur Shiroian in Aghtamar and Mkrtich Kefsizian in Cilicia—exploited legal pluralism to establish positions of privilege in networks of power. In the hopes of repelling the centralization efforts, Shiroian and Kefsizian both adopted networking strategies in an effort to preserve their prerogatives. Such strategies, I argue in Part 3, culminated in the peripheralization of Armenians and their institutions in imperial governance.

PART 1: THE IDEOLOGY OF THE TANZIMAT

While there is some disagreement, historians of the Ottoman Empire usually agree to the following periodization for the state's final century of existence: Tanzimat (1839–1876), Hamidian (1876–1908), and Young Turk (1908–1923).[5]

Events of significant import mark the transition from one period to another, each bearing its own ideological mark. Ottomanism, a fluid term typically meant to connote the fashioning of a supranational imperial political identity, marks the Tanzimat period. Islamic (or pan-Islamic) is used to characterize the reign of Sultan Abdülhamid; and nationalism—most important, the Turkish iteration thereof—was the leitmotif of the final years of the empire as it violently splintered into nation-states. There is significant reason to interrogate both this periodization and the subsequent ideological categorization it suggests. Such categorization merits scrutiny because it unproblematically reproduces arguments advanced in a series of articles originally published in 1904, collectively entitled "Üç tarz-ı siyaset," by the Turkish nationalist Yusuf Akçura.[6] Reducing the ideology of the Tanzimat to an ill-defined Ottomanism provides us with little analysis of either. Framing that ideology as legally centric, however, does.

What does it mean to describe the Tanzimat's ideology as legal centralism? How can we think about it productively in an imperial context? Legal scholarship, particularly the work of the late John Griffiths, defines legal centralism as an ideology that consciously seeks, without exception, the uniformity of law for all people subject to its authority. Moreover, law is—according to a legal centralist prescription—top-down, hierarchical, and predicated on some set of prevailing norms.[7] Griffiths conceded that legal centralism, with its emphasis on uniformity, is largely a feature of nation-states; such a formulation does in fact cohere to Benedict Anderson's well-known observation that national communities are "conceived as a deep, horizontal comradeship."[8] A normative and unified legal order would produce similar sets of experiences between those who had never met and thus provide them with a shared cultural script allowing them to imagine themselves as part of a unified national community. Such an approach appears to conflict with the very premise of empire, which was a political enterprise predicated on the enforcement of difference to inscribe its legitimacy. As a concept, legal centralism implicitly conjures its other: legal pluralism. The compulsory heterogeneity of empire meant that its subjects would possess access to a variety of legal mechanisms to adjudicate grievances. Describing this state of affairs as legal pluralism, however, would mean to describe the whole of any imperial project as such; doing so runs the risk of having the term lose its explanatory purchase. It is therefore possible, I contend, to think of an imperial legal centralism that aims to reject deviant legal orders while accommodating and enforcing difference.

The Tanzimat did not, as the proponents of Ottomanism-as-ideology suggest, attempt to forge an Ottoman nation.[9] Nor did dictates against discrimination in public service entail the abolition of structures or norms that precluded the establishment of social equality between those of different confessions. The ambiguity of some reform policies may have created problems for bureaucrats on the ground, but the general tenor of the Tanzimat remained top-down. The Tanzimat is more productively understood as an Ottoman restoration.[10] In this respect, it extended the policies introduced during the reign of Mahmud II (r. 1808–1839) that strove to subordinate all social and political forces that might challenge the sultanate to the authority of the official state. Legal centralism thus took aim at the alternative legal orders dotting imperial society that were crucial to the fashioning of a polity where sovereignty was shared. Legal centralism in this setting retained its imperial character as centralization ultimately enshrined and reinscribed confessional difference. Uniform law and unified legal practice need not presume equality between subjects in an imperial context.

Beyond Courts: Millets *and Ottoman Legal Pluralism*

What was legal pluralism in the Ottoman context? How did it interact with the imperial organization of difference? And why would Khachadur Shiroian and Mkrtich Kefsizian ultimately bid to preserve it? Given that these battles would be fought through the institutions of the Armenian Church, finding answers to these questions entails exploring how Ottoman non-Muslims engaged with the category of *millet* and the idea of a *millet* system. Properly grappling with the nuances of non-Muslim experiences with Ottoman legal pluralism requires confronting a powerful obstacle—namely, that of court-centric analysis. The study of legal pluralism in the Ottoman context to date has largely built upon histories based on Islamic court records.[11] Recourse to these court documents is understandable. As guarantor of justice, the Ottoman authorities placed special emphasis on their court system. In some contexts, courts were the central state's primary institution for making its presence felt in regions outside the capital. The state thus made a special effort to record, preserve, and organize the testimonies and deliberations made in Islamic courts. These records have provided scholars unique opportunities to peek into the lives of those who petitioned the court. Social and gender historians, in particular, have expertly used these records to open up new vistas for studying the cultural history of the Middle East.

That non-Muslims engaged in a legal dispute with a coreligionist theoretically enjoyed the privilege of selecting a venue—either the Islamic court or one from their own community—is crucial for such analyses. Forum shopping, particularly by non-Muslim women seeking redress in divorce or inheritance disputes, tells us a great deal about the agency of Ottoman subjects and how they might navigate imperial society and rule. It also offers us a vantage point on the limits of non-Muslim communal control within the field of Ottoman law. Moreover, because they allow us to see what issues predominated in a given area for a fixed period, these records produced by the Islamic courts also make it possible to sketch out social, economic, and cultural histories of Ottoman life. Only non-Muslims, it should be noted, enjoyed the privilege of forum shopping.[12] This, it would appear, made the Ottoman legal system plural: because different religious rules applied to different imperial subjects, multiple legal orders therefore occupied the same social field. Was this the case? Taking this tack requires exploring how the institutions of non-Muslim communities figured into the Ottoman legal world. This is a cumbersome endeavor. Although we do have the voluminous records of the Islamic court records, we lack a similar corpus of materials from the non-Muslim communities. In the case of the Armenian community, for example, only the records for a few cases adjudicated before Armenian Church authorities are available to us.[13] Therefore we know very little about what issues Armenians sought to resolve when petitioning their own courts. Absent a trove of such material to make comparative analysis, satisfactorily contextualizing non-Muslim appeals to the Islamic court becomes problematic insomuch as we hope to understand how actors used access to different regimes of law.

Being privy to such information would still fail to resolve a tension central to our understanding of Ottoman legal pluralism as deployed by scholars to this point. The argument that forum shopping made the Islamic court the ultimate arbiter of justice by giving it the final say in legal matters reinforced the superiority of Islam—particularly that of the Hanafi school of jurisprudence favored by the Ottomans—vis-à-vis Christianity and Judaism is convincing.[14] Making the Islamic court available to non-Muslims as the preeminent forum—and therefore investing those communities and their institutions in Muslim institutions of rule—was an important Ottoman imperial strategy. In other words, this was the design of the system; it was not so much plural as it was hierarchical, where a Muslim institution functioned as something akin to an appellate court. Moreover, describing this state of affairs as legal pluralism is predicated on assumptions about both the imperial state and *millet* as normative orders that enjoyed uniformity in their practice across the empire. This was demonstrably not the case. Important to note, it is not until the nineteenth century that we see both the reformers engaging with the ideology of legal centralism for the first time and the non-Muslim communities producing documents that purportedly demonstrated the existence of a *millet* system as part of a bid to claim prerogatives during a period of social, political, and legal reconfigurations. Ottoman legal centralism and the *millet* system developed in tandem as they were mutually constitutive of one another. For this reason, contending that the *millet* system is an example of legal pluralism is, ironically, predicated on a legal centric and functionalist view of Ottoman law and society.

Engaging Ottoman Legal Regimes
Reducing non-Muslim engagement with Ottoman law to an analysis of the courts thus precludes taking a broader view of how Ottoman subjects, particularly non-Muslims, perceived legal regimes and how to interact with them. It also prevents us from understanding what exactly was plural about the legal system. Courts were not the only—in fact, probably not even the primary—venue for pursuing legal grievances and seeking redress. Based on available documentary evidence, the Armenian tool of choice for addressing those grievances was the petition. The petition was a prominent feature of Ottoman political and legal culture across communities.[15] While some may have been presented to a governor or prelate, the majority of Armenian petitions available to us were appeals made to the Patriarchate of Constantinople. Petitions, adorned with the colorful seals and choppy signatures of the community on whose behalf they were submitted, afforded Armenians greater latitude for expressing how they had been wronged. The number of endorsees attaching their name to a document could convey its importance more efficiently than the text itself. Secretaries at the Patriarchate of Constantinople scribbled the words "a *takrir* was drawn up" either on the reverse side or along the margins of many of these documents, recording that the issue had been referred to the Sublime Porte for redress.

The presence of these petitions tells us multiple things about how Armenians understood and perceived Ottoman law in the nineteenth century. First, they saw a legal system that extended beyond the courts. Armenians believed they could make claims on the coercive force of the Ottoman state to mete out justice against those whom they had accused of transgressions. That they could circumvent the Islamic court to make such appeals—particularly when the accused was a Muslim—is actually quite understandable. This was how Armenians shopped for a forum. Armenian Church institutions were integrated into the empire's political and legal systems. Church canon, law, and tradition thus belonged to imperial law; Church decisions regarding members of its flock, expressed through the pronouncements of clergymen, enjoyed the force of Ottoman law. The design of this system was not only to coopt indigenous institutions and place them in the service of the state but also to ensure the supremacy of the Islamic religion in imperial law. Islam ultimately welded these disparate parts together as part of a unified legal system. It also meant that Armenians experienced much of that system through their own institutions and would, consequently, turn to them to pursue legal matters. In the course of doing so, they actually reinforced this system by making a legal centralist claim on it. Working through *millet* institutions contributed to the centralization of the state.

Legal Centralism's Other: Ottoman Legal Pluralism
Armenians, particularly those of lower social standing in the provinces, thus had ample incentive to throw their weight behind the reform efforts. The reorganization of their own communal institutions offered them a tool for eliminating the legal orders that the centralizing imperial state now castigated as deviant or non-normative. The introduction of the *millet* system was therefore crucial to dismantling the networks that had fostered an Ottoman legal pluralism that operated along multiple fault lines of which the confession of religion was only one.

Scholars of colonial empires were among the first to make legal pluralism a subject of intellectual inquiry.[16] The geographic organization of the imperial project in these contexts makes it possible to read legal pluralism along a center-periphery axis. This highlights a peculiarity of approaches to Ottoman legal pluralism. A historiographical tradition that has treated the center-periphery binary as an orthodoxy has been strangely content to relegate legal pluralism to religious difference. Although Ottoman imperialism did not claim overseas colonies, the state was still a composite political formation marked by regional variation.[17] This variation had made it possible for local power brokers to craft repertoires of action to preserve prerogatives they had claimed for themselves and to wield extensive influence over a local population.

I contend that it is possible to reconcile these divergent approaches and to think of an Ottoman legal pluralism that accomodates both geography and confession. In his seminal article on the phenomenon, John Griffiths described legal pluralism not as a system but as a concomitant of social pluralism; legal pluralism emphasizes the policing of individuals' action.[18] A complex mélange of forces came together to produce the structures that socialized people into this policing. In this case, the description of *millet* as a networked communal space that I advanced in the first chapter is a useful tool for tracing out these structures by allowing us to locate non-Muslim actors and institutions in confessional, imperial, and local contexts. Unburdened from essentialist assumptions about *millet*s in turn makes it possible to move beyond the functionalist and positivist assumptions implicit in thinking about Ottoman legal pluralism. A legal plural order of things was more likely to bring pressure down to bear on the structurally disadvantaged than it was to provide subalterns with instruments of resistance. Resistance was more likely to find expression in "hidden transcripts."[19] Pro-reform Armenians thus embraced the Tanzimat's ideology of legal centralism and transmitted it through their communal institutions.

Legal pluralism was not only about multiple religions functioning in one hierarchical and unified imperial system; it was about how people experienced and made law on the ground. Those laws were not communicated only as written texts but also as social and cultural codes. The law that people made and experienced through these interactions constituted a legal regime unto itself, one that operated in contention with the normative order imagined by the Tanzimat. Still, these regimes theoretically occupied the same social field; as such, they afforded actors resources to make legal, political, and social claims. Yet they could do so only within the parameters that had been disproportionately delineated by the structurally privileged. Brokerage across networks within this social field—which linked actors and institutions from multiple ethnic and confessional backgrounds—was a key component in determining who would enjoy that disproportionate say. Contestation over ecclesiastical jurisdiction unfolded within this larger context and over these stakes.

PART 2: OTTOMAN LEGAL PLURALISM IN PRACTICE

Court-centric analyses of Ottoman legal pluralism have overstated the positive consequences of such an order for the empire's non-Muslims. Rather than use legal pluralism as a frame for writing history from below, by moving away from the courts I look at how actors who enjoyed a privileged social location—in this case, high-ranking clergymen—navigated and enforced a legal plural order to preserve their positions and the prerogatives associated with them. Because Ottoman Armenian ecclesiastical jurisdiction in the nineteenth century rested at the intersection of overlapping points of contention—intercommunal relations, intraconfessional politics, state centralization, and armed campaigns against Türkmen *derebey*s and Kurdish leaders—clergymen enjoyed access to multiple regimes of power. These, in turn, facilitated their ability to maintain a plural legal order that occupied the same social field as formal imperial law, including the legally-centric Tanzimat. Preservation of the prerogatives furnished by legal pluralism required the defense of networks that brought Armenian clergymen together with regional powerbrokers. They dealt violently with anybody who challenged the configuration of these networks.

Killing a Catholicos
On October 2, 1864, the prelate of Van, Iknadios Kakmajian, wrote to Harutiun Vehabedian, his counterpart at Erzurum, to convey the news that the Order of Aghtamar had elected a new catholicos.[20] The Order of Aghtamar had done so without prior authorization from the Patriarch of Constantinople. At the community's request, the government in Van dispatched a colonel and four *zaptiye* to prevent the consecration ceremony on September 26; their efforts failed. Midway through his letter, Kakmajian noted that the previous catholicos, Bedros Bülbül, had been banished by the Aghtamar Order to his nephew's home in the village of Pshavank to contemplate the missteps he had taken during his tenure. While there, an armed assailant entered the home and shot and killed Bedros. The police colonel brought a number of Armenians back to Van with him for questioning, including four clergymen (two bishops and two celibate priests), the village head of Pshavank, and the late catholicos's nephew. He also brought one Kurd. Out of respect for the Armenian Church and its role in imperial governance, the colonel decided against bringing Khachadur Shiroian, the newly consecrated Catholicos of Aghtamar, to the mainland despite his suspicion that Shiroian had played some role in the murder.

Kakmajian's letter is curious for several reasons. As discussed in Chapter 4, the Patriarchate of Constantinople had originally dispatched him to Van as prelate to support the reforming efforts of the trailblazing Mkrtich Khrimian. Yet the information he shared with the Patriarchate typically repeated points sympathetic to antireform actors such as Vehabedian and Shiroian. In particular, Kakmajian laid blame at the feet of Bedros Bülbül for his own demise. The letters to Constantinople accuse Bedros of failing to implement reform and of poisoning the community's relations with the local Muslim population. In a letter composed more than a year after the murder, Kakmajian claimed it was the Muslims whom Bedros had offended who ultimately pulled the trigger.[21] Kakmajian's discursive strategy in these letters, unwittingly or not, was a persuasive defense of Shiroian and his allies; Kakmajian casts Shiroian not as a usurper, but as a deft social entrepreneur who would have otherwise been a protector of his predecessor.[22] Eventually, the Patriarchate ordered Kakmajian and Vehabedian to participate in the investigation on the community's behalf. The report they produced in 1865 reiterated the negative traits ascribed to Bedros and reemphasized their belief that Shiroian and his allies had no hand in the murder.[23] A report composed by the governor of Van, under whose jurisdiction the investigation fell, conceded the possibility that two Kurdish bandits had dealt the final blow to Bedros, but insisted that Shiroian and his allies were probably implicated in the murder.

The most authoritative account of the killing emerged nearly nine years after it had occurred. Bishop Eremia Tevkants, a reformer originally from nearby Van, traveled through the dioceses of Aghtamar in 1873 as part of his inspection tour of Armenian communities of eastern Anatolia.[24] Tevkants's reports detail his own interactions with the provincial Armenian elite, as well as their relationships with local Muslim communities and the provincial government. His own familiarity with provincial culture, however, allowed him to maneuver beyond whatever reality the elite wished to project and access local knowledge. The story Tevkants reconstructed in his report describes how Shiroian plotted to have himself enthroned as Catholicos of Aghtamar. Bedros, who was on the mainland when word reached him, attempted to rush back to the island to thwart Shiroian. Bishop Hagop, a Shiroian ally, intercepted Bedros. He and his comrades then beat the catholicos and left him for dead on the sand of the beach before making their way back to the island.[25] Bedros somehow managed to reach his nephew's home in Pshavank, where he would later die.

A Kurd did, in fact, deliver the coup de grâce. But the killer who broke into the house and used a pistol to finish off what the priests had started was no simple bandit as suggested in earlier reports; the assailant was Gülihan, a son of Derviş Bey and the grandson of Khan Mahmud, the powerful Kurdish tribal leader and rebel who had joined forces with Bedirkhan Bey in the failed 1840s uprisings. As early as 1865, Kakmajian had informed the Patriarchate that Gülihan and Derviş Bey may have played a role in the killing but noted that the suspected killers had been associates of Bedros. This latter claim is dubious, but it served the rhetorical purpose of placing Bedros in league with known rebels and therefore in opposition to the Tanzimat program and an enemy of state. The murder arose from disputes connected to how Bedros engaged with local Muslims, a recurrent theme in Kakmajian's letters to the Patriarchate. Kakmajian's failure to describe those Muslims in satisfactory detail—particularly when the governor himself suspected Khachadur Shiroian—casts suspicion over whatever claims he made about Bedros.

Motive for Murder
The use of generic or essentialist terms such as "Kurds" or "Muslims" to describe non-Armenian communities tells us little—which was precisely the point. Doing so was a tactic used by Armenians embedded in networks of power to defend their prerogatives from actors invested in policies of state-centralization.[26] The aforementioned Bishop Hagop, who was also implicated in Bedros's murder, tried this tactic in an unsuccessful attempt to intimidate the peripatetic Bishop Eremia Tevkants; Tevkants's simple response that he, too, was *hayastantsi*, or a native of Armenia, made clear that reductive binaries would not fool him so easily.[27] The percolation of this terminology into official correspondence with the Patriarchate reflects the prejudices of many reformers, particularly those with an Istanbul-centric worldview, who were only too happy to frame deviant legal orders in essentialist terms; antireform Armenians embedded in local structures of power exploited this tendency to conceal the connections they had forged to integrate themselves in those power structures. Intercommunal relations, such as the one that Kakmajian had accused Bedros of forging with Derviş Bey, were reduced to the level of the individual rather than the institutional. However, those precise connections enjoyed an institutional quality that ultimately dictated how people made law at this edge of the empire. Contention over ecclesiastical jurisdiction underwrote a good deal of these institutional connections. Revealing these connections and the context within which they were forged will help to establish the different parties' motives for killing Catholicos Bedros Bülbül.

The Catholicosate of Aghtamar had originally been established to challenge the ecclesiastical hierarchy of the Armenian Apostolic Church in the context of Armenian dynastic politics of the Artsruni kingdom during the late Bagratid period (750–1045). It was originally founded as a bishopric in the tenth century and then elevated to a catholicosate in the twelfth century. From that point it began to contest the Catholicosate of All Armenians in Etchmiadzin for control of dioceses throughout Anatolia. Although Aghtamar did tender letters of submission to Etchmiadzin, occasional rebellion against the Mother See continued into the eighteenth century.[28] One such episode, which unfolded between 1737 and 1748, led to the excommunication of the reigning Catholicos of Aghtamar. Etchmiadzin later reversed that decision but issued an anathema that forbade any future election of a Catholicos of Aghtamar. Ultimately, Etchmiadzin was unable to enforce this anathema and in 1762 opted to recognize the reigning Catholicos of Aghtamar and his right to bless the holy chrism on condition of submission to Etchmiadzin and Church canon.

This recognition afforded the Brotherhood of Aghtamar institutional autonomy that facilitated its integration into local networks of power. Although information for the Catholicosate is lacking, a reading of its known interactions with Constantinople and the various Kurdish political formations in the area allows us to identify how Aghtamar participated in those relationships. While the Catholicosate rested on the island of Aghtamar in Lake Van, its jurisdiction was recognized over dioceses located south of the lake in the Kurdish borderlands. Aghtamar's holy see was spread over several of these areas, including parts of Siirt; Botan-Cizre; Hakkâri; and, perhaps most important, Müküs (Moks). Prior to their defeat by Ottoman forces in 1847, these regions were organized as a series of principalities and emirates ruled over by hereditary dynasts.

Leaders in these areas did not necessarily reject Ottoman sovereignty—a point they were often quick to highlight. Their actions—whether refusing calls for troops or appointing their own judges—did constitute a rejection of the central state's authority. Such stances invited predictable responses from the government. As a result, the imperial authorities ultimately compelled many Kurdish leaders, as well as their men, to join the Ottoman army in the 1830s. Unfortunately for the Ottoman state, this meant that many of these Kurdish leaders were present at the disastrous Battle of Nezib in June 1839, in which Egyptian troops under the command of Ibrahim Pasha routed the Ottoman army.[29] This episode galvanized many Kurdish leaders, particularly Bedirkhan Bey of Botan-Cizre, who had come to resent Ottoman interference in their affairs; the tempo of this interference increased following the proclamation of the Tanzimat in October 1839. Under the loose leadership of Bedirkhan Bey, a low-level rebellion subsequently broke out in the Kurdish emirates. The Ottomans' effort to undermine Bedirkhan Bey's influence by redrawing administrative boundaries in the area in 1842 and 1843 catalyzed the uprising's pace by providing the incentive for more Kurdish leaders to join him. The abolition of tax farming only a few years earlier had already signaled the empire's shift away from indirect rule—which had allowed local social and political order to flourish—and toward something more rigidly top-down and intrusive. In summer 1843, Bedirkhan Bey began making overtures to other Kurdish leaders, most notably Khan Mahmud of Müküs, to work collectively to resist the influence of Ottoman governors. Khan Mahmud and Bedirkhan Bey managed to repel Ottoman advances until their eventual defeat in 1847. Both rebel leaders would later die in internal exile.

In the northern regions of the Kurdish emirates, Armenian merchants and clergymen used their communal institutions to connect the Kurdish economy to regional centers in Diyarbakir, Erzurum, Mush, and Van. The clergy were thus instrumental in fashioning the networks that facilitated a legal and political order in the region, as their relationship to Khan Mahmud's family demonstrates. Thus, in 1843, the same year that Bedirkhan Bey and Khan Mahmud agreed to take more strident action against the Ottoman governors in the region, Aghtamar reenters the historical record when the reigning catholicos was murdered by "some Kurds."[30] A group of clergymen, led by Bishop Khachadur Mokatsi (from Müküs), approached Khan Mahmud to request permission to elect a successor. Despite protests from the Patriarchate of Constantinople, which expressed its wishes to Khan Mahmud directly, the election proceeded and resulted in the installation of Khachadur Mokatsi as Catholicos of Aghtamar in 1844. Constantinople's desire to end the catholicosate was almost assuredly connected to the Sublime Porte's active military campaign against the Kurdish rebels and targeted their allies among the clergy. Constantinople subsequently secured an order from the Porte for Khachadur Mokatsi's exile to Şebinkarahisar, where he would remain for two to three years. He received an imperial pardon and returned to Aghtamar, where he reigned until his death in 1851.

Without their patron Khan Mahmud, a more recalcitrant Brotherhood of Aghtamar was compelled to request permission from Constantinople to hold new elections. Although the Patriarchate initially denied permission, Constantinople gave its consent for elections following threats by some at Aghtamar to convert to Islam should they be left without a catholicos. Aghtamar subsequently selected the prelate of Van, Kapriel Shiroian, a powerful figure in regional politics and society who enjoyed good relations with both the Armenian merchants in Van and various Kurdish tribal leaders. He also sponsored the careers of other entrepreneurial clergymen, such as Boghos Melikian and Khachadur Shiroian. Melikian rose to the level of vice prelate under Kapriel Shiroian and used his position to establish relations with the leadership of the powerful Haydaranlı Kurdish tribes. Khachadur Shiroian, who was already allied with the family of Khan Mahmud, adopted Kapriel's surname to convey proximity to his patron in the Armenian Church. The selection of Kapriel Shiroian thus permitted Aghtamar to maintain its relations with Kurdish elites in the region and to preserve the catholicosate's location in local regimes of power. Kapriel's decision to remain at Van until 1856 afforded Khachadur Shiroian and his allies within the Brotherhood of Aghtamar both time and support to consolidate their positions within the catholicosate and to navigate the fallout stemming from the exile of Khan Mahmud in 1847, on one hand, and furnished some connections to Kurdish power brokers and notable Armenians outside their own dioceses, on the other.

Those connections located the Catholicosate of Aghtamar in network structures that ultimately regulated people's actions—albeit largely through informal mechanisms. In this environment, clergymen such as Khachadur Shiroian could exploit tax collection, come to amass fortunes, and leave no viable recourse available to those whom they wronged. Appealing to the normative order imagined by the legally-centric Tanzimat and Armenian Constitution was in many cases the only option that aggrieved parties could pursue for redress. They could appeal to inspectors dispatched by the center—either the Sublime Porte or the Patriarchate of Constantinople—or use labor migrant networks to open cases in the capital. In other words, actors were aware of the different available forums and consciously made political choices when selecting one avenue over the other. The Armenian National Constitution and related efforts to centralize imperial governance thus threatened those connections and, by extension, the legal order of things structured by those connections that existed on the ground throughout the dioceses of Aghtamar. Ensuring that those legal orders remained plural was paramount to Khachadur Shiroian and his clergy partners and ultimately motivated them and their allies in Khan Mahmud's family to conspire to commit murder.

The Catholicosate of Cilicia
Like Khachadur Shiroian in Aghtamar, Mkrtich Kefsizian—who would be made the Catholicos of Cilicia in 1871—would intervene in the implementation of reform projects as part of a bid to maintain a social and political order and,

in turn, perpetuate a plural legal order. In this regard, it is notable that Cilicia in the nineteenth century bore some similarities to Aghtamar. As a catholicosate, it enjoyed authority over its own clergy, consecrated its own bishops, and blessed and distributed the holy chrism throughout its dioceses. As I discuss below, this autonomy mapped onto a local political culture, which afforded the stewards of the Church the means to forge long-standing connections with regional power brokers. In the case of Cilicia, these were Türkmen *derebey*s.

The differences between the two catholicosates are perhaps more important. Unlike Aghtamar, the Catholicosate of Cilicia was not originally formed as a challenger to the Mother See; rather, the Catholicos of All Armenians settled there in 1293 after the seat of the Church had floated around other parts of Anatolia following the collapse of the last independent Armenian kingdom in the eleventh century at the hands of the Byzantines. Contrary to the wishes of the Mother See, the monastery at Cilicia elected to retain the title and prerogatives of a catholicosate following the return of the Catholicos of All Armenians to Etchmiadzin in 1441. While this initially precipitated conflict with Etchmiadzin, harmony between the two seats reigned by the middle of the seventeenth century. The comparable absence of conflict between Etchmiadzin and Cilicia actually made the latter a greater threat to Constantinople's claim to represent Armenians before the Ottoman government. The circulation of Cilician clergymen, including bishops, throughout the Ottoman Empire portended the possibility that some members of the community—including those outside Cilicia's dioceses—might find sufficient incentive to pledge their allegiance to Cilicia rather than Constantinople. Though strife was generally absent between Constantinople and Cilicia from the beginning of the eighteenth century forward, ecclesiastical tension between the two remained a distinct possibility; this tension was renewed in the nineteenth century when the Patriarchate of Constantinople allied with the Sublime Porte to project central power into regions it now viewed as a periphery.

Centralization in its various iterations had been a hallmark of imperial legal politics in the decades that preceded the declaration of the Tanzimat. The existential threat to the empire posed by Mehmet Ali and Ibrahim Pasha of Egypt, however, made the need to unify legal and social orders—in the view of the imperial center, at least—overwhelmingly apparent. Ibrahim Pasha's incursions into Anatolia, which as stated earlier had galvanized Kurdish notables such as Bedirkhan Bey, had a similar impact on many of the Türkmen *derebey* families, who now felt emboldened in taking increasingly antagonistic stances against the imperial government. As was the case in the Kurdish emirates, displacing a legal plural regime required reordering the social structures that had given that regime shape in the first place. The Catholicosate of Cilicia played a central role in brokering the networks that structured that legal regime. By the middle of the eighteenth century, the Catholicosate had come under the control of an Armenian clan, the Ajapahians, who allied with *derebey*s, particularly the Kozanoğlu clan, to produce an order of things that would rest in contention with the legally centric reform policies of the Tanzimat state and the Armenian Church.

The Ajapahian Dynasty

As stewards of the Armenian community of Cilicia, the Ajapahians played a seminal in brokering the networks that structured regional society. The family was a large clan composed of multiple branches that operated throughout Cilicia.[31] Many members of the clan entered the clergy, as both celibate and married priests. The inclusion of married priests among their number was critical to giving the clan a dynastic quality. This allowed Armenian elites an opportunity to marry into the Ajapahian family and for offices reserved for celibate priests to pass from uncle to nephew. Although their most prominent branch was based in Sis (Kozan), the location of the catholicosate and its primary monastery, the family was also in places such as Hajin (Saimbeyli) and Adana, which allowed it to become a force within the church administration with all the extramural privileges that this entailed. By 1731, with the blessing of the Patriarchate and the consent of the Porte, the family established its control over the catholicosate itself with the ascension of Ghukas I Ajapahian as Catholicos of Cilicia. An Ajapahian would sit on the throne until 1866.

As leaders of the community in Cilicia, the Ajapahians interacted with the Türkmen *derebey*s, who enjoyed a degree of autonomy in the region that bordered on independence. *Derebey*s did not hesitate to thumb their noses at the Sublime Porte or its expressions of central power. They controlled access to the region, operated their own militias, oversaw infrastructure, and collected taxes. At first glance, it would appear that their stance toward Armenians in the region was unaccommodating; this would corroborate some Armenian sources, which claim the Ajapahians submitted complaints to the Porte against the *derebey*s, particular the Kozanoğlu. *Derebey*s were in fact responsible for the murder of multiple Ajapahians: Mikael I (1758), Kapriel I (1770), Teotoros

III (1791, 1796, or 1801), and Giragos I (1822). Except for Kapriel, all died at the hands of the Kozanoğlu clan.[32] Much like the case in Aghtamar, this projects a binary view of Christian-Muslim enmity that belies larger social, political, legal, and economic dynamics.

Rather than intercommunal discord, the deaths of Ajapahian catholicoi connote the difficult role they played in maintaining a legal and political order and that, most likely, an individual catholicos had taken a position inimical to the interests of one power broker or another in that order of things. The Ajapahians' control of the catholicosate was recognized by an imperial berat, and Ajapahians or their representatives made trips to the imperial capital, which suggest that the catholicosate acted as an intermediary between the Kozanoğlu and the Sublime Porte.[33] While convincingly establishing that suggestion proves difficult, the evidence more persuasively demonstrates that the Armenian community led by the Ajapahians played a significant intermediary role in the social, political, and economic life of Cilicia. Armenian merchants, who could operate as such only with the tacit approval of Church leaders, enjoyed greater freedom of movement than most others in the area, which allowed them to circulate goods and capital within Cilicia and to connect its economy to regional markets.[34] Armenian clergymen similarly appear to have enjoyed freedom of movement into and out of the region, even at times when *derebey*s were fighting either with one another or with the central government. Moreover, Armenian merchants and *sarrafs* were tasked with procuring ceremonial garb donned by the Kozanoğlu elite, which required traversing territory held by rival *derebey* clans.[35]

Ajapahian stewardship of the community thus ensured that Armenian institutions and capital were deployed to furnish connections between the Kozanoğlus and others—be those rival *derebey*s, the imperial government, merchants, or markets. The Ajapahians were thus unequal partners in the creation and maintenance of a political, social, and legal order from which they benefited. They enjoyed recourse to Kozanoğlu coercion, which helped them to intimidate rivals and, in at least one notable case, expel Protestant missionaries.[36] Perhaps most important, they and their Armenian allies were free to engage in brutally exploitative tax farming that ensured the upward redistribution of community resources to the clergy, merchants, and *sarrafs*.[37] The diffusion of their influence through the ecclesiastical institutions of the catholicosate ensnared local notables and village headmen, who ultimately found themselves invested in perpetuating the status quo of Ajapahian and Kozanoğlu rule.

The Dynasty's Last Stand

Ajapahian rule of the catholicosate adds a layer of complexity to the center-periphery binary typically used to explore the relationship between the imperial government and provincial notables. Contextualization of Ajapahian stewardship of the Cilician Armenian community and its relationship to Kozanoğlu preeminence in the region instead lends support to the more recent historiographical intervention that frames the relationship between the imperial government and other forces as a partnership.[38] The onset of centralization in the eighteenth century changed that partnership; the introduction of the Tanzimat in response to Ibrahim Pasha's successful incursions transformed it entirely. *Millet* reform, as it would in other places, meant placing Armenian community institutions in the service of the Tanzimat's centralization project and partnering them with state institutions. The Ajapahian dynasty thus found itself targeted by the reformers.

The abrupt shift in the tenor of relations between Cilicia and Constantinople is telling. Constantinople issued an encyclical in 1839—the same year the Tanzimat was proclaimed—that admonished Catholios Mikael II for consecrating bishops.[39] Mikael ignored the encyclical at first and instead continued to rely on Kozanoğlu patronage to preserve his prerogatives. Over the following years, however, Mikael's resistance to center-imposed controls waned; successful government assaults on the *derebey*s probably weighed on his mind. With their patrons compromised, the Ajapahians found themselves less inclined to challenge the authority newly claimed by Constantinople as they were now compelled to navigate the shifting of loyalties between the *derebey*s and the Porte that had come to mark Cilician politics.[40] In 1851, for example, Mikael formally requested the Patriarchate's permission to consecrate a bishop.[41]

The Patriarchate seized the opportunity to apply more pressure on the Ajapahians. In 1854, the Patriarchate unilaterally composed a set of regulations for the catholicosate and dispatched a two-man committee to Cilicia to implement it. One of the members, a teacher originally from Van named Mkrtich Khrimian, would later become perhaps the most important Ottoman Armenian clergyman of the nineteenth century. Khrimian's reports on Cilicia are revelatory.[42] He was critical of Ajapahian rule and leveled sharp criticism at Mikael for his collaboration with the Kozanoğlus. Notably, he laid blame at the feet of the Ajapahians for widespread conversions to Protestantism and contended that their continued rule of the catholicosate would compel more Armenians to follow suit. Some Armenians, Khrimian seemed to imply, saw conversion as a novel method for engaging a legal centric order that sought to partner the imperial government with non-Muslim religious establishments. Unable to pursue grievances through the formal institutions of the Church, which officially connected them to the imperial state, or through the informal relationships that were likely to adjudicate such issues, Armenians could simply elect a new legal category to mediate their subjectivity as Ottomans by becoming Protestants. Conversion theoretically emancipated them from the reach of the Ajapahians. Protestantism also would have provided them access to a community capable of presenting issues before the Sublime Porte.[43] Newly converted Armenians were ultimately making a strategic decision about which legal order they wished to activate as part of an effort to circumvent the informal networks central to the Ajapahian-Kozanoğlu alliance.

Mikael's begrudging acceptance of Constantinople's terms did not lead to their immediate implementation. Giragos II Ajapahian, who came to sit on the throne immediately after Mikael's death in 1855, assumed a stance similar to that of his predecessor. According to Gould and others, the election of Giragos II—if one even took place—was carried out quickly and in secret.[44] Giragos II relied on his Kozanoğlu allies to silence any bishop who might voice opposition to the hastily organized consecration. Together they continued their abusive tax farming practices. Yet the die had been cast. The Sublime Porte's armed actions against the *derebey*s, spearheaded by special military units organized as part of the Reform Division (*fırka-ı islahiye*), ultimately defeated the Türkmen leaders. With the exception of one minor uprising during the 1877–78 Russo-Turkish War, the Porte had largely defeated the *derebey*s by 1865. Giragos II passed away that same year. With the Kozanoğlus defeated, the Ajapahians found themselves without the connections that had previously integrated them into political and social structures in Cilicia. They would need to take more drastic measures to perpetuate the Ajapahian dynasty. A group of notables led by Shahen Agha, the Kozanoğlus' Armenian advisor, convened a secret consecration at which they made Bishop Nigoghos Ajapahian the new Catholicos of Cilicia.[45] The passing of that social world, however, meant that Nigoghos's consecration would not even enjoy ceremonial importance. In 1866, the Patriarchate of Constantinople ruled Nigoghos's election illegal and the catholicosal seat vacant, and with the support of the Sublime Porte and its military, the patriarchate dispatched a bishop to Sis to serve as locum tenens catholicos.[46]

PART 3: PERIPHERALIZATION

Military victories and Armenian ecclesiastical reform undermined the networks that had structured the social field of which the legal pluralist order was an attribute. Reform efforts bid to complete the transformation of that field through the introduction of a center-periphery binary. The transmission of a legal centralist ideology through the empire's political institutions—including the Armenian Church—legitimized reform and encouraged actors of all faiths to adjudicate legal matters through officially sanctioned bodies. In so doing, the state hoped to undermine the network structures that had brought together *derebey*s, Kurdish emirs, and Armenian catholicosates into alliances as part of a provincial ruling class by redirecting social and political action toward formal institutions of state.

To disrupt the implementation of reform in their own dioceses, and thus preclude the introduction of a center-periphery binary in imperial governance, the leadership of the Armenian catholicosates deployed divergent network strategies to safeguard the legal plural order that had afforded them and their allies wide-ranging authority. Ironically, the methods they used to resist categorization as a periphery in a top-down bureaucracy facilitated the peripheralization of the communities they shepherded in the context Ottoman imperial governance. Peripheralization as discussed here describes the process by which Armenian actors and institutions became increasingly isolated in a network setting. The reform program's enticement that actors resolve disputes through institutions of state not only shuffled network connections and the relationships that made them but also weakened the social capital of provincial notables and Armenian clergymen alike. The network strategies used by the Armenian catholicoi—Mkrtich Kefsizian in Cilicia and Khachadur Shiroian in Aghtamar—as part of an effort to preserve their own social capital further severed the threads that connected Armenians to other forces in Ottoman society. Although their strategies ensured that as individuals they would continue to enjoy place of privilege—both enjoyed tenures that lasted until their deaths from natural causes—the communities they led became increasingly disconnected from other groups, including other Armenians, and thus pushed them to the margins of both imperial governance and Ottoman Armenian society.

Kefsizian in Cilicia

The Patriarchate of Constantinople treated the two catholicosates as a single comprehensive issue. The reformers may have had in mind the robust interpersonal connections between many of the prominent individuals involved.[47] Yet if we wish to understand the intersection of confessional difference and the composition of local structures of power in the production of plural legal orders, the failure of Cilicia's equivalent to Shiroian—Nigoghos Ajapahian, not Kefsizian, was the institutional heir to a preexisting set of arrangements—suggests that we instead explore the manners in which the two issues differed. Shiroian and Ajapahian wished to maintain network structures that helped to produce a legal order. Mkrtich Kefsizian would try to rearrange connections to produce a new order of things. When he was finally elected Catholicos of Cilicia six years after the passing of his predecessor, Kefsizian entered a social and political world where the meaning of the *millet*—as both a community and a legal category—was contested by a variety of forces, including Armenian notables, Ajapahian opponents, pro-reform Armenians, and the ecclesiastics of the Armenian Church. Kefsizian's deft manipulation of those forces allowed him to construct and maintain a type of legal pluralism that very nearly ripped the *millet* in two. As discussed below, he would pursue brokerage across networks to structure new connections that would link the Catholicosate of Sis to the government but cleave it from much of the Ottoman Armenian community.

The actual election of Kefsizian brought these forces together. The Armenian National Constitution, which had been the official law of the *millet* since its reintroduction in 1863, imagined a gridded political formation that unified practice through the creation of a series of prelacies subordinate to the Patriarchate of Constantinople. In theory, the Constitution changed how Armenians experienced imperial law by providing them new mechanisms for pursuing resolutions to their grievances. It could do so only if it enjoyed, on the one hand, the ecclesiastical legitimacy afforded it by the Catholicos of All Armenians in Etchmiadzin and the political authority offered by the Sublime Porte, on the other. Local structures of power—which were integrated into trans-imperial network structures—challenged this implementation. To ensure there would be no interference by the Ajapahians or their allies in the selection of a new catholicos, the Patriarchate ordered the 1871 election to be held in

Adana rather than at the seat of the catholicosate in Sis. At the request of the Patriarchate, the Porte also sent Hurşit Efendi, a military commander who had participated in the campaigns against the *derebey*s, to help oversee the election. Upon his election as Catholicos of Cilicia, the Patriarchate required Kefsizian to sign a letter that reaffirmed both his submission to the laws of the Church and his recognition of the supremacy of Etchmiadzin.[48] As the newly elected Catholicos of Cilicia, Kefsizian thus found himself at the intersection of imperial state power, networks, and contention over ecclesiastical jurisdiction. How he navigated these would dictate how he could consolidate his position.

Kefsizian's election signaled the formal conclusion of the Ajapahian dynasty. The significance of this must not be understated, as no non-Ajapahian had managed to claim the throne over the preceding century and a half. As both Shahen Agha's intervention and the Patriarchate's decision to move the election to Adana demonstrate, the Ajapahians retained influence throughout much of Cilicia. Kefsizian thus worked to expunge their presence. Using the powers now available to him, Kefsizian set about persecuting any Ajapahian who continued to serve in the clergy. One of them, Bishop Harutiun Ajapahian, converted to Islam to escape to Kefsizian's harassment.[49] Kefsizian also published a booklet entitled *Kilikya'nın Esrarı ve Sefaleti* (The Mystery and Misery of Cilicia) in Armeno-Turkish, which he authored under the pseudonym Bir Adana'lı Hay Eridasart ("An Armenian Youth from Adana") and addressed to his "*vetanperver kardaşlar*" ("patriotic siblings" [or "brothers"]).[50] The booklet appropriates the language of Mkrtich Khrimian, the Patriarch of Constantinople (r. 1869–1873) who enjoyed great popularity as a champion of the peasantry and the labor migrants, to criticize the Ajapahians for the wealth and power they had accumulated thanks to their partnership with the Kozanoğlus.

Kefsizian's choice of pseudonym—a nod to his alliances in Adana—was part of a strategy for marginalizing the Ajapahian stronghold of Sis. Kefsizian was a native of Marash and enjoyed connections in other parts of Cilicia. His decision to stoke intra–Cilician Armenian rivalry was not without basis. The Porte's armed incursions into Cilicia brought long-simmering differences among Armenians into the open. While the Armenian notables of Zeytun (modern-day Süleymanlı) had decided to take up arms to preserve the old social order, their counterparts in other parts of Cilicia—such as the Armenian notable who hosted Reverend E. J. Davis—actually joined the Porte in its assault on Zeytun.[51] In fact, many Armenian notables from towns and villages outside of Sis were open to the Porte's overtures and chose to ally with the government. For some, entering the government's service was an opportunity to preserve the prerogatives and social standing they had enjoyed under the *derebeys*.[52] For Kefsizian, this meant the apparent groundswell of anti-Ajapahian sentiment was not part of (or at least not confined to) a lower-class reaction to the end of *derebey* rule. The government's decision to produce the appearance of working central institutions through brokerage provided Kefsizian with a line of access to the government. This helped Kefsizian consolidate his rule in Cilicia and benefited him later when the stakes were raised.

Major transformations followed the government's defeat of the *derebey*s in Cilicia. The forced sedentarization of regional Türkmen and Kurdish tribes ushered in social, economic, political, and environmental changes. Moreover, Cilicia found itself host to a multitude of seasonal labor migrants—many of them Armenians from regions of eastern Anatolia such as Harput—as the region's plains were put in the service of cotton production to satiate world demand in the wake of abolition and the embargo of the South's economy during the American Civil War.[53] A cadre of Armenian notables who had opted for government patronage thus provided Kefsizian with stable bases of support for navigating these transformations. As an important clergyman in the Ottoman Empire, however, Kefsizian would ultimately have to contend with the ecclesiastical jurisdiction of the Armenian Church. As demonstrated in Chapter 2 by the case of Khanjalis, simple confession of faith alone did not define how Christians participated in imperial governance; ecclesiastical jurisdiction (and its recognition by the government) was paramount for enjoying access to institutions of imperial rule. To this end, the Catholicos of All Armenians in Etchmiadzin delivered Kefsizian a gift.

As was the case with both Jerusalem and Aghtamar, early versions of the Armenian Constitution—particularly the original 1860 document—failed to give precise definition to the relationship between the Catholicosate of Cilicia and the Patriarchate of Constantinople. The proponents of state centralization in the National Assembly were largely content to consider the catholicosate a prelacy unto itself.[54] This arrangement could work only with the blessing of the Catholicosate of All Armenians in Etchmiadzin, which had recognized the Patriarchate of Constantinople as its deputy in the Ottoman Empire; Cilician submission to Constantinople thus constituted recognition of Etchmiadzin as the Catholicos of *all* Armenians (*katoghikos amenayn hayots*) and a repudiation of Cilicia's history as a rival claimant to that title. The reformers in the capital considered a letter of submission from Kefsizian sufficient for ensuring that these arrangements remained in place. The Catholicos of Etchmiadzin—none other than Kevork Kerestejian, who as an Ottoman Armenian bishop had engineered the suspension of the Armenian Constitution a decade earlier—viewed Kefsizian's letter as insufficient and therefore a threat to the integrity of the Armenian Church. A pontifical bull issued in December 1871, which placed Constantinople and its patriarch in violation of Church law for its handling of the Cilician election, created a new opportunity for Kefsizian.[55]

Etchmiadzin's interference undermined the Patriarchate; weakened its claims to ecclesiastical jurisdiction and authority; and, by calling into question the legality of actions it had taken in accordance with constitutional rule, cast doubt over the legitimacy of the relationship between the Patriarchate and the Sublime Porte. With the Patriarchate thus compromised—the fallout contributed to the resignation of Patriarch Khrimian in 1873—Kefsizian felt emboldened to make demands of Constantinople. He instructed the Patriarchate to permit him to move the seat of the Catholicosate of Cilicia from Sis to elsewhere in the region, to expand Cilicia's jurisdiction, and to elevate his position in the eyes of the government; it was viewed as no more than a prelate at that point. The Patriarchate offered Kefsizian some concessions in 1874 in its *Instructions for the Dioceses of Cilicia*, which made the catholicosate a sort of super prelacy.[56] While other prelacies were directly subordinate to the Patriarchate in accordance with the "spoke-and-hub-without-the-wheel" model, Constantinople signaled its willingness to recognize the Catholicosate of Cilicia as the intermediate between it and Cilicia's dioceses. Constantinople's acquiescence on this point would not only have provided Kefsizian a measure of autonomy but also recognized a distinctly Cilician Armenian political culture.

Kefsizian, who understood the strength of his position, ignored the *Instructions*. He consecrated bishops without Constantinople's permission, and as the rolls of the National Assembly show, never sent delegates to the capital to participate in its deliberations. Meanwhile the Patriarchate found itself burdened with a full agenda that, in addition to the tumult between Constantinople and Etchmiadzin, relegated Cilicia a secondary matter. On the one hand, this allowed Kefsizian time to drag his feet with whatever orders he might receive from a distracted Constantinople. The Patriarchate did not give meaningful attention to the catholicosate again until late 1880. On the other hand, the tumult compelled Constantinople to demonstrate its loyalty to Etchmiadzin. Given that the latter seat was located in the Russian Empire, this proved burdensome for Constantinople—particularly in the wake of the Russo-Turkish

War of 1877–78—which rightly feared the Ottoman government may, in turn, question its loyalty.

Kefsizian thus found himself with multiple tools at his disposal when he arrived in the capital to negotiate with the Patriarchate. In talks that lasted nearly a year, Constantinople pressed Kefsizian to honor the ecclesiastical organization of the Armenian Church in the Ottoman Empire by remembering the name of the Catholicos of Etchmiadzin during the liturgy, consecrating and distributing the holy chrism only to Cilician dioceses, and barring the circulation of Cilician-ordained clergy beyond the jurisdiction of the catholicosate. Kefsizian refused the Patriarchate's requests and, in so doing, conveyed his rejection of Constantinople's claim to ecclesiastical supremacy within the Ottoman Empire. He also did not recognize the second principal relationship that endowed the Patriarchate of Constantinople with its authority. While in the capital, he held meetings with the Sublime Porte, where he argued that, as a subordinate of Etchmiadzin, the Patriarch was "little more than a Russian agent." Kefsizian, meanwhile, was allied with Armenian notables who had enlisted with the government and taken arms against their co-religionists in Zeytun. Sympathetic to this view, the Porte issued Kefsizian a new berat that omitted the proviso that "the Catholicosate of Sis [Cilicia] is subject to the authority of the Patriarchate of Constantinople."[57] In other words, the imperial government now regarded Kefsizian an equal to the Patriarchate of Constantinople. For the moment, Kefsizian had orchestrated Cilicia's de jure secession from the *millet*.

Constantinople ultimately convinced the imperial government to reverse its decision and subordinate Cilicia to the jurisdiction of the Patriarchate. Constantinople's victory was, however, symbolic at best. The Armenian Constitution had imagined the community as an active partner in governance and an agent of imperial reform; Armenians' contributions to the reform effort were to be realized through the ecclesiastical reorganization of the community in the empire. The Kefsizian episode, however, made it clear that the government no longer viewed the community as a partner in governance. When viewed from the vantage point of network analysis, the connection that Kefsizian had forged with the Porte—even if it was only temporary—constituted a bridge that bypassed Constantinople. Kefsizian's actions demonstrated the extent to which the collective social capital of the community—as headed by the Patriarchate—had weakened. Rather than submit to the authority of the Patriarchate and benefit from access to an empire-wide community, Cilicia chose to make itself a periphery in the network structures of imperial governance, thereby weakening the *millet*. Although the Constitution still ruled in Cilicia on paper, Kefsizian had made it clear that it was little more than a dead letter in his holy see.

Closure: Exoneration as Peripheralization
Khachadur Shiroian, the Catholicos of Aghtamar, would also claim victory over the reformers and evade any consequence for the murder of his predecessor, Bedros Bülbül. Shiroian formally pronounced his innocence at a session of the Religious Council in Istanbul on December 4, 1875, and on October 20, 1876, he departed the capital for Aghtamar as a free man.[58] Shiroian's masterful exploitation of the ecclesiastical jurisdictions, networks, and interconfessional alliances at the core of a legal plural order in the Kurdish-dominated borderlands had laid the groundwork for his eventual exoneration. These provided Shiroian with the means necessary to begin reordering the connections that had made the Armenian communities of Aghtamar as part of a bid to preserve his position in that order. Although his methods reveal an ingenious exploitation of the normative orders that contended for jurisdiction, the strategy that he ultimately chose to pursue was network closure. In the process, however, he disentangled Aghtamar's institutional connections to local structures of power, contributed to the removal of Armenian social capital in local society, and thus facilitated the peripheralization of Aghtamar in both Armenian and imperial governance.

The vicissitudes of monastery culture that marked life at the Patriarchate of Jerusalem were a staple of Ottoman Armenian politics and thus present at Aghtamar. Constantinople warned the clergy at Aghtamar to postpone the consecration of their own catholicos until a new Catholicos of All Armenians had been installed at Etchmiadzin. Bedros, who had already been selected, conveyed his willingness to wait for permission from both Constantinople and Etchmiadzin.[59] Forces among the clergy, including Khachadur Shiroian and his partners Hagop and Ghazar, pressured Bedros to proceed with the consecration. Their ally, Boghos Melikian, who was serving as acting prelate of Van at the time, ordered the consecration to proceed. Melikian's intervention signaled to Bedros Bülbül that many of the forces to which Aghtamar was connected through local power structures wished for the ceremony to be carried out immediately. Faced with such opposition, Bedros suspended his opposition and agreed to their terms. His first act as Catholicos of Aghtamar was to consecrate the clergymen Khachadur Shiroian, Hagop, and Ghazar as bishops; elevation to the rank of bishop was a prerequisite for eventual consecration as catholicos.

Aghtamar's decision to proceed with the election angered the Patriarchate of Constantinople, which refused to procure a berat from the Sublime Porte that would ratify the election of Bedros in the eyes of the imperial government until Aghtamar first agreed to a set of conditions.[60] These stipulated that Aghtamar recognize Etchmiadzin as the "eminent catholicos and supreme patriarch of the Church of the East and the legal successor of Saint Gregory the Illuminator."[61] To do this, Aghtamar was required to denounce its rebellious history against the Mother See and tender a formal letter of submission to the Catholicos of Etchmiadzin. In other words, ecclesiastical centralization, as part and parcel of the Tanzimat, once more posed a challenge to the informal prerogatives of the clergy. In particular, ecclesiastical centralization threatened to bridge the legal orders present in the Aghtamar's dioceses. Bedros Bülbül's willingness to agree to Constantinople's terms signaled that centralization had been extended to the region and thus marked him as an enemy of local power brokers—particularly those who may have had a vested interest in the recent rebellion against the imperial state.

This is the context against which we must read the reports and petitions critical of Bedros Bülbül's rule. Khachadur Shiroian and his allies strategically recognized the normative order claimed by the legally-centric aspirations of the imperial government and the Patriarchate of Constantinople by submitting such petitions; their goal was to engage that order to demonstrate its limitations in practice. Slandering Bedros called into question the agreement between Etchmiadzin and Aghtamar (which ultimately formalized Aghtamar's subordination to Constantinople), but more important, deflected attention from the catholicosate and its holy see and onto the individual of the reigning catholicos. With Bedros Bülbül caught between monastery pressures and local notables on the one side and the Patriarchate of Constantinople and the legally-centric Tanzimat on the other, Khachadur Shiroian and his allies enjoyed the freedom to use Aghtamar's ecclesiastical institutions—its clergy, monasteries, and parishes—to strengthen their connections with powerful Kurdish families, Armenian merchants, non-Aghtamar clergymen in neighboring prelacies, and local government officials. In the immediate aftermath of the killing, these institutional connections permitted the killers to confuse the police investigation and obstruct any subsequent inquiry in the future to uncover the role played by either Khan Mahmud's family or the Aghtamar clergy.

Khachadur Shiroian and Bishop Hagop then focused their attention on the ecclesiastical management of the dioceses. They first removed Bedros Bülbül's allies from all posts in the catholicosate, going so far as to exile one. Yet it was through the monasteries that they projected their power. Only clergymen may serve as monastery abbots in the Armenian Church; throughout Aghtamar's dioceses, however, village heads and other laymen loyal to Khachadur Shiroian assumed this role. Tevkants's analysis of this strategy is a smoking gun. He wrote that making village heads and other laymen monastery abbots ensured that nobody would lodge complaints "against the actions taken by Bishops Khachadur or Hagop, nor would anyone focus their attention on the Aghtamar Monastery to request reform or demand accountability."[62] In effect, this maintained the pluralism of the legal order: the law of the Tanzimat and the Armenian Constitution was theoretically available but contended with a rival normative order.

The efforts taken by Shiroian to defend his place of privilege consequently reified the nexus of connections that had anchored Armenian political life in borderlands governance. As we have seen in other cases, the institutions of the Armenian Church had facilitated brokerage across networks that anchored the community in Ottoman governance and society. They did not simply integrate the community into governance; they facilitated a movement of capital that helped to weld the empire together as a polity. Shiroian's reconfiguration of connections into a top-down structure atop which he sat constituted a different networking strategy: closure. While this concentrated power on his person, it had the unintended consequence of stripping the community of its social capital. Aghtamar thus became a place largely impervious to penetration by the centralization of the Patriarchate, but one that was also losing its footing in a local context.

As early as 1866, the Patriarchate of Constantinople had procured an order from the Sublime Porte demanding that Khachadur Shiroian appear before the National Administration in the capital for questioning in the matter of Bedros Bülbül's murder. The Patriarchate would wait two years until Shiroian finally arrived in Istanbul. Another eight years would pass before he was permitted to return to Aghtamar, recognized as its catholicos by both the Patriarchate and the imperial government, as confirmed by berat and his conferral with a *Mecidiye* medal of the first order.[63] But to what did he return? The concentration of power in the person of Khachadur Shiroian had precluded Armenians throughout Aghtamar's dioceses from employing either of the legal systems theoretically available to them to pursue grievances. Many voted with their feet to find a different order of things. Without an Armenian population to shepherd, Aghtamar's properties gradually fell into the hands of Muslim notables. The seat of the catholicosate was reduced to a simple destination for pilgrims, overseen by monks whom one traveler regarded as little more than hoteliers.[64] Shiroian's paranoia prevented him from consecrating any other bishops for fear that they might emulate their master. Following Shiroian's death in 1896, the remaining bishop at Aghtamar left the catholicosate in hopes of receiving recognition from Etchmiadzin. Meanwhile, the jurisdiction over the catholicosate's dioceses gradually fell to the Prelacy of Van. Increasingly bereft its connections to local forces while actively severing its links to Constantinople, Shiroian's dioceses became peripheral in the network structures to which they belonged. Aghtamar essentially died with its last catholicos.

CONCLUSION

As Griffiths instructs us, legal pluralism is an attribute of a social field, not a legal system.[65] This is not to say that a social field stands in opposition to a legal system, but to highlight that social relations produced a socially constituted normative order that enjoyed legitimacy in a given setting.[66] An investigation of legal pluralism in the context of Ottoman non-Muslims should, as this chapter has argued, thus turn away from a focus on the courts or non-Muslim access to communal institutions and instead emphasize the making of social structures that contributed to the policing of people's actions. This, in turn, invites us to consider the ways in which the elite of those communities were able to forge connections by which they could integrate into and consequently remake network structures.

Ottoman legal pluralism was therefore not a tool that afforded non-Muslims—at least the overwhelming majority of them—a competitive advantage vis-à-vis Muslims. Legal pluralism and the nexus of network structures that helped to produce it brought the weight of the empire down that much more forcefully on the majority of those communities' members. Legal pluralism did provide actors access to multiple legal mechanisms and regimes. These were, however, interconnected and largely in the service of the structurally privileged. For most Ottoman Armenians, particularly those in the provinces, interaction with these regimes and mechanisms was less about forum shopping and more about the encounter with variable forms of coercion that would place sanctions on behavior that either transgressed norms or otherwise threatened the status quo. That is why many of these provincial Armenians found themselves allied with the reformers in the capital: the legal centralist ideology promised both legibility. For the reformers, this meant the implementation of a normative order that regarded other legal regimes as illegitimate. For provincial Armenians, this promised an interaction with one legal regime over which, through the institutions of the Constitution, they would enjoy some formal control.

Elimination of the plural legal order required the elimination of its concomitant, social pluralism, and the structures that had made them both possible. The project of the Tanzimat and the Armenian Constitution was thus not simply a question of what texts would enjoy the force of law but rather one of competing agendas over how Armenians would deploy their collective social capital in Ottoman governance. For the proponents of legal centralism, Armenian social capital should have been deployed to help produce a legible top-down order that helped to project the authority of the central state into the provinces. Opponents of reform in the provinces, including a large segment of the clergy and their allies among the upper classes, sought to preserve the networking world in which Armenian social capital was deployed to help sponsor pan-imperial network structures and, by extension, produce regimes of power that policed the behavior of Armenians and others. The institutions of the Armenian Church had provided them the tools by which these Armenian elite could integrate into structures of power and enjoy a stake in preservation of the status quo.

To challenge the reform program, Shiroian and Kefsizian turned to two social capital strategies: closure in Aghtamar and brokerage in Cilicia. The consequences of each strategy were significant for the community. While they were able to produce obstacles to the implementation of reform projects and, as a result, maintain a privileged location in local structures of power, they peripheralized their dioceses in both imperial and community governance. Unbeknownst to Kefsizian, Shiroian, or the reformers at the time, the tension produced by their conflict chipped away at the institutional and structural moorings that had anchored the community in imperial governance and society.

It did so because the reform program shaped how Armenians could imagine Ottoman politics and their role in it. By reframing the ideology of the Tanzimat as legal centric, we can see more clearly the stakes over which Armenians clashed within their own community and its implications for imperial governance. This was nothing less than a reinterpretation of what the politics of difference could mean in the Ottoman context. Armenians' appropriation of the state ideology afforded them a political language for participating in this reimagined politics as they could now denounce the legal orders they were likely to encounter as illegitimate or deviant. Finally, the reframing of the Tanzimat's ideology as legal centralism has allowed us to decouple Ottomanism from the top-down policy initiatives of the Sublime Porte. This is not to say that Ottomanism was not an important feature of the Tanzimat period. In fact, the ideology of legal centralism was a primary component of it. Properly understanding what it was, however, requires focusing our attention on the reformers on the ground in the provinces.

4 OTTOMANISM

WHAT, THEN, IS OTTOMANISM? As discussed in Chapter 3, historians have largely followed the pan-Turkist ideologue Yusuf Akçura's description of Ottomanism as a political ideology—juxtaposed against either (Turkish) nationalism or Islamism—that, as a part of the Tanzimat reform program, sought to integrate the empire's subjects with one another. Akçura's identification of Ottomanism as such in 1904 suggests that it may have enjoyed some currency in political and intellectual circles as an ideology in the early twentieth century. Yet Akçura was himself an ideologue who, in the course of advocating for a political community predicated on exclusion, had ample incentive to cast Ottomanism as an ideology that had failed to weld together the seemingly disparate communities across the empire under the Ottoman banner. Unsurprising, some ideological stances implicit in Akçura's formulation—the immutable otherness of Ottoman non-Muslims and the boundedness of their communities—have found expression in professional historiography. Non-Muslims, according to this line of thought, had been presented a choice: shed ethno-confessional identities for the sake of the empire or pursue secession.

Subsequent scholarship has problematized this approach by demonstrating that nascent nationalist or patriotic sentiment among non-Muslims (or, in the case of the Arabic-speaking regions, non-Turks) could nestle alongside loyalty to the Ottoman state without any apparent contradiction.[1] Despite these interventions, the pervasiveness of an Ottomanism/nationalism binary persists in a good deal of the historical literature. I contend that this is so because of a positivist reading of Ottoman history that reads ideology as a causal or motivating force for interpreting social action. Deploying such an approach introduces a teleology that treats outcomes—such as the collapse of the empire—as inevitable. The retroactive application of ideology as causal force in turn produces a coherent narrative that, as self-fulfilling prophecy, absolves the state or its sociological majority of any complicity in those outcomes, on one hand, and robs non-Muslims of any real agency by ignoring the cultural contingencies they mediated while making claims on imperial governance, on the other.

This chapter responds to these challenges by arguing that historians conceive of Ottomanism as a repertoire or cultural tool kit. My focus in this chapter and the next centers largely on Armenian clergymen with ties to Van, an important provincial town near the Russian border. While these clergymen sparred with their opponents in a largely local context, the Ottomanism repertoire that they crafted and deployed relied on a set of cultural tools that blended together the imperial, local, and ecclesiastical. It is precisely because of their location in Ottoman society as Armenian clergymen that they were positioned to make a nuanced reading of the organization of Ottoman society and to understand how that organization constrained and facilitated social action. The cues they took from that reading signaled opportunities for probing the structures—namely, networks—that contributed to the organization of politics and society. In the course of doing so to make claims on imperial politics and local society, clergymen at the eastern edge of the empire made state centralization a primary facet of Armenian politics and a preferred method for justifying reform policies.[2]

To explain how an Armenian articulation of Ottomanism made state centralization a principal component of Armenian politics during the reform period, I first describe how local actors in Van deployed a variety of social, cultural, and economic resources to extend their control over community institutions and participate in imperial governance. The tension between these notable Armenians and their less privileged coreligionists helps us to understand which opportunities were available to those seeking to challenge the status quo. Subtle shifts in structure and the distribution of capital presented reformers new possibilities for taking and justifying action. Here, we are introduced to the early decades of a decades long war between Boghos Melikian, a clergyman infamous for his abuse of the flock that he shepherded, and Mkrtich Khrimian, a popular reformer from the provinces who would later serve as

Patriarch of Constantinople and thereafter as Catholicos of All Armenians in Etchmiadzin.

THE EDUCATION OF A PRELATE

Center and periphery, as discussed to this point, are terms that historians should treat as contingent and fluid rather than fixed and defined. The use of these terms has helped to amplify the otherwise fading echoes of modernization theory and structural-functionalism in Middle East historiography, which were highly influential during the field's formative years in the North American academy, by ensuring that the imperial center remains at the forefront of historical analysis. More recent cohorts of scholars have pushed back against this privileging of the central government and its agency by using tools from multiple intellectual traditions. This revisionist body of scholarship has, among other things, provided a framework for critically reading documents—particularly those produced by the state—to identify the agency of actors located at the margins of imperial society.[3] This has entailed understanding how the imperial center "made" peripheries to justify policy initiatives. It has also demonstrated that, rather than a passive receptacle, in certain contexts peripheries did influence the elaboration of said policy, if they did not dictate terms outright.

The case of Iknadios Kakmajian, who was made prelate of Van in 1859, exemplifies much of this inherent tension between center and periphery. Kakmajian was a native of Istanbul whose experience as a clergyman prior to his appointment in Van had been largely confined to the capital. His appointment was part of a broader effort made, on the eve of the introduction of the Armenian National Constitution, to reform and reorganize the Armenian community in the provinces. In particular, he was sent to Van to aid the efforts of a local clergyman, Mkrtich Khrimian, who had just returned to the town of his birth after spending time in the capital. Khrimian had encountered resistance in his efforts to introduce educational reform, primarily at a monastery just outside of Van, where he had been appointed abbot by the Patriarchate. Both Khrimian and his opponents understood, of course, that education was the opening salvo in the contests of reform. The stakes were, as the Constitution would soon make abundantly clear, about state centralization and a reformulation of non-Muslim engagement with imperial governance.

Khrimian and Kakmajian both enjoyed the support of the Porte-employed Armenians reformers in the capital. Yet significant differences marked the two.

Their published works are a case in point. Khrimian's body of work, which I discuss below in more depth, occasionally explored religious themes. It more frequently showcased a provincial Armenian cultural ethos through its discussions of labor migration, family life, and the community's ties to the land of Armenia. Kakmajian's lone known publication was a booklet that explained and interpreted the Holy Communion and the Divine Liturgy, published in 1862 while he was Prelate of Van.[4] These contrasts in outlook reflected the divergent cultural scripts available to each. Although the careers of each were forged in the crucible of the Tanzimat and the culture of the Armenian Church, and although they were allied in the project of imperial reform, they were consigned to making very different readings of politics and society in Van.

Kakmajian thus arrived in Van with much of the intellectual and cultural outlook that we would associate with a representative of a metropole descending upon a periphery. He exuded erudition and cosmopolitanism; moreover, he had been dispatched to the edge of the empire to eradicate legal nonconformity through the introduction and enforcement of a normative order. The records of his experience as prelate—available to us largely in the form of letters and reports that he had submitted to the Patriarchate in Istanbul—reflect the underlying assumptions that informed his reading of the politics that he had been charged with reforming. He of course bemoaned the lot of his flock, particularly their suffering at the hands of Muslims, yet also made a point to make multiple references to provincial Armenians' ignorance of their own religion and its ceremonies.[5]

Most important, however, his correspondence used language palatable to the Armenian reformers employed by the Porte. His paternalistic view of provincial Armenians as backward extended to his interpretation of their politics. In an 1866 missive to the Patriarchate, for example, he noted that provincial Armenians were inexperienced in matters of governance, as they had begun to enjoy freedom only twenty years ago—an invocation of Bedirkhan's failed revolt and the consequent destruction of the Kurdish emirate.[6] This allowed Kakmajian to make an implicit juxtaposition of provincial Armenians against Armenians in Istanbul or other urban centers in western Anatolia who had crafted the normative order that he now sought to introduce and to define the former order as an anachronism. It also allowed him to cast local Muslims, particularly the Kurds, as antireform and enemies of the state. Here, he made very clear that the Church and his flock were, in fact, the Porte's true allies.

As I argue in preceding chapters, pro-reform Armenians viewed their own communal reform as part of a larger effort to reorganize imperial governance. The interest in collaborating with pro-reform clergymen from the provinces, such as Khrimian, his acolytes, or others such as Bedros Bülbül or Mkrtich Dikranian of Diyarbakir, stemmed from a desire to access local knowledge and develop partnerships in the periphery that could be placed in service of the state. Despite being an outsider to Van, Kakmajian did manage to procure such information and sent detailed reports on various Kurdish rebels and their allies in the local government—namely, members of the Timurzade clan.[7] Yet how he came to possess such information, despite not knowing the lay of the land, reveals the constraints placed upon Kakmajian's ability to really learn or explore how Armenian politics were an endemic feature of Ottoman society in and around Van.[8]

Here it bears recalling that we were first introduced to Kakmajian in Chapter 3, when he appeared to have cooperated with Harutiun Vehabedian, the Armenian Apostolic prelate of Erzurum, to produce a report that masked the involvement of Khachadur Shiroian in the murder of the Catholicos of Aghtamar. Knowing that Kakmajian went to and returned from Van with the blessing of the Armenian reformers at the Sublime Porte—he was elected Patriarchate of Constantinople by them in 1869, which prompted him to leave his post as prelate of Van, but he passed away before his reign could commence—begs us to ask why he appears to have collaborated with individuals opposed to reform. It seems this way because the individuals best positioned both to access such information and to convey it to Kakmajian were clergymen and their merchant allies opposed to reform. As an outsider and reformer, Kakmajian's outlook, as suggested by a reading of his letters, was governed by three binaries: center/periphery, non-Muslim/Muslim, and state/antistate. The Armenians on whom he had to rely for information and local know-how played on his prejudices about provincial life. Clergymen from Aghtamar, who had likely conspired to kill Bedros Bülbül, were among Kakmajian's informants. His letters also express similar gratitude to local Armenian notables for making him privy to machinations within the local government. In the course of doing so, these antireform actors consciously deployed monoliths that reinforced the categories to which Kakmajian was predisposed. As a result, they were able to present to him an Armenian politics of Van that argued for the status quo—and the delegitimation of lower-class political aspirations—by convincing Kakmajian that accord between the well-to-do and the artisans was what afforded the community status in the eyes of the local government. Intracommunal accord and the consequent association with the state was what, in this line of thought, distinguished Armenians and their politics from those of the rebellious Kurds.

Kakmajian thus arrived in Van in 1859 with preconceived notions of what a periphery was. Those prejudices precluded him from understanding the integrated nature of imperial politics and consequently made it possible for local Armenian power brokers to teach him only what they wanted him to learn. He thus found himself acting as an advocate for the very people against whom Khrimian—with the tacit consent of the Porte—was ready to go to war.

CONSTITUTING ARMENIAN POWER IN VAN: MERCHANTS AND *MÜTEVELLIS*

Kakmajian's rote deployment of binaries failed to account for the fluidity that marked the networked world of Ottoman governance. More specifically, his letter suggests he failed to comprehend that Armenian institutions had already been placed in the service of exercising Ottoman sovereignty and ensuring that imperial authority did, in fact, emanate from the central government in the capital. This inability explains, in part, why he ultimately found himself at the mercy of local fixers in the clergy and open to the information that they provided him; to a certain extent, the notables' politics did share points of convergence with those of the reform project. As elsewhere in the Ottoman Empire, the Armenian well-to-do of Van and their allies in the Church exploited their location in this order of things to mobilize a variety of resources not only to participate in imperial governance and society but also to exert pressures on the Armenian community to perpetuate the status quo.

British consular officials used the term "notable" to describe the lay Armenian elite of Van. In local discourse, they were called either "the twelve" in Turkish (*onikiler*) or "the princes" (*ishkhank*) in Armenian. In some cases, they claimed prerogatives that dated back to Safavid control of the region in the sixteenth century. They may also have belonged to the so-called *vangulis*—Armenians who supposedly enjoyed the right to wage war on the Ottomans' behalf.[9] It is just as likely that they, like their *amira* counterparts in Istanbul, wished to endow the prestige they already enjoyed with noble descent. As non-Muslim well-to-do in Ottoman politics and society, the notables in Van and the *amira*s in the capital shared networks, buttressed by the ecclesiastical structure of the Armenian Church, as well as a politics that sought to maintain those connections. These politics of course revolved around the mechanisms of tax collection, which allowed the empire-wide Armenian elite to realize as much as a fivefold return on their investment.

The wealth that the notables generated from tax collection went hand in hand with other forms of capital that they possessed. Many of them were engaged in some form of trade and had offices throughout the region. In the second half of the nineteenth century, two of the affluent in particular—Kevork Bey Kaljian and Sharan Bey—controlled most of the bazaar in Van. At least two of the families, the Hamamjians and the Eramians, had extended their trade networks to include Tiflis and Istanbul. Others, such as the Terzibashians, were landowners. The economic imprint that the notables left on the region placed them in relationships with other local power brokers, such as Muslim notables, and government officials. Armenian merchants were particularly well placed to serve as economic brokers between Kurdish groups in the area and the cities and towns. The empire-wide commitment of the Armenian well-to-do to imperial governance, as discussed in Chapter 1, allied the Van notables as well with local governors and other officials. It should come as little surprise that members of the notables sat on local government councils.[10]

As Armenians in the Ottoman Empire, the endurance of the notables' power was predicated on their ability to extend their influence over their own community, the exploitation of which ultimately underwrote most of their enterprises. This influence was projected through the institutions of the Armenian Church. Local community councils, which enjoyed prerogatives that were not checked by elections prior to the introduction of the Constitution, oftentimes selected a prelate or communicated with the either the Patriarchate or the local government on the community's behalf. The signatures on a document produced by such a council in May 1851 reveal that eight of its members hailed from the local Armenian elite.[11] Yet even if a prelate had been appointed by the Patriarchate and with the backing of the Sublime Porte, as was the case with Kakmajian, the infusion of notable capital into the institutions of the Armenian Church made it such that the notables' influence would be brought to bear upon whatever clergyman was charged with shepherding the community.

The notables did this by using monasteries' status as pious foundations in the Ottoman imperial system. As pious foundations, or *vakıf* (*waqf* in Arabic), Armenian monasteries and their properties were not subject to the same rules of taxation as were other enterprises. This made them potential sites of money laundering. In the Muslim context, abuse of this system became so rampant that the Sublime Porte was compelled to create a special ministry for auditing Muslim pious foundations. As discussed in Chapter 2, the individual most likely to benefit from intervention in the activities and finances of a monastery was its trustee, or *mütevelli*. The *mütevelli* was thus positioned to exert tremendous influence on the abbot of a monastery and to dictate, in part, how he could interact with his flock or the local government. Kaspar Agha, a patriarch of the aforementioned Hamamjian family, is a case in point. Hamamjian was a native of Van who had relocated to Istanbul to oversee his business interests in the capital. Yet he retained his position as the *mütevelli* of two important monasteries near Van—Lim and Gduts. Correspondence between him and one of the abbots, Hagop Topuzian, reveal the extent to which a *mütevelli* could impact a monastery.[12] When Topuzian had difficulties with the local government concerning ownership of a salt mine that had been bequeathed to the monastery, for example, he had to appeal to Hamamjian to request that the Patriarchate intercede with the Sublime Porte on its behalf. He likewise had to request Hamamjian's permission to expend money to repair a door.

The example demonstrates how oversight of a monastery's finances dictated how communal institutions could be used to determine who participated in imperial governance and how. That an abbot had to request a *mütevelli*'s permission to repair a door, for example, reveals how fleeting the likelihood that community funds might be used for something approximating a public good was. As argued earlier, the Armenian share of Ottoman sovereignty condensed around the institutions of the Church; the *mütevelli* system thus created bridges to the Patriarchate (and, by extension, the Porte) and local officials that were commanded by the well-to-do and could be crossed only at great cost. Because most Armenians could not afford the toll, they were effectively disenfranchised from governance and had to find alternative mechanisms to access it. Such arrangements appear to have continued into Kakmajian's term as prelate. His letters inadvertently reveal that nonelites had to rely on labor migrant networks to bring concerns to the attention of the Patriarchate. He used his position as prelate not only to make the Patriarchate aware of the notables' grievances but also to use the ecclesiastical structures of the Church as a collection agency directed at individuals—Armenian and Muslim alike—who had slipped out of the region without settling their debts with the notables.[13]

The influence that a *mütevelli* enjoyed over an abbot was projected even further through the latter's monastic order. Before the reorganization of the community into a series of discreet prelacies, monasteries—particularly larger ones—functioned as smaller dioceses that were charged with furnishing the spiritual needs of their flock and representing them before the government. Many of the larger monasteries, such as Lim and Gduts, came to administer smaller monasteries in the area. Topuzian, the abbot of Lim, thus enjoyed the right to determine who would head smaller monasteries, such as Skanchelagorts or Metsopay. He appointed priests only he had himself ordained, thus bringing these smaller monasteries into Lim's orbit; this strengthened Topuzian's position while enhancing the institutional reach of the *mütevelli*. Moreover, many of these monasteries, small and large, shepherded communities in areas where Muslim power brokers, particularly Kurdish tribesmen, held more sway than the local government. Clergymen forged relationships with these powerful actors, which they sometimes consummated by becoming *kirve* to a chief's sons by participating in the Muslim circumcision ceremony. Thus, the clergy networks that helped lace together the Church's ecclesiastical organization at the local level afforded affluent members access to yet other sites of power in imperial governance. Monasteries and their clergy thus functioned as far-reaching conduits for the projection of notable power and influence that precluded nonelite access to governance.

Unlike Khrimian who, as the son of a local guildsman, understood perfectly well the structures of power in Van, Kakmajian seems not to have realized just how entrenched notable power was, how it was distributed through the very institutions of the Church that he led, or how that furnished connections with the Muslims whom he freely criticized. Coming from the capital, he had his own idea of center and periphery, something that the well-positioned clergy and notables were only too happy to indulge. By doing so, they flipped the tables on Kakmajian. Although he had come from the capital to transform a periphery, it was the provincial elite who would define the center—its role and its limits in the politics of Van—and place it at their service.

THE RESILIENT ARMENIAN SHAYKH

Their investment of capital in the institutions of the Armenian Church meant that the notables could bring immense pressure to bear upon the clergy. This pressure could be applied, directly or indirectly (as was the case with Kakmajian), to preserve the status quo. Clergymen may have had to negotiate the influence of the well-to-do, but they were not passive actors. At the end of the day, it was the clergy that operated the institutional moorings by which the communal space was ultimately woven into imperial governance; that is, after all, why the lay elite invested so heavily in the Armenian Church. The clergy, which already bore the responsibility of collecting some taxes, thus found itself allied with the notables—and other non-Armenians—in perpetuating the connections that facilitated imperial governance. And in fact, as the examples of Khachadur Shiroian, Harutiun Vehabedian, and Mkrtich Kefsizian make clear, enterprising clergymen were especially well positioned to reap the benefits of brokering the different groups of actors that connected across the communal space. The structural pressures that the notables could exert on priests thus did not encourage passive behavior but instead provided immense incentives to clergymen to maximize their positions in these network structures by precluding their flocks from challenging the extant arrangements.

Arguably, no one was more effective at this than Boghos Melikian. Much of the available evidence of Melikian's life conjures the image of a classic villain. A transcription of a Lenten sermon delivered in 1885, for example, describes how Melikian turned the *bem* into a literal bully pulpit by berating his parishioners and threatening his opponents in vulgar Armenian laced with colloquial Turkish.[14] That he was even delivering such a sermon as late as 1885 speaks to his ability to survive the challenges his opponents would mount. These would be frequent: one of the very first items addressed by the newly formed National Assembly at its opening session in 1860 was a complaint against Melikian. The Armenians of Van anointed Melikian with the epithet "*hayanun sheykh*," or "the shaykh with an Armenian name." He hailed from the village of Noravank, where he was born in 1820, likely into poverty. Per a British consular report, he is alleged to have been conscripted into an irregular military force in the 1830s to fight against Muhummad Ali.[15] He was captured near Acre and returned to his native region only in the early 1840s. Shortly thereafter, he became a deacon at the Lim monastery. His relationship with Kapriel Shiroian—a prelate of Van who ultimately sponsored the careers of a number of important clergyman—began here. Melikian's standing as a clergyman advanced quickly. He accompanied a delegation, possibly headed by Topuzian, to Tiflis—likely for fundraising. In 1850, he was made the abbot of Varak. Two years later, he was called to serve as Kapriel Shiroian's vice-prelate. Later that decade, he was made abbot at Gduts. Finally, the notables installed Melikian as prelate in 1857 following the passing of Kapriel Shiroian. Over the objections of the guilds, the Patriarchate confirmed his installation and the imperial government conferred him with the Fifth Order Mecidiye.[16]

Despite enjoying the apparent support of the Church hierarchy and the government, Melikian would find himself under near constant assault by pro-reform forces over the next two decades. In addition to formally bringing him to the attention of the National Assembly, reformers managed to open a court case against him in the capital.[17] They would inundate the Patriarchate with requests that Melikian receive some kind of punishment for his transgressions against the flock. In an anti-Melikian booklet entitled *The Accusations Against Boghos Vartabed of Van*, the reformers dated Melikian's daily abuse of the flock to his ordination as a celibate priest and contended that he was "the cause of the moral and material death of the [Armenian] community of Van."[18] Even the brotherhood at Gduts, where he was abbot, petitioned the Patriarchate for his removal.[19] That the brotherhood, which was itself thoroughly enmeshed in local politics, dared to challenge Melikian speaks to the degree of his unpopularity in Armenian circles. The notables in Van, of course, countered with their own petitions that defended Melikian, attempted to laud his more positive attributes, and published their own booklet that included a series of letters authored by pro-Melikian clergymen, such as Harutiun Vehabedian, and slandered his opponents.[20]

For the most part, Melikian won a decades-long war between him and pro-reform forces that generally coalesced around Mkrtich Khrimian. In the course of prosecuting this rebellion against the reform program, however, Melikian revealed the extent to which he and the community's institutions were not just constituent components of imperial governance but in fact influential in its politics. Melikian's aggressive policing of community boundaries positioned him to broker multiple sites and actors through community institutions. In so doing, he demonstrated the limits of the center-periphery vision that informed pro-reform advocates such as Kakmajian. This is why the aforementioned anti-Melikian booklet argued that it would be "impossible for Boghos [Melikian] to go to the [Lim] Anapat or another of Van's monasteries and not interfere in National issues."[21] Real reform required local knowledge, cultural know-how, and a willingness to sever the connections that anchored the community in networks of governance. The simple introduction of an electoral politics via the implementation of the Constitution and its representative councils was not sufficient for provincial Armenians to realize the transformative potential of the Tanzimat so long as governance remained nodal.

THE *ACCUSATIONS* OF CRIMES AGAINST THE FLOCK

The *Accusations* present a straightforward accounting of transgressions committed by Melikian against his flock. They describe in some detail the specific actions Melikian took, when and against whom he took them, and with whom he may have conspired. Yet they reveal much more. To this point, we have seen the stakes over which the politics of reform played out—namely, access to governance, tax collection, and privilege—and why the clergy and the notables guarded these prerogatives jealously. The vivid descriptions of Melikian's activities presented in the booklet in fact reveal how the network structures responsible for anchoring the community in imperial governance and local society were constructed. Melikian's strategic use of violence ensured that he would marshal the power and capital that condensed around community institutions and could use them to broker difference by connecting to other social formations in Ottoman society, which in turn he could use to negotiate in local politics and society.

Many of the crimes described in the *Accusations* smack of corruption and arbitrary discipline.[22] According to the booklet, Melikian once took a large bribe to force a twenty-year-old woman to marry a seventy-year-old man. He forced another woman to be wed to a suitor; while Ottoman Armenian social convention meant a woman did not always enjoy a say in selecting a husband she could reasonably expect to avoid being forced into an unwanted marriage if, as was the case of this particular woman, she already happened to be married. In another case, he and his servant (described simply as a "barbarous Kurd") kidnapped a woman and beat her after hearing a rumor that her child had stolen a ring. Yet another time, he broke into a home in the village of Aliur, near Van, and attacked a woman. She was rescued by her husband. For his troubles, Melikian returned with a posse that beat the husband to the brink of death and left only after extorting a 300-kuruş bribe from him.

Terrorizing the flock, as Melikian and his associates did, intimidated the community and dissuaded them from making claims on the empire's politics. This was done most effectively by striking at those with some institutional wherewithal. Married clergymen, who usually occupied the lowest rung on the ladder of the hierarchy of the Armenian Church, were primarily tasked with tending to the spiritual needs of the communities from which they hailed. Their ministry was not their primary vocation, as they had either to tend to their field or ply a trade to provide for their families. Like Khachadur Shiroian in Aghtamar, Melikian ensured their acquiescence—and the consequent disenfranchisement of their communities from *millet* politics—by either pressuring them or leaving them to their own devices when confronted by bandits. Melikian also strove to intimidate village headmen (*reis*). The case of Yeranos, the headman of the village Daghveran, is instructive. Yeranos married a woman whom he had met while traveling. He then brought her back to his home village. Word of his nuptials and his return reached the priest Partughimeos, one of Melikian's close associates. Given that Yeranos, as a native of the Van region, fell under his spiritual jurisdiction, Melikian declared the wedding illegal and ruled the nuptials void. He then had the newlyweds brought to the prelacy, where they were imprisoned. The *Accusations* imply that Partughimeos and Melikian then raped the woman over the course of several nights. As a final insult, Melikian arbitrarily fined Yeranos twenty-five lira for the disruption he had caused.[23]

Cowing local clergymen and village headmen ensured the resilience of structural barriers to popular participation in governance and that Melikian and his allies could continue to reap the benefits of operating at the intersection of multiple networks. Without access to networks of power or governance, the bulk of the community found itself with little leverage in its dealings with Melikian. Just as important, the structural impediments made it highly unlikely that word of these transgressions would reach the ears of either the Patriarchate or the local government. Kakmajian's inability to read local society closely meant that the responsibility of alerting the *millet*'s administration to Melikian's actions fell to labor migrants who, now beyond the reach of Melikian's coercion, felt empowered to do so. To circumvent such problems, the Patriarchate would later begin dispatching fact-finding missions to the provinces to procure local knowledge inaccessible to outsiders like Kakmajian, such as the one led by Eremia Tevkants that was discussed in Chapter 3.

LOCAL GOVERNANCE

A rote center-periphery binary fails to capture the tension that marked Ottoman Armenian politics during the Tanzimat period. The Armenian community of the capital and its upper classes, as discussed earlier, were invested in a politics of governance that extended the presence of the Sublime Porte into the provinces. The notables and the clergy were thus already predisposed to establishing positive relations with the local government and participating in its projects. By extracting resources from the community, enterprising clergymen such as Melikian provided the notables a valuable asset in negotiating those relationships. The most immediate benefits of these relationships was the exploitation of tax collection. Yet it also extended to public works projects.

Two such projects merit attention. Melikian and the notables at one point pledged community support for the construction of a military barracks in Van.

Kakmajian's letters to the Patriarchate stressed the importance of the military's presence for the Armenians of Van. Kakmajian placed particular emphasis on the military's ability to safeguard rural communities from assaults by Kurdish tribes.[24] Moreover, the construction of a barracks would free Armenians from the burden of having troops quartered in their homes. To deliver on the community's pledge of support, Melikian placed the onus on lower-class Armenians whom he forced to liquidate assets and provide unpaid labor. On another occasion, the government tasked Melikian with building and repairing bridges in the area; he once more compelled local Armenians to provide their labor without remuneration.

The community's share of governance was predicated, in part, on the ability of its leadership to police the community's activities and ensure its loyalty to the state. Melikian accomplished this by placing the community and its institutions in the service of projects that were underwritten by the notables' capital. This increased the return on the notables' investment in projects of governance and demonstrated their reliability to the government. It also fostered closer interpersonal relationships between Melikian and the clergy, on one side, and government officials, on the other. This connection decreased the likelihood that he would ever be sanctioned for his abuse of the community, should anyone dare to file a complaint in the first place. Most important, good relationships with members of the government positioned Melikian to act as broker between multiple groups in provincial society.

BROKER

The history of Kurdish-Armenian relations during the late Ottoman period has garnered attention in recent years. New scholarship has pushed back against the Orientalist framing of two monolithic groups locked in conflict with one another and instead highlights the complexity that marked these relations. Asymmetries of power did exist and frequently culminated in Kurdish oppression of Armenians in the form of double taxation, banditry, or the *kışlak*, the quartering of semi-nomadic Kurdish families with Armenians during the winter. Episodes of oppression were of course the product of a complex set of dynamics. Most Ottoman Kurds lived in poverty and had to navigate divisions that fractured along religious, tribal, and linguistic lines. As the alliance between Khan Mahmud's Müküs-based clan and the Armenian clergy at Aghtamar demonstrated, Armenians and Kurds comfortably collaborated with one another to craft local regimes of power. The Ottoman state's destruction of the Kurdish emirate in the wake of the failed rebellion of the 1840s created an opportunity for the establishment of new partnerships. Kör Mustafa, the Timurzade clan's patriarch, did just that when he defected from Bedirkhan Bey's side and joined with the government.[25]

Kör Mustafa was not alone in searching out new relationships that might fill the power vacuum in the Kurdish borderlands and the southern regions of historic Armenia created by the defeat and exile of Bedirkhan Bey and Khan Mahmud. The collapse of Kurdish political power coincided with the retreat of the Qadiri Sufi orders that had helped perpetuate family dynasties. They instead gave way to Naqshbandi networks through which new Kurdish elites could forge relationships with the government.[26] Others continued to seek Armenian mediation. According to Hagop Shahbazian's 1911 book, many Kurdish leaders appealed to the Armenian prelacy at Van to settle disputes, submit complaints to the governor, and transfer criminals.[27] While Shahbazian's discussion may have overstated his case, it clearly described Boghos Melikian (and possibly also Kapriel Shiroian). Melikian's close relations with the government and the lay Armenian elite—both in the region and the imperial capital—allowed him to wield tremendous influence over rural Armenian clergymen and village headmen who most frequently interacted with Kurdish tribes. Such influence in turn reinforced Melikian's standing before both the government and the Kurdish elite, thus positioning him to broker relations among the three groups.

Multiple important Kurdish tribes dotted the borderlands regions that reached as far as Cilicia in the west, modern-day Iraq to the south, Qajar Iran in the east, and the Armenian Plateau in the north, including the Modki, Celali, Cibranlı, and Hasananlı.[28] Among Melikian's most important relationships were those with Kurdish beys hailing from Shadakh and Müküs, territories that once fell under the influence of Khan Mahmud, and others who had allied with Armenian clergymen at Aghtamar. This included Derviş Bey, whose family had likely participated in the murder of Bedros Bülbül described in Chapter 3. More important were Melikian's fraternal ties to the Haydaranlıs, a powerful tribe that resided in the areas between Van and Başkale. Their leader, Ali Agha, referred to Melikian as his "father."[29] After an aborted uprising against the government, Ali Agha only agreed to return to the Ottoman Empire after Melikian personally guaranteed the authorities would take no action against him. From that point forward, travelers seeking safe passage through territories controlled by Ali Agha needed first to procure a letter of introduction from Melikian. With such a privilege in hand, Melikian acquired that much more influence with Armenian merchants spread across the region whose long-distance trade was critical to the region's economy.

RULING THE FAITHFUL

As part of the imperial reform program, the Armenian community transformed itself into a diocese wherein the Patriarchate of Constantinople presided over a series of prelacies in a largely top-down fashion. Istanbul-based reformers, who viewed community and imperial politics through this lens, not only were at the mercy of their interlocutors on the ground, as was the case with Kakmajian and Melikian, but also were less likely to understand how community politics extended beyond the geographic limits of the prelacy. In other words, Kakmajian and others may have known that they were helping to introduce a center-periphery relationship but they failed to realize that they were transforming the community's organization to center-periphery *from* a nodal organization. Coupled with his relationships to the Kurdish elite, the government, and the Armenian notables, Melikian navigated the nodal organization of governance to project his influence into other jurisdictions and to establish connections with allies in his rebellion against the Patriarchate.

Melikian's relationships with the Kurdish elite associated with Khan Mahmud of Müküs portended such influence in the dioceses of Aghtamar. In fact, Melikian was a friend and ally of Khachadur Shiroian, the Catholicos of Aghtamar suspected of conspiring to murder his predecessor.[30] Likely, their alliance owed to their mutual patron, Kapriel Shiroian, the prelate of Van who had been appointed locum tenens Catholicos of Aghtamar. Kapriel Shiroian's death had precipitated the 1858 election and consecration of Bedros Bülbül that had caused problems with Constantinople. As acting prelate of Van, it was Melikian who falsely informed Aghtamar that it had Constantinople's permission to proceed with the consecration. By burning Bedros Bülbül's bridge with Constantinople, Khachadur Shiroian and Melikian placed the newly consecrated catholicos in a structurally disadvantageous position that left him compelled him to rely on the support of those Armenian clergymen who enjoyed closer relations with regional power brokers.

The connections to Aghtamar provided Melikian access to other networks. In particular, the influence he wielded over merchants, whose goods had to traverse the dioceses of Aghtamar, positioned him to enjoy the goodwill of the well-to-do and their allies among the clergy in both the Plain of Mush and Erzurum. Most of these actors in Mush and Erzurum were already predisposed to supporting Melikian; he did, however, possess the tools necessary to dissuade any potential challengers to his authority. In particular, Melikian found a ready ally in Harutiun Vehabedian, the Prelate of Erzurum who was introduced in Chapter 2. Like Melikian, Vehabedian enjoyed partnerships with the local government and Armenian notables. These connections had helped him weather multiple instances of internal exile as he returned triumphantly to his post after each one. As we have seen, it was Vehabedian who took the lead in engineering the acquittal of Melikian's friend, Khachadur Shiroian. In the course of the proceedings, however, Vehabedian used his authority as an investigator to return Melikian to work at the prelacy in Van. When Melikian was exiled to Erzurum in 1871, Vehabedian authored letters on his behalf to argue for Melikian's return to Van. Finally, Vehabedian appears to have connected Melikian to the St. James Brotherhood at Jerusalem, which was engaged in its own rebellion against Constantinople and the implementation of the Constitution. A member of that order, Melikset, falsely accused one of Melikian's enemies, Eremia Tevkants, of taking bribes to ordain Protestants as Armenian clergymen as part of a bid to disrupt Tevkants's work as a reformer.[31]

Swayed by the influence of the notables, Kakmajian initially found himself advocating on Melikian's behalf in his letters to the Patriarchate. His time in Van, however, taught him how much of an obstacle to reform Melikian in fact was. Kakmajian subsequently sought to have Melikian confined to one of two monasteries on islands in Lake Van, thinking this would remove his influence from community politics. Here, Kakmajian demonstrated once more his inability to comprehend the constitution of Ottoman social power. Here, the *Accusations* admonished the late Kakmajian and his supporters in the capital when the anonymous author argued that simply moving Melikian to a different monastery would not prevent him from interfering in communal affairs. The anonymous author, most probably Khrimian's student Karekin Srvantstiants, understood that Melikian was a fixer par excellence whose power and influence derived from an imperial dynamic that transcended the binaries, such as center/periphery and Muslim/non-Muslim, that were implicit in the political vision of many in Istanbul.[32] Simply removing him from a position at the prelacy or placing him in a different monastery would not change the fact that the interpersonal relations he had forged, which had helped to anchor the community and its institutions in one type of imperial governance, would continue largely unabated. In 1872, for example, as reform efforts in Van were arguably at their peak, Ali Agha and other members of his branch of the Haydaranlı Kurdish tribe entered the city and began intimidating and harassing Armenians on Melikian's behalf.[33] It was a reminder to the reformers and their potential allies that, no matter how much Constantinople might provide support to its people on the ground, the politics of the Armenian community extended beyond its own boundaries and that actors outside of it were just as invested in preventing its reorganization as some of those within it.

LIMITS OF REFORM

Melikian's example demonstrates how the structures that facilitated the networked world of imperial governance afforded actors opportunities to forge relationships that wove the community that much more completely into Ottoman politics and society. Armenians, Kurds, and the government were invested in one another's politics and enjoyed the ability to influence each, albeit on largely unequal terms. It might be tempting to juxtapose the reform program and Ottomanism against this order of things and treat the two in opposition to each other. As we have seen, however, the networking world into which well-to-do Armenians across the empire had invested their capital did, in fact, ally the community with efforts to centralize the state in the vein of Bayrakatar Mustafa Pasha, the *Sened-i İttıfak*, and earlier iterations of reform that had predated the Tanzimat decree. This is of course why actors such as Melikian in Van—but also Vehabedian in Erzurum or Kefsizian in Cilicia, among others—enjoyed the ability to collaborate with the imperial government, local Armenian notables, and regional Muslim power brokers. They were structurally positioned to forge such alliances and broker among these groups, but could do so only because the reproduction and perpetuation of the networks they created was predicated on overlapping political interests between those groups. Initiatives to which Armenian reformers were committed thus did not necessarily contradict the aims of those whom they claimed to oppose. The example of Hagop Topuzian, a highly regarded Armenian clergyman from Van with ties to both Khrimian and Melikian, offers an opportunity to trace out the range of politics available to provincial Armenians during the reform period and to understand the context in which Ottomanism-as-repertoire, as understood by Khrimian and his allies, was deployed.

Khrimian is rightly regarded as a significant figure for the reform period. Yet it was Topuzian who arguably laid a foundation upon which the better-known Khrimian would later build in Van. Like many of the reform-inclined clergymen, Topuzian hailed from an artisan family. He was born in Van in 1800 and raised by his mother and brother, the latter of whom eventually became a goldsmith.[34] As was usually the case for provincial Armenians of artisan background, the Church provided Topuzian the only access he might have to a formal education. He received his early education at the foot of a bishop in or near Van. Later, his brother would earn enough money to have Topuzian sent to the ancient St. Garabed monastery in Mush to continue his studies. Despite the religious education he received, he did not initially join the clergy. In fact, he returned to St. Garabed to work as a lay teacher following the completion of his studies. During the five years he taught there, he curried the favor of Zakaria Vartabed and Bishop Bedros, two leading members of the Order of St. Garabed. It was through their sponsorship that the order at Lim, near his native Van, would accept Topuzian into their ranks. The order was only too happy to receive a teacher of his caliber and arranged for his ordination as a celibate priest by Hovhannes VIII (r. 1831–1842), the Catholicos of All Armenians at Etchmiadzin.

Topuzian's renown as a teacher afforded him opportunities and provided him access to people. Shortly after his ordination, for example, Yeprem II Ajapahian (r. 1822–1833) called Topuzian to Cilicia to teach in Sis.[35] After teaching there, he traveled across the Ottoman-Russian frontier to work at the Catholicosate of Etchmiadzin. While there, he also traveled to Tiflis, where he secured donations for Lim in the form of large tracts of land. He later left Etchmiadzin to return to St. Garabed in Mush at the request of his patron, Zakaria Vartabed. He briefly interrupted his work at St. Garabed to travel to Jerusalem for study. He returned to his teaching position at Mush and then later made his way to Istanbul. In the imperial capital, he preached throughout the city at churches that were attended by labor migrants from the eastern provinces. With their assistance he began to raise funds for the construction of schools in Van. Most of the money he collected for the effort, however, appears to have come from the upper classes in capital. In the end, he raised enough money to settle the debts accrued by Lim and Gduts, and the rest appears to have been used to build schools. Topuzian's efforts benefited from his relationship with Hagop Grjigian, the *loghofet* of the Armenian Patriarchate, who was himself a high-ranking bureaucrat with influence at the Sublime Porte. Topuzian eventually had a hand in opening six schools in or near Van.

By the time Topuzian returned to Van, he had proven himself an exceptional teacher, but also a competent fundraiser and politically deft. He had won the favor of esteemed people throughout the Armenian world. His renown made him a potential candidate to take over the prelacy in Van. The position would instead pass to Kapriel Shiroian, whom Topuzian replaced as abbot at Lim. In fact, Topuzian would never advance far beyond that position, though the National Assembly did consider him for Catholicos of Aghtamar in the course of the murder investigation. Although it made him eligible to become Patriarch of Constantinople, even his consecration as bishop in 1861 appears more ceremonial than substantive, a reward conferred for achievement rather than a harbinger of greater political responsibilities to come, as was the case with Khrimian and others. How, then, do we explain Topuzian's inability to advance too far beyond the walls of the monastery?

Topuzian's contributions to community life largely revolved around education and fundraising. Though he succeeded in his endeavors, his projects did not fundamentally challenge the networked world of governance that had helped propel Vehabedian, Melikian, and others to the fore. While reform in education oftentimes meant challenging social hierarchies within the community, it could just as easily fall into the hands of the well-to-do. As was the case with the Üsküdar school discussed in Chapter 1, some schoolmasters in Van were reactionaries. Notable among these was Koloz *Varzhapet*, a teacher whom the notables used to discredit and intimidate reformers. Education provided conservatives an opportunity to hide their abuses behind a curtain of enlightenment and patriarchal benevolence. Vehabedian and the Order of St. James resorted to this tactic on multiple occasions. In theory, educational reform meant using Church properties and other community institutions to create pathways to social advancement for the families of artisans and peasants. In practice, however, the opening of the schools, much like the resolution of the monasteries' debts, placed Topuzian at the mercy of the notables of Van and the *amira*s in the imperial capital.

This speaks to the larger structural issues that would have plagued Topuzian had he ever tried to challenge the nodal governance sponsored by Armenian capital. Although he enjoyed a strong reputation and connections to every major seat in the Armenian Church, as well as a number of highly placed individuals, he failed to develop any social capital, because the scope of those connections was limited to the communal space of the *millet*. We find, for example, no evidence of Topuzian attempting to connect with regional power brokers or the local government. Although he had his relationships within the community, he did not broker among groups in the way that Melikian and others did. Topuzian instead deferred that role to Kapriel Shiroian. Part of this decision may have been due to decorum among the Armenian clergy; as a patron, Shiroian commanded respect and even a certain degree of obedience from Topuzian. Topuzian's location in network structures thus precluded him from forging the relationships he would have needed to act as a broker. Those prerogatives instead remained in the hands of Kapriel Shiroian and other clergymen who had remained in Van, such as Melikian. Thus, Topuzian could not even enjoy the benefits typically associated with serving as abbot. With little to leverage, Topuzian and his projects ultimately remained dependent on conservative clergymen, the notables, and their capital, and therefore failed to challenge the status quo.

HAYR ARTSIV

Mkrtich Khrimian is a somewhat misunderstood actor in both Ottoman and Armenian historiographies. Presentations of his life and work produced in Armenian occasionally border on the hagiographic.[36] Perhaps more persuasively, he is presented in the context of the development of Armenian national identity or Armenian nationalism. Khrimian did of course express patriotic sentiments and, as others have discussed, advanced an articulation of Armenian identity that transcended the parochialism of religion by prioritizing timeless roots in historic Armenia. This should not be conflated with the territorialization of identity, particularly as a precursor to some form of Wilsonian claim-making, nor should his well-known "Iron Ladle" sermon, where he contrasted Armenian misfortune during the Russo-Turkish War of 1877–78 with the concessions the Treaty of Berlin had granted Balkan Christians who bore arms. Although they differ in their judgments—was he a potential liberator or a secessionist?—there is general consensus between the two historiographies that Khrimian pursued the establishment of an Armenian political entity of some sort.[37] Such conclusions are, however, predicated on ripping Khrimian from the larger context of Ottoman politics and society in which he operated. We find that, when returned to that context, he was a very active proponent of imperial reform and state centralization. Ottomanism was a repertoire he deployed in his attempts to help reshape imperial governance and the networks that made it possible. Unlike others, Khrimian was positioned to make a unique reading of imperial politics that would justify the actions he would take over the course of several decades in Ottoman and Armenian public life.

Khrimian enjoyed perhaps the most consequential—and almost certainly the most eventful—career of an Ottoman Armenian clergymen during the Ottoman reform period. When he returned to his native Van in December 1856, he did so armed with tools that would set him apart from many of his contemporaries. He brought a printing press with him from the capital. His journal, *Artsvi Vaspurakan*, relocated with him to Van, becoming the first periodical published in historic Armenia.. More important, however, his return marked his forceful entry in the politics of Van and the onset of a conflict between two divergent visions of imperial governance. Thus began the so-called forty-year war between him and Melikian, which would conclude with Khrimian in exile and Melikian dead at the hands of Armenian revolutionaries. Yet Khrimian would also spar with Topuzian and other members of the clergy. Based on his reading of imperial politics and communal reform, Khrimian felt no compulsion to accommodate the cultural niceties that reinscribed the elites' social standing.

Topuzian and Khrimian shared similarities. Khrimian was born into an artisan family in 1820 in Aygestan, a district immediately north of the city walls of Van. His father died when he was young, and he was raised by his mother and uncle. With his uncle's support, he received some formal education at the local monasteries.[38] Eventually, he followed in the footsteps of his father and became a tailor. Only when he made his way to Istanbul in May 1848 would Khrimian finally find opportunities for significant advancement. He had initially hoped to further his education in the capital, but instead found himself navigating labor migrant networks to find work as a cobbler. Later that year, and for reasons that are not entirely clear, he took a job as a teacher at a girls' school in Hasköy. There, his charged lectures on the land of Armenia won him the moniker "*hayastantsi varzhapet*" (the teacher from Armenia). The renown he enjoyed afforded him access to the Armenian upper classes of Istanbul; this included work as a private tutor in the homes of some *amira* families. In particular, he found the opportunity to establish close ties with the Ayvadian, Odian, and Balian families, each of which held positions at both the Patriarchate and the Sublime Porte. These relations, particularly with the Odians, would be of great importance to Khrimian throughout his career in Ottoman public life.

These connections helped Khrimian gain entry to Armenian intellectual circles. His standing among them, as well as the Armenian world in general, benefited greatly from the publication of a poem in the widely read Mkhitarist journal *Bazmavep* in October 1849.[39] He then published his first book, *Hravirak Araratean*, the printing of which was sponsored by Hovhannes Amira Ayvadian. The patronage of Porte-employed *amira*s continued. Later in 1850,

Boghos Odian—the father of Krikor Odian, who would later collaborate with Midhat Pasha on the Ottoman Constitution—sponsored Khrimian's pilgrimage to Jerusalem. Two years later, the Porte-employed Armenian reformers had Khrimian appointed to a committee that was dispatched to Cilicia to investigate Ajapahian rule. Elite patronage continued after both Khrimian's initial return to Van as well as his ordination to the holy orders. The notables of Van seem to have initially welcomed Khrimian back on account of the pomp and small fortune, earned during his time in Istanbul, that he now enjoyed. Upon his return home, for example, he found a business partner in the notable Mkrtich Agha Terlemezian. Finally, when the recently ordained Khrimian returned to the capital, *amira* sponsorship allowed him to begin publication of his journal, *Artsvi Vaspurakan*. Perhaps most notable was a 200-kuruş donation made on behalf of the dispossessed banker Mkrtich Jezayirlian, who had been the personal financier of the former Grand Vizier and father of the Tanzimat, Reşit Pasha.

The publication of *Artsvi Vaspurakan* began only after Khrimian had once more returned to Istanbul. While in Van, however, he had formally entered the clergy. During his absence, his wife and young daughter had passed away. Contrary to his family's wishes that he remarry, Khrimian decided to enter the clergy. He took a boat to Aghtamar in February 1854 where the acting catholicos, Kapriel Shiroian, ordained Khrimian as a celibate priest. Although the ordination took place at Aghtamar, Khrimian was made a member of the brotherhood at Varak. While at Aghtamar, however, Khrimian attempted, with the support of his allies in the Patriarchate, to introduce some modest educational reform. Frustrated, he left his home region for the capital. His return in late 1856 would be far more consequential.

OTTOMANISM: REPERTOIRE AND NETWORKS OF GOVERNANCE

Framing Ottomanism as an ideology reduces the scope of non-Muslim politics and engagement with imperial governance to a false binary: loyalty to the empire or nationalism and secession. Non-Muslim communities were too deeply woven into the fabric of imperial society to perceive these as options; subjectivity was a given and secession an impossibility. These dynamics may be more productively observed from the vantage point of the communal space introduced earlier, which makes it possible to identify the points of intersection—economic, political, religious, and geographic—between individuals, institutions, and networks that connected Armenians to imperial governance. Social actors enmeshed in these politics and its culture intuitively grasped how these points of intersection figured into the complexity of empire. Their own location in network structures, however, dictated how they viewed these politics, how they articulated their own interests, and how structures might constrain or facilitate social action.

Thus, the differences between Topuzian and Khrimian come into relief. Both, as we have seen, enjoyed support from the well-to-do. Each had been deployed in official capacities throughout the empire. They were also natives of Van from artisan families, earned notoriety for their teaching, and enjoyed the patronage of Kapriel Shiroian, Prelate of Van and acting catholicos of Aghtamar. Khrimian's location in network structures, however, meant that he experienced these similarities much differently from Topuzian. Topuzian had already entered the clergy and found himself subject to its rules, hierarchies, and culture when he began interacting with the well-to-do. He was therefore not positioned to benefit from these exchanges as significantly as he might have otherwise. Ultimately, as I argued above, his location in these network structures precluded him from brokering among groups or finding methods for leveraging concessions from any of them. Khrimian, on the other hand, found himself positioned much differently. In particular, his relationships with the Porte-employed Armenians at the Patriarchate afforded him connections that circumvented the decorum of the Church, but more important introduced him to the Tanzimat ideology of legal centralism. The cultural tools on which Khrimian could draw to craft strategies of action thus diverged greatly from whatever Topuzian might possess.

Here, Khrimian's experience as part of the commission deployed to investigate Ajapahian rule in Cilicia in 1852 assumes importance in our analysis. The Patriarchate had charged the commission with overseeing the implementation of some regulations for the dioceses of Cilicia that the Ajapahians had, with the support of the Kozanoğlus, resisted. Khrimian thus found himself in conflict with members of a local ruling class, but along a center-periphery axis rather than a guildsmen-notable divide. He confronted the Ajapahians and contested their power not as a tailor or teacher but as the representative of state officials from the Sublime Porte. Khrimian's reports, which describe irregularities in the Ajapahians' consecration of bishops and appointment of prelates, were presented to the Supreme Council in July 1852, which in turn began to interfere in the ecclesiastical work of the catholicosate. This experience seems to have left a lasting impression on Khrimian. The visible shift in imperial governance from networking to Tanzimat centralism allowed Khrimian to juxtapose the politics that had propelled—but also restrained—Topuzian against a normative order that theoretically enjoyed the coercion of the imperial state.

Ottomanism, therefore, was a repertoire that drew on these tools to form strategies of action. Khrimian could now see a set of alternative networks with direct lines of contact to the Sublime Porte that framed and justified whatever political or social action he might take. By repertoire, I am borrowing a concept from cultural sociology arguing that individuals draw on bits and pieces of culture that they have consumed to form strategies of action.[40] These strategies of action depend on habits, moods, sensibilities, and views of the world. For Khrimian, Ottoman Armenian politics bundled the community's share of imperial sovereignty as a non-Muslim community in the Ottoman Empire together with class tension, interethnic and interconfessional relations, and imperial legal centralism. His location in network structures, however, differentiated him from both Topuzian and Kakmajian. Like Kakmajian, Khrimian's strategies of action were predicated in part on a view of imperial politics that placed the central state (or, in the Armenian context, its partner the Patriarchate of Constantinople) at the fore. Like Topuzian, however, he also possessed a local knowledge of the networked world of governance and how Armenians and their institutions interacted with other forces in Ottoman society. Khrimian's nuanced knowledge of Ottoman politics that merged the imperial with the local permitted him to craft strategies of action that linked center and periphery through Armenian political contention. Ottomanism, which guided the action of Khrimian and other Armenian reformers, oriented their politics toward the capital and the Sublime Porte. Neither they nor their detractors were seeking a way out of empire. Rather, they each produced cultural scripts to justify one vision of empire and governance over the other.

THE DECLARATION OF WAR

Taking Khrimian as a champion of the imperial center and its policies may appear perplexing at first glance. Khrimian's brand of Armenian patriotism, *hayrenasirutiun* ("homeland loving"), diverged sharply from the more popular *azgasirutiun* ("nation loving") that was popular with the Istanbul elite. The latter enshrined an abstract cultural identity that revolved around language and religion, while the former, as noted above, rooted identity in the land of Armenia. Khrimian's prioritization of the land, which he propagated in the pages of *Artsvi Vaspurakan*, placed agency in its inhabitants and ascribed them an active political role. Provincial Armenians, in Khrimian's view, bore the responsibility of reforming their community to partner with the state. They took on this project of state centralization by hacking away at the alliances that prevented Istanbul from introducing a normative order in its periphery. The presence of the state on the horizon emboldened Khrimian and his allies, who set about wresting the community's share of sovereignty from the elite.

Upon his reentry into Van in December 1857, Khrimian seized the offensive against the notables and their allies in the clergy. Likely at Khrimian's urging, Boghos Odian and the Supreme Council had dispatched another clergyman, Bishop Hagop Edesian, to investigate Shiroian and Melikian.[41] To announce their arrival, Khrimian went directly to Surp Nshan Church in the city center to read aloud his instructions from the Patriarchate. The lone description of Khrimian's storming of the pulpit fails to describe the content of those instructions—only that a line had been drawn with the notables, Shiroian, and Melikian on one side, and Khrimian and the people on the other. Khrimian likely announced the investigation into Shiroian and Melikian, the Patriarchate's decisions to sever Varak from Van's jurisdiction, and his own appointment as its new abbot. He probably also produced the imperial ferman that would have signaled the government's ratification of the Patriarchate's course of action. The notables would have failed to see this as anything less than a declaration of war. Khrimian, in turn, would target the semiotics that marked the integration of Van's Armenian community into networked governance.

Here, Khrimian's decision to challenge Shiroian publicly cannot be understated. As discussed earlier, clergymen forged powerful bonds of fictive kinship that imposed mutual obligations on each party. Khrimian's disregard for clerical decorum not only escalated the tension between him and the notables who correctly understood his contestation of hierarchy but also brought him into confrontation with Topuzian. Topuzian must have taken issue with the upstart Khrimian's success. Twenty years Topuzian's junior, Khrimian had been made an abbot by order of the Patriarchate only a few years after his ordination as a clergyman. Moreover, the Porte-employed Armenians of the capital, who all hailed from *amira* families, seem to have regarded Khrimian less as a supplicant begging for alms and more as a partner in reform. Their sponsorship of his activities was about state politics rather than patriarchal benevolence. Khrimian was thus able to open a school at Varak and carry out repairs of the monastery without the notables' interference, something that Topuzian, mired as he was in a web of local networks, would never succeed in doing.

The differences between the two became public as Shiroian approached death. On his deathbed, Shiroian called his three "sons"—Topuzian, Eremia Tevkants, and Khrimian—to his side.[42] Despite their differences, Shiroian had continued to view Khrimian as his "blood son," a point that must have antagonized Topuzian, who had respected the hierarchy likely to his own detriment, that much more. Topuzian and Khrimian openly sparred over where to inter Shiroian after he passed. Topuzian wanted to bury Shiroian at Lim, where both had served as abbot. Lim, however, had remained under the notables' influence. Khrimian thus argued that Shiroian be interred at either the prelacy—which was now being brought more fully under the authority of the Patriarchate—or Varak, where Khrimian now operated largely independent of local networks. Khrimian scored yet one more symbolic victory over the notables when Shiroian was buried at the prelacy.

CONVERTING THE FAITHFUL

Much like their *amira* counterparts in Istanbul, the notables of Van were no monolith. Although they ultimately benefited from the nodal governance underwritten by their capital, they had diversified interests that, against the backdrop of the Tanzimat, portended a reconfiguration of their politics. In Van and elsewhere in the provinces, many Armenian notables, particularly those who had government contracts, gradually found themselves receptive to Khrimian's overtures. Members of notable families, generally through either matriculation to the school at Varak or the shifting allegiances of their relatives in the clergy, gradually came to Khrimian's side. Among these were the Terlemezian, Natanian, Tevkants, and Kaljian families. Others, such as Sharan Bey's clan, would eventually embrace the reform program a decade later. The notables' shift toward Khrimian was gradual and uneven. Throughout the 1860s, several continued using their influence to pressure Kakmajian and support Melikian in the hopes of disrupting Khrimian.

Still, the possibility that some were now willing to place their capital, connections, and wherewithal in the service of institution-building meant that Khrimian would enjoy access to networks and other resources. In turn, he could pass those connections on to his acolytes studying at Varak to continue the work of building those institutions in his absence. This enabled Khrimian to leave Van for Mush in 1862, where he had won appointment as prelate and abbot of the St. Garabed monastery. There, he was afforded the opportunity to practice, recalibrate, and disseminate the Ottomanism repertoire. Like in Van, he encountered initial resistance from locals. Clergymen, who were the least bashful when expressing their dislike of Khrimian to the Patriarchate, offered the most potent resistance to the implementation of reformist policies in the administration of the monastery and the prelacy.[43] The brothers of St. Garabed may even have tried to murder him. Yet Khrimian's view of imperial politics continued to reap dividends. He made his overtures to the governor, which in turn allowed him to integrate into local society and to hack away at the connections that had entangled the monastery and the prelacy in larger networks. His actions won him the adoration of the peasants and earned him the nickname *hayrik*, or papa, a term that would conjure his image in the mind of most any Ottoman Armenian over the following forty years.

CONCLUSION

In 1869, the National Assembly elected a new Patriarchate of Constantinople. Krikor Odian, the son of Khrimian's patron Boghos Odian, excited many of the delegates when he announced his nomination of the Prelate of Mush for the highest position in the Ottoman Armenian Church hierarchy. He left the assembly in a raucous mood, as shouts of "Long live Odian! Long live Khrimian!" reverberated throughout the hall. Khrimian was duly elected. As Patriarch of Constantinople, Khrimian attempted to make Ottomanism a more salient feature of Ottoman imperial governance. With his acolytes and allies now deployed all across the empire, particularly on the Armenian Plateau, Khrimian would oversee the aggressive implementation of the Armenian National Constitution. He and other Armenians of provincial backgrounds understood perfectly well that the Constitution was the tool they needed to sever the links responsible for weaving the community and its space into the networked world of governance.

5 A CATASTROPHIC SUCCESS

SCHOLARS INCLINED TO LAY BLAME at the feet of nationalism—particularly that of subject communities—for the collapse of the Ottoman Empire might look no further than Bishop Mkrtich Khrimian. The Russo-Turkish War of 1877–78, which was fought in both the Balkans and eastern Anatolian provinces of historic Armenia, had brought Armenian-Muslim polarization into stark relief. The war was concluded when Russian armies, storming through the Balkans, reached the Istanbul suburb of San Stefano. Russian officers there were hosted by the influential Armenian *amira* Dadian family, which owned a substantial amount of the suburb's real estate, while they negotiated terms of the Ottomans' surrender. The belligerents signed the Treaty of San Stefano, which granted the Russians significant concessions, including provisions that would allow them to project their influence into Ottoman territories in the Balkans and Anatolia. European powers, which had their own desires for dismembering the Ottoman state, balked at the expansion of Russian power in the region and, in response, compelled a renegotiation of terms at the Berlin Congress about three months later in 1878. Although they were uninvited, the Armenian Patriarchate of Constantinople dispatched a delegation to negotiate on behalf of the Ottoman Armenian community, which included Khrimian, a former Patriarch of Constantinople.

The Armenian delegation, which lacked any diplomatic standing in the eyes of the Congress's other participants, found itself ignored by the Europeans; the delegation's members thus returned to Istanbul frustrated and dissatisfied.

Shortly after his return, Khrimian delivered a sermon at the Patriarchate of Constantinople where he explained European diplomacy to his flock. The Europeans, Khrimian said, had placed a cauldron of *harisa*, a stew traditionally made of barley and chicken, before the Christian communities of the Ottoman Empire. Each approached and, with ladles made of iron, took their portion and ate. Khrimian, armed with only a paper ladle fashioned from requests Armenians had wished to present to the Congress, was unable to take his share. The weak paper ladle stuck in the stew and fell apart, leaving the Armenians to watch jealously as Christians from the Balkans feasted. In a later retelling of the sermon, Khrimian left no room for misinterpretation of his metaphor: the iron ladles belonging to the Balkan Christians were weapons. Armenians, too, would need arms to defend themselves against their Muslim neighbors if they ever hoped to win concessions from either the Europeans or the Ottomans.[1]

Khrimian was therefore a nationalist advocating for armed revolution against the Ottoman state, secession from the empire, and collaboration with European imperialism. His sermon is thus further evidence that the experiments with the Tanzimat and Ottomanism, as they are typically understood, are failures in their attempts to integrate non-Muslims into the imperial body politic. The rush to such conclusions would not only misread Armenian politics and its role in Ottoman governance, but also misrepresent the history of Ottoman Armenian discourse on arms and legitimate violence. Though Islamic law theoretically prohibited non-Muslims from wielding weapons, Armenians and other Christians found themselves pressed into military service at different points in Ottoman history. The Armenian National Assembly actually devoted several sessions to discussing Armenian access to arms—in the military or otherwise—in the years preceding the Russo-Turkish War of 1877–78 that resulted in the Congress of Berlin.

These discussions on weapons and legitimate violence were only one part of a larger politics that sought to understand how Armenians and their institutions participated in imperial governance and as partners of the Ottoman state in the Tanzimat period. Khrimian and others pursued these politics in an Ottoman framework—which they refashioned as they pursued these politics—as part of a bid to make claims on the empire's politics. Armenians such as Khrimian did not envision the future of their Armenia as an independent country and were perfectly comfortable with Ottoman rule. In fact, those whom we would expect to play the role of insurgent—namely, Khrimian and the reformers—were already engaged in a largely successful campaign to orient Armenian institutions and politics toward the capital and make them partners in state centralization. Yet, as we see with Berlin, Armenians felt increasingly isolated in the nexus of relationships and institutions that constituted imperial governance. Herein lies the ironic success of Armenian engagement with the Tanzimat: the integration of community institutions into formal state politics through Armenian reform policies had the unintended consequence of disenfranchising the community and those institutions from imperial governance. If Armenians found themselves on the way out of empire, it was not a path of their own choosing.

Historians' explanations for the collapse of the Ottoman Empire have emphasized various strains of nationalism and external forces such as the public debt owed to European lenders, the activist work of expatriate groups, and other pressures exerted by the international political system.[2] These forces were of course intertwined with one another. They were also connected with the reconfigurations of power ushered in by reform that had restructured the networks through which Armenians engaged with governance and society. Ottoman Armenians both participated in and navigated these reconfigurations. This chapter follows the final decade and a half of Mkrtich Khrimian's public life in the Ottoman Empire—beginning with his election as Patriarch of Constantinople in 1869 and concluding with his banishment to the St. James Monastery as an internal exile in Jerusalem in 1885—to understand how Armenians tried to engage with an empire that was pushing them further to the margins. This period witnessed Khrimian not only in Berlin but also in Istanbul and his native Van, as he operated at multiple levels of the empire's political system. His allies and acolytes, meanwhile, spread across the empire to wage battles for the implementation of reform programs. Armenians appear to have felt that the comparatively successful implementation of reform in their own community justified their expectation that the Ottoman state's efforts yield similar results. When it became obvious that this was not the case, they were compelled to adopt new strategies to find their footing in a quickly shifting political and social landscape. For Khrimian and his allies, this ultimately meant trying to reverse their victories in a desperate bid to restore the networked world of governance they had fought so hard to unmake.

THE PEOPLE'S CHAMPION

Khriman curated his image. Still, there is little doubt that his sentiments were genuine; the political risks he had taken won him the adoration of wide swathes of the Ottoman Armenian community, particularly among the poor from the provinces, who called him *hayrik*, a diminutive perhaps best translated as "papa" or "dad." As is clear from his literary work, Khrimian reveled in provincial Armenian culture, which he viewed as markedly distinct from that of his coreligionists in the imperial capital.[3] Rarely did he miss an opportunity to showcase his provincial roots. Yet it would be misleading to view his politics or his term as patriarch through the lens of a center-periphery binary. As the pomp and circumstance surrounding his election and inauguration as patriarch would show, his politics defy easy categorization. The baptism by fire that he was about to receive in the imperial capital would further test those politics.

Khrimian's election was no simple coronation. Following the resignation of Boghos Taktakian, the patriarch who had overseen the reintroduction of the Armenian National Constitution, the Sublime Porte's Armenian employees who shepherded the community's administration wished to replace him with Iknadios Kakmajian, the Prelate of Van. They considered Kakmajian's strengths. He was a proponent of reform, had gained valuable practical knowledge about Armenian provincial life in Van, and was an Istanbul native familiar with the conservative culture of the *amira*s and the clergy. The reformers failed, however, to account for his death; Kakmajian passed away shortly after his election and would never be enthroned.

On September 4, 1869, the Armenian National Assembly in Istanbul reopened discussion on Taktakian's successor. The reformers advanced their second candidate: Nerses Varjabedian. Like Kakmajian, Varjabedian was an Istanbul native who supported the reform program. His knowledge of ecclesiastical precedent had helped the reformers defeat the challenge authored by Jerusalem. While Varjabedian hailed from a family of artisans in the capital and remained attuned to the concerns of lower-class Armenians, he also possessed the skills to find common ground with the upper classes and clergy. Before coming of age politically in the capital, he had studied at the Armash monastery near Bursa, which regularly produced conservative clergymen. His consecration as bishop by the Catholicos of Cilicia, however, disqualified his candidacy for the position of Patriarch of Constantinople.

Only after they had failed to install either of their first two choices did the reformers make an effort to elect Khrimian. A year earlier, in 1868, Khrimian had been consecrated bishop by the Catholicos of Etchmiadzin, thus paving the way for his potential election as Patriarch of Constantinople. Krikor Odian, the Ottoman statesman whose family had sponsored Khrimian's earlier efforts at provincial reform, rallied the representatives in the National Assembly; Khrimian's name appeared on forty-two of the forty-eight ballots cast. Khrimian received word of his election at the ancient St. Garabed Monastery (called *Çanlıkilise* in Turkish), where he had sat as Prelate of Mush since 1862. Nearly two months after the election, on November 3, 1869, he embarked for the capital.

The authorities provided him a horse and an imperial escort for the journey.[4] As he left Mush for his first stop, the garrison town of Erzurum, villagers feted him with cries of "long live *hayrik*." Keeping with tradition, some brought him bread and salt; meanwhile, those of some means tried to curry God's favor for their heroic bishop by performing the ritual *matagh* sacrifice that harkened back to Armenia's pagan past. As he neared Erzurum, a welcoming party—which included the governor, lower officials, and Armenian clergymen—awaited Khrimian at the town's outskirts. In town, an Armenian notable family threw a lavish feast in Khrimian's honor. Similar scenes played out at Bayburt, Gümüşhane, and Trabzon. From Trabzon, Khrimian boarded a steamship that Sultan Abdülaziz himself had dispatched for the final leg of the journey.

The steamship arrived in Istanbul's Kumkapı district on September 6, 1869, where throngs of Armenians had gathered to greet Khrimian. Many, if not most, were labor migrants from the eastern provinces who had traveled to the imperial capital, oftentimes in violation of the law, to work menial jobs such as porters in the nearby old city. Shortly after he disembarked, Khrimian met with his old ally, Krikor Odian. The following day, Sultan Abdülaziz granted him an audience. Five days later, on November 12, 1869, Khrimian made his first appearance before the National Assembly. As an artisan from the provinces who had come to the clergy late in life, Khrimian was accustomed to operating in a political and social world where interpersonal relationships got things done. The National Assembly, he would soon understand, was a different animal.

As the newly elected Patriarch of Constantinople, Khrimian was required to take an oath to uphold the Constitution as part of his enthronement. Khrimian reasoned that he alone could not uphold the Constitution and invited the members of the two councils to join him.[5] He did, however, express his willingness to do as the National Assembly wished. That was all the justification the National Assembly needed to debate the mostly symbolic gesture exhaustively. They eventually concluded that the language of the Constitution permitted only the Patriarch to take the oath and prohibited anyone from joining him. Khrimian did not object to their decision, marched to the main church at the patriarchate, Surb Astvatsatsin, and prepared to swear the oath alone before God. A large crowd assembled; many of them were labor migrants originally from the provinces, overjoyed to see their champion reach the pinnacle of Ottoman Armenian society. To their astonishment and dismay, a conservative deputy interrupted Khrimian as he began to speak. The deputy, Garabed Efendi Panosian, spoke over Khrimian and demanded that he swear to uphold each individual article of the Constitution.

Those assembled may have found Panosian's intervention inappropriate. Yet the whole day—both the deliberations in the National Assembly and the interruption—was a harbinger of what awaited Khrimian during his term as Patriarch. Panosian had wanted Khrimian to commit himself to a literal interpretation of the Constitution, knowing full well that the document was being rewritten; Panosian was also likely aware that, based on his practical experience in the provinces, Khrimian desired to introduce changes to the Constitution that would give the people greater control over their communal institutions and, consequently, more robust tools for making claims on Ottoman politics and participating in governance. Panosian's challenge therefore embodied a principal frustration of the reform period: opponents of reform would attempt to make its institutions or initiatives, such as the Constitution or the ecclesiastical organization of the Armenian Church, into obstacles to reform. The people adored Khrimian. Many of the elite, both in the provinces and the capital, deeply respected him. That would never be enough.

AN OTTOMAN BISHOP

Khrimian took his oath. He swore to God that he would uphold the laws and traditions of the Church of Armenia and be true to the *spirit* and principles of the Constitution.[6] Juxtaposed against Panosian's insistence on the specific, Khrimian's decision to use more flexible language offers a glimpse into his political framework. The bishop from Van wished to address the larger structural issues confronting provincial Armenians. His political speeches, sermons, personal correspondence, and literary work reveal someone carefully attuned to the larger overarching themes that marked Ottoman Armenian life in the nineteenth century. This work highlighted, among other things, the economic and moral anxiety caused by labor migration, education, corruption, and interconfessional relations. Khrimian placed these concerns under the wider umbrella of the province-focused *hayrenasirutiun*, the "fatherland loving" patriotism introduced in the last chapter.

Many people have been content to situate Khrimian and his projects in the context of nation-building or, more ominously, nationalism. Scholarship produced in the Armenian Soviet Socialist Republic and its successor state, which is arguably the most polished on the subject, overwhelmingly frames Khrimian in a national-liberation struggle. Although they generally hesitated to call Khrimian a true revolutionary, their prioritization of class struggle actually highlights many of the forces against which Khrimian battled.[7] Emphasis on the "national," however, predetermines the aims of those projects. Scholars working outside the Marxist-Leninist tradition similarly locate Khrimian in the progressive development of a national identity. For the political scientist Razmik Panossian, Khrimian belonged to a national "multi-local awakening."[8] Based in the provinces, he and other Anatolian Armenians were the "ground point" of this awakening that was buttressed by intellectual forces at the other points—namely, the west (Istanbul) and the east (Tbilisi).

Such an approach coincides with the seemingly unending quest—of Abdülhamid's agents and historians alike—to identify non-Muslim nationalists (and secessionists) in the Ottoman Empire. Here, commerce and economics come to the fore. Christian and Jewish advancement in commerce in the late eighteenth and nineteenth centuries, we are told, stoked Muslim resentment of Ottoman non-Muslims. These, in turn, exacerbated structural cleavages between communities. The ensuing volatility compelled non-Muslims to look inward; as one scholar has commented, "given the vagaries of commerce," non-Muslims "chose to *revert* to a community based on ethnic and religious ties," which tied them to emergent nationalist discourses.[9] Merchant capital thus underwrote patriotic or nationalist agitation among the non-Muslims. As non-Muslim communities found themselves increasingly distant from their Muslim neighbors, they forged "closure around communal ties" in response to those increasingly widening social cleavages.

Ascribing nationalism to any of this puts the cart before the horse. Given the organization of difference in the Ottoman world, it should come as little surprise that non-Muslims would look to their friends, family members, or communal institutions to navigate the changing landscape of imperial governance; none of this justifies presupposing their political ambitions. Moreover, scholars of the early modern period have demonstrated that ethnic or religious ties could be used to ensure bonds of trust among merchant communities. In many cases, the bases for these connections were more narrow than religion or ethnicity. This was arguably the case of the Armenian *amira*s with ties to Akn. As we have seen, there was nothing remotely nationalist (or even patriotic) about their political or social aspirations. Arguably, aspects of this explanation apply to the Balkans, where Greek merchants were compelled to choose sides as local disturbances surrounding notable politics developed into the Greek War of Independence. Their support of any national movement, therefore, had less to do with ideology and more with conjuncture. Applying this analysis to the Armenian case is problematic. Although some Armenian merchants may have supported the reform projects, they were more likely to join with their conservative allies among the clergy to oppose Khrimian's efforts in their bid to preserve the networked world of imperial governance.

Khrimian and his allies saw themselves engaged in the project of Ottoman state-building and state centralization. He was no "middle point" in the development of Armenian political discourse but rather operated very much in accordance with the goals of the Armenian employees of the Sublime Porte. Their shared politics derived from a critique of the networked world of governance that centralization bid to displace. As we have seen, Khrimian's political career began prior to his ordination to the holy orders as a lay teacher, dispatched to Cilicia by the reformers to introduce institutions of educational reform. As a clergyman in Van, Prelate of Mush, or Patriarch of Constantinople, he bid to expand the scope of this reform through the introduction of a normative order governing Armenian institutions. This reform would extricate those institutions from dense sets of networked connections by turning their control over to the people who would then partner them with imperial structures. This, in turn, would make it possible for Armenians, via their institutions, to make direct contributions to imperial policy as formulated in the capital. Khrimian was not seeking a way out of empire; rather, he sought the opposite. He probed the extent to which manifestations of difference, as rearticulated during the Tanzimat period, could be deployed to make claims on governance.

THE REPORT

Khrimian's Iron Ladle Sermon was not the first time he or the community publicly discussed the possibility of Armenians possessing arms. In his capacity as Patriarch of Constantinople, Khrimian used the introduction to the controversial document *Report on Provincial Oppression* to suggest that the government provide instruments of self-defense to those provincial Armenians subjected to the predations of Kurdish or Circassian tribes, assuming the government continued in its unwillingness to disarm the latter.[10] Khrimian did not seek an interethnic civil war; rather, he was throwing down two challenges. First, he was pushing the government to make itself a Weberian state and establish a monopoly on the legitimate use of violence. Second, he urged Armenians to recognize their own political agency so that they, too, could assume an active role in developing Ottoman statecraft. He was encouraging them to make centralization a part of their cultural tool kit.

The Patriarchate had, throughout the nineteenth century, received petitions or other correspondence from the provinces requesting help for resolving issues that should have been addressed at the local level of government. With the introduction of the Armenian National Constitution, these issues were delegated to the Political Council of the National Administration, which was led by Armenian employees of the Porte. The Political Council not only enjoyed broad autonomy in administering communal affairs but also had clear connections to the highest levels of the imperial government. It was therefore an institution ideally located for making claims on Ottoman governance. From here, Khrimian would try to make the community not just a tool of reform but a source for elaborating policy.

At Khrimian's request, the Political Council began to prepare the *Report on Provincial Oppression*. Khrimian issued an encyclical to all provincial prelates that instructed them to compose and submit detailed reports of all known episodes of violence or exploitation to which their flock had been subjected. Importantly, the encyclical also requested the prelates' suggestions for remedying provincial Armenians' concerns. The Political Council collected the records and used them to compose their own report, a full version of which was then presented to the National Assembly in December 1871. Versions of the report were reproduced in the minutes of the assembly's subsequent sessions. A final, published version of the report was not completed until 1876, but an initial copy, endorsed by the community's leadership, was submitted to Grand Vizier Mahmud Nedim Pasha on April 11, 1872.

Controversy and skepticism had swirled around Khrimian even before his election as Patriarch of Constantinople. His conservative opponents had girded themselves for his policies and were prepared to contest his proposals. The final version of the report from 1876 comprised three sections. The second and most substantial portion was a list of incidents that the Political Council had submitted to the Sublime Porte for redress; the government had remained indifferent to the overwhelming majority of these. There was little to argue here. Instead, the discussions in the National Assembly focused on the first section, where Khrimian had proposed his remedies for fixing the Ottoman Empire.

As previously discussed, Khrimian had brokered the idea of Armenians possessing arms. He and others therefore proposed that the community make Armenians eligible for conscription into the army. In so doing, they sought to resolve multiple issues. First, they worked to relieve the community from paying the *bedel-i askeri*, the military exemption tax that had replaced the *cizye* during the Tanzimat period. Taxation, in its official and unofficial forms, had constituted a primary source of frustration for provincial Armenians. Reformers could reason that fewer interactions with tax collectors would help to alleviate, in part, provincial Armenians' burdens. Moreover, participation in the military would provide Armenians familiarity with arms and place them on a more equal footing with their Muslim neighbors; after all, the Tanzimat had promised equality between subjects. Bandits would be far less inclined to raid an Armenian village if they knew that its residents had demonstrated their willingness to shed blood for the homeland.

Others joined conservative opposition to the proposal in the National Assembly. The idea of Armenian soldiers serving under the Ottoman flag portended wholesale disruption of the markers of difference that had structured imperial society to that point. Conservatives, even among the Armenians, understandably found this proposal to be unsettling. The most convincing counterarguments were made on economic grounds. The removal of able-bodied men from the provincial workforce via conscription, others argued, had had deleterious effects on Muslim agricultural production. To avoid harming Armenian economic output, the delegates agreed to strike Khrimian's proposal from the suggestions.

Although Khrimian may have lost the debate on this point, the motivations that informed his broader framework for community and imperial politics still echoed throughout the first and final sections of the report. Armenian political agency and imperial reform were, for Khrimian, inextricably intertwined. Provincial Armenians and the central government needed to work with each other to realize their mutual goals, a point that he and the reformers did not shy away from making to the Sublime Porte.

PREACHING TO THE PORTE

Khrimian composed the introduction to the report. The community leadership authored the conclusion collaboratively. Each of these may be read as a guide for the Ottoman state on how to help empower Armenians and partner with their community institutions in imperial governance. They also represent a direct and public attempt on the part of Khrimian and the reformers to integrate Armenian experiences and local knowledge into the corpus of texts that constituted the Tanzimat.

The report's introductory pages made great effort to establish the stakes of imperial reform and the role of the Armenian community in it. Khrimian described the Kurdish tribes that imposed unofficial taxes on Armenians and raided their villages as disloyal Ottoman subjects.[11] As noted earlier, he therefore called on the government to disarm those Kurds (as well as Circassians and other *derebey*s) and to exile their leaders. Khrimian would not have his Armenian soldiers, but this did not prevent him from requesting the government to expand its coercive presence in the provinces by increasing the number of soldiers and police stations there. The police, he contended, should include Armenians on its force "as both high- and low-ranking officials."[12]

The inclusion of Armenians in policing belonged to a broader desire to familiarize Armenians with the law and its enforcement. In the report, Khrimian had identified three new forms of taxation introduced during the Tanzimat period—the military exemption (*bedel-i askeri*), property (*emlak*), and income (*temettü*)—as sources of abuse.[13] Economic exactions aside, the report stated that tax collectors were the more odious imposition on the community. Perhaps more important, the work of tax collection remained in the hands of those who pursued their profession zealously. Tax collectors would obtrude on families, demand care for their horses, beat people, and in some cases even "dishonor the women."[14] They were, however, largely insulated from any possibility of prosecution, as Armenians had little or no real access to the formal legal system.

Notable Armenian families, as we have seen, controlled access to the community institutions that enjoyed the right to petition the government. They were also more likely to sit on nominating committees (*meclis-i tefrik*) that, in accordance with the 1864 Vilayet Law, were tasked with selecting candidates for positions at the provincial and subprovincial levels of government. In so doing, the Armenian notables and their allies packed government posts with their own appointees to ensure that those of less privileged backgrounds—Muslim or Armenian—would not find anyone wielding any authority that might hear their grievances. Yet lower-class Armenians did not simply lack the tools necessary to access the legal system. In the instances that these Armenians did access the courts, their testimony as non-Muslims remained—contrary to the dictates of the Tanzimat—inadmissible against Muslim defendants, which was troubling for Khrimian. To remedy this state of affairs, Khrimian suggested that orders from the imperial government sent to local governors be published in official periodicals; thus the people would know when government officials violated the law. He also requested that the Düstur (Code of Laws) be made publicly available in the languages spoken by non-Muslims.[15]

Making the law less esoteric and accessible to the people would, Khrimian hoped, help them understand when officials were in violation of the empire's wishes. He was, consonant with the legal centralism ideology of the Tanzimat, presenting a normative order from which deviation should not be tolerated. Yet he was also preaching to the Porte the necessity of engaging its subjects directly. Armenians wishing to participate in imperial governance needed to know not simply that tools had been made available to them but also that the central government had partnered with them in implementing the reform program. Khrimian and the community leadership thus included thirty-three pages of individual reports previously submitted the Sublime Porte, the vast majority of which the government had ignored. The Armenian reformers did so in order to convey the Armenian expectations that the state take more concrete steps to demonstrate its partnership with the community.

The final section of the report, appended in 1876 during the patriarchal reign of Nerses Varjabedian, was even more explicit in its stance that the government assume a more proactive role in the support of Armenian reformers. In particular, it laid blame at the feet of the government for Armenians' need to bring so many issues to the attention of the Porte. Had the government not contented itself with appointing officials who were incompetent, corrupt, or religious zealots, the report argued, Armenians would have been able to resolve issues locally; in other words, the Tanzimat would have succeeded. On this point, the Armenian leadership in the capital implored the central government to have local governors collaborate with Armenian administrative bodies in the provinces and to take the complaints and information they presented seriously.[16]

Armenian reformers such as Khrimian had, by 1876, been engaged in the hard work of extending constitutional order over those community institutions with the express intent of providing provincial Armenians more direct access to the government. Their efforts met with opposition from not only fellow Armenians but also those Armenians' allies in the local government and among the local power brokers. The reform project as pursued by Khrimian and his allies—which put their lives and careers in jeopardy—linked Armenian political agency with the Tanzimat. They impatiently awaited some signal from the government that this was in fact the case.

PROSELYTIZING THE TANZIMAT

As we saw in Chapter 4, Khrimian and other Armenian reformers had fashioned an Ottomanism repertoire, or cultural tool kit, that located the imperial center and reform policies in webs of cultural meaning as part of their effort to build a social movement. Khrimian, in particular, expertly blended the semiotics of power available to him—imperial, ecclesiastical, and local—to communicate his programs or his vision to the flock. Privately, he met with people of all backgrounds. Publicly, he used the pulpit to challenge the well-to-do who had used informal relationships to cast their influence over community institutions. This partly explains why Khrimian and his allies implored the Porte to make strong remonstrations on their behalf. While battling to redistribute Armenian power and social capital from the informal relationships that located the community in networked governance and into the formal institutions of the Tanzimat state, Khrimian and his allies ultimately found themselves reliant on their own personal relationships.

Both Khrimian and his successor, Nerses Varjabedian (r. 1874–1884), relied on a few close associates among the clergy whom they trusted. During his frequent bouts with illness while serving as Patriarch of Constantinople, Varjabedian tasked Hovhannes Mgrian, a married priest from Istanbul, with overseeing the patriarchate's day-to-day affairs. His other close associate was Matteos Izmirlian, a celibate priest who hailed from a family of craftsmen, as had Varjabedian and Khrimian. Izmirlian, who had played a key role in advising the patriarchate during its conflict with the Catholicosates of Cilicia and Aghtamar, later served his own explosive tenure as Patriarch of Constantinople; his populism, like Khrimian's, would earn him banishment to Jerusalem as an internal exile at the hands of Sultan Abdülhamid II. Khrimian also relied on Mgrian and Izmirlian, particularly during his time in the capital. Yet for the work of seeing reform through on the ground in the provinces, Khrimian turned primarily to the connections he himself had forged.

The epicenter of Khrimian's political and religious world remained Varak, the monastery just outside of Van where the Patriarchate of Constantinople, at the urging of the Odians, had sent him in 1856 to introduce educational and centralization reform policies. He ensured that the students he trained at Varak were equipped with not only a command of their religion but also the knowledge necessary to strike at the informal networks targeted by the reform project.[17] During his tenure as either abbot at Varak or in Mush, or as Patriarch of Constantinople, Khrimian installed his students in key positions both to preserve the victories they had scored previously and, it was hoped, to build on them. Here, Khrimian's first class of students at Varak, admitted in 1859, is the most important. Almost all the pupils were, like Khrimian, children of artisans who resided in the Aygestan district of Van, located immediately north of the city walls. In preparation for their eventual entrance into the clergy and the need to assume a new identity, Khrimian assigned each student a new first name.

Three members of this first class merit notoriety: Krikoris Aghvanian, Arsen Tokhmakhian, and Karekin Srvantstiants. Tokhmakhian, who later assumed the responsibilities of abbot at Varak, won prominence in some circles for his fundraising for public goods and speeches that unflinchingly advocated on behalf of Armenian peasants.[18] His efforts earned him the attention of the Ottoman authorities who eventually imprisoned and tortured him. He was later the victim of a brutal murder, his killer dismembering and incinerating his corpse. Aghvanian and Srvantstiants, as I discuss below, were also subject to threats and intimidation. Khrimian brought them with him to Mush when appointed prelate and abbot of St. Garabed in 1862. There, they were handed important duties; Srvantstiants had the responsibility of overseeing the newspaper *Artsvik Taronoy*.

Khrimian sought to profit from the investment of time and trust he had made in his students from Van. As Patriarch of Constantinople, he appointed them patriarchal vicars and cast them across the empire. Backed by imperial fermans, they enjoyed wide authority to introduce reform policies and enforce their implementation. In addition to Aghvanian and Srvantstiants, these included two men from comparatively affluent backgrounds—Boghos Natanian and Eremia Tevkants—whose families had embraced the reform program. Eremia Tevkants's mission to the provinces in 1872–73, as discussed in Chapter 3, revealed important details on Khachadur Shiroian's involvement in the murder of his predecessor as Catholicos of Aghtamar, Bedros Bülbül. During his travels, Tevkants also instituted Constitutionally mandated assemblies and elections, much to the dismay of Armenian notables and clergymen who benefited from their location in local networks of power. He and other pro-reform clergymen were missionaries: they spread the good word of reform; dispelled myth and rumors surrounding the policies; and, perhaps most important, made the presence of the Patriarchate tangible.

THE EAGLE AND THE NIGHTINGALE

Among Khrimian's associates, Srvantstiants commands the most attention. Although the ethnomusicological work of the genocide survivor Komitas is better known, Srvantstiants's ethnographic tracts arguably did more to preserve and record our knowledge of provincial Armenian culture. He was the first to record the famous *Sasuntsi Davit* epic. His ethnographic work, however, was fully intertwined with his work as a clergyman and reformer, which required him to travel frequently throughout the provinces. Moreover, Khrimian loved him as a son. Before the people began calling him *hayrik*, Khrimian was known as the "eagle." Srvantstiants was the *sokhak*, or nightingale. A reading of their correspondence, much of which is now housed at the Charents Museum of Literature and Art in Yerevan, captures the frankness with which they communicated.

Srvantstiants began touring the provinces as early as 1868, when, during Khrimian's tenure as Prelate of Mush, the younger student bore the responsibility of reporting on the relationships of the Armenian clergy with local power brokers, such as the leadership of the Kurdish Cibranlı tribe.[19] As the economic interests of Armenian notables in Erzurum extended into the Plain of Mush, Srvantstiants's attention was also directed to the north. Srvantsiants's interactions with people in Erzurum, however, actually allowed him to project Khrimian's presence into the provinces. Notables in Erzurum, for example, conveyed their greetings to Khrimian through Srvantstiants. He was therefore uniquely positioned to collect reliable information on actors operating at all levels of society, which he communicated to Khrimian in rather straightforward terms, who could then deploy that information to formulate policies. Here, we can better appreciate the frustration that Khrimian and the reformers must have felt when their *takrirs* to the Porte failed to make an impression on the stewards of the central government; they had placed their hard-won local knowledge at the disposal of the Porte, which ultimately disregarded it.

Having eyes and ears on the ground was important for Khrimian, particularly during his term as Patriarch of Constantinople. But it would be wrong to think that Srvantstiants was only that. Khrimian's trust in him was due in large part to his knack for forging relationships and disrupting networks. This is why, of all the clergymen from Van in whom he had invested a great deal of his trust,

Khrimian assigned Srvantstiants with what he must have considered the most important task of all: toppling Boghos Melikian.

"THAT OLD OBSTACLE"

As discussed in Chapter 4, Boghos Melikian was a clergyman from Van who had used his position in the Church hierarchy to forge connections with Armenian well-to-do and non-Armenian actors, such as Kurdish leaders or government officials in the area. He was a broker in the networked world of imperial governance, an order of things he aggressively bid to preserve. He defended both this order of things, as well as his position in it, through acts of violence and intimidation that permitted him to exploit both the wealth and labor of his flock. Given the interconnectedness of commerce, politics, and the Armenian Church, Melikian was ultimately able to influence Armenian merchants as far away as Erzurum and to forge de facto alliances with fellow clergymen across the Ottoman Empire.[20] It was from Van that he engaged in a rebellion against Khrimian's patriarchate by attempting to disrupt the introduction of communal reform policies at as many levels as possible.

The Patriarchate's early attempts at reform in Van, spearheaded by Khrimian and Kakmajian, were part of a larger effort to transform community institutions into sites of formal (and popular) politics. The possibility of turning community institutions over to popular control directly challenged the integration of the Armenian community into the networked world of imperial governance and thus precipitated the formation of two "parties" (*kusaktsutiun*) in Van: one, in favor of the status quo, was called the *Poghoseank* (those who rallied around Boghos Melikian). The other, *Apoghoseank* (anti-Boghos Melikian) or *Khrimeanakanner* (pro-Khrimian), bid to pursue the reform policies as part of a larger imperial effort to centralize the government through the introduction of a normative order. As noted earlier, a good deal of the reform policies seem to have been designed specifically with the contention between Melikian and Khrimian in mind. Khrimian had been originally sent by the Patriarchate in the 1850s to combat Melikian, and the Political Council—where Khrimian's allies, the Odians, were particularly influential—began investigating him almost immediately after its formation in 1860.[21] The reformers, in fact, secured Melikian's temporary banishment from Van later that decade. Khrimian's ascent to the patriarchal throne, however, meant that the provinces would feature more prominently on the agenda of the National Assembly in Istanbul. The increasing focus on the role of prelacies in Armenian and imperial governing structures, which the reformers wished to standardize, attests to this. Perhaps more important, Khrimian began circulating his allies with the task of implementing reform. Srvantstiants was thus sent to his hometown of Van.

The first of Srvantstiants's letters to Khrimian from Van in the course of his mission, and available to us, is dated December 28, 1871.[22] In it, he mentions that the monastery at Varak, a symbol of Khrimian's power and influence in the region, had been targeted unfairly for taxes. Subsequent letters convey the greetings of allies and minor details on the convening of constitutionally mandated assemblies. Perhaps most interesting among these early letters are the overtures made by Sharan Bey to Khrimian.[23] Sharan Bey, who owned the bazaar in Van, had traditionally been allied with Melikian and had actually opposed Hagop Topuzian's efforts to build schools in the city in the 1850s. Now, instead of activating his networks to resist the presence of the central state as projected through the Armenian community, he was signaling a willingness to help Srvantstiants introduce it. Possibly an entrepreneur such as Sharan Bey understood the shifting landscape of Ottoman society and sensed that the best option for preserving his influence and capital was to reinvest it in the normative order as pursued by Khrimian and Srvantstiants. As shown later, he and others who had endeavored to delegitimize Khrimian would become his allies.

Sharan Bey's overtures suggest a growing realization on the part of some affluent Armenians that significant shifts in the configuration of imperial politics and society, which to this point had provided them clear incentives for defending the status quo, were afoot. Still, Melkian retained a great deal of power and influence into the 1870s. In response to a question posed by Khrimian about "that old obstacle [to reform]," Srvantstiants first mentions Melikian in a February 29, 1872 letter.[24] Srvantstiants explained that "since the day of my arrival" he had heard nothing but "insults and curses from the mouth of Boghos *vardapet*." In the same letter, Srvantstiants was even more explicit about Melikian and the implications of reform for the Armenians of Van and the Ottoman state. Melikian, he informed Khrimian, was working against "your Patriarchate and the execution of our office, [and] finally the Ottoman *Tenzimet* and the Armenian Constitution."[25]

Srvantstiants proceeded to describe the methods Melikian had deployed to resist the Tanzimat. First, he suggested that Melikian was "of the same blood" as the Timurzades (or Temuroğlus), a notable Turkish family that occupied many positions in the local government; this was, of course, an allusion to the connections that had propped up the local ruling class. The Timurzades would, for example, harass and intimidate Armenian peasants if their village dared to submit a petition against Melikian. Much of the Timurzades' work was financed by three local Armenians: Banirian, Isajanian, and Marutian.[26] Melikian brokered among these Armenians and the Timurzades. Together they marshaled spiritual and institutional authority, coercion, and capital to intimidate those who might sponsor the implementation of new state institutions. This posed a particularly significant challenge to Khrimian and the reformers. The reform programs had bid to introduce a normative order that, by placing legitimacy in the people, would link the provinces and the imperial center and produce a gridded polity. Melikian made clear that he still possessed the tools to remind provincial Armenians just how far away the central state truly was. Srvantstiants concluded that exiling Melikian from Van was the only meaningful option available to the reformers. He therefore requested that both the Patriarchate and the Sublime issue order to this effect and that a locum tenens prelate be appointed.

Melikian's opposition to Srvantstiants's attempts at implementing the Constitution became more entrenched. The pro-Melikian "bigwigs" approached Srvantstiants and told him that creating new councils and overseeing the election of a prelate were responsibilities that belonged to Melikian, the reigning prelate.[27] The anti-Melikian party, meanwhile, grew increasingly impatient while waiting for the Patriarchate to do something more than simply dispatching a Khrimian acolyte to introduce the formal institutions mandated by the Armenian Constitution. Srvantstiants urged the Patriarchate to take immediate action, as inaction by the center emboldened Melikian. He thus recommended that Khrimian reassign Krikoris Aghvanian from Mush to Van. Aghvanian, unlike Srvantstiants, came from a moneyed family in Van, which might afford him better connections locally for challenging Melikian and his allies. The other high-ranking clergy of well-to-do background from Van—Eremia Tevkants— was not suggested, as "it would appear [the people] are startled by him."[28]

Melikian's rebellion against the Patriarchate, and by extension the Tanzimat state, was joined by his allies and continued during Srvantstiants's time in Van. Supporters of Melikian frequently approached Srvantstiants to express their willingness to go directly to the Sublime Porte on behalf of the embattled clergyman; they were, of course, suggesting that their informal and semiformal connections trumped the institutions the reformers were working to establish.[29] Possibly, they recalled Jerusalem's largely successful resistance of Constantinople in 1862, as discussed in Chapter 1. They also demonstrated the other tools at their disposal. An unnamed Kurdish official, ostensibly a Melikian ally, intimidated a priest named Eghiazar from assuming control over the prelacy on a temporary basis, although both the governor and the Church authorities were on his side; Melikian, for his part, continued to ignore calls that he step down from his post.[30] Marutian, Banirian, and Isajanian, the aforementioned financiers of the Timurzade clan, made regular visits to the offices of the prelacy with the intention of interrupting Srvantstiants's work. In another case, Ali Agha, the Kurdish Haydaranlı leader introduced in the previous chapter, entered the city of Van with some of his men where they asked every Armenian they encountered whether they were Melikian's enemy or friend. By manufacturing disincentive for investing in the reform project at as many levels of society as possible, the pro-Melikian faction aimed to remind people where real power and coercion in Van lied. Even as some Armenians defected from Melikian's camp in the hopes of establishing more official sets of relationships with both society and the government, the structure of Melikian's network proved resilient. Reform, however, was the official law, and Melikian's power continued to rest outside it. Srvantstiants, therefore, reiterated to Khrimian the plea he had made to him earlier: appoint Aghvanian as patriarchal vicar and secure an order from the imperial government for Melikian's exile.

The Patriarchate still moved too slowly for Srvantstiants. He had yet to receive a ferman from the government that would have officially ratified his appointment. Without that, he lacked any formal standing with the provincial authorities, without whose support he would struggle to introduce communal reform. Despite this, the governor privately expressed his shock that Khrimian and the reformers in the capital had yet to secure Melikian's banishment.[31] Srvantstiants thus reiterated his demand that the order for Melikian's exile come from the Sublime Porte rather than the Patriarchate of Constantinople; bold action by the state could undermine Melikian and his supporters.

Srvantstiants's inroads did worry Melikian and his allies. Melikian retreated to the Lim monastery on Lake Van, where he had somehow managed appointment as abbot at some point in 1870. There he could conduct business with his Kurdish allies away from the prying eyes of his Armenian enemies. Back in the city, Melikian's supporters continued to cause problems for Srvantstiants and openly cursed him in the streets.[32] Victory, however, seemed at hand for Khrimian and Srvantstiants, as the Patriarchate had finally sent a *takrir* to the Porte that requested Melikian's expulsion from Van. In response, Melikian's allies increased their public attacks on Srvantstiants's character in an effort to undermine him.[33] They also sought out new ways to challenge the legitimacy of Khrimian's rule. One of Melikian's associates, the priest Partughimeos, traveled to Etchmiadzin for an audience with the Catholicos of All Armenians in the hopes that Etchmiadzin would use its ecclesiastical authority to further undermine Khrimian and the reform program. Catholicos Gevorg II had just cast a cloud of doubt over the legitimacy of the Constitution the previous year for its handling of the Cilicia and Aghtamar issues. Partughimeos returned from the Mother See with a bull; however, it made no reference, indirect or otherwise, to Melikian. Melikian and his allies sought other options. They placed their hopes in news of Istanbul-based banker Simon Bey Maksudian's election to the National Assembly. Melikian's allies believed that Maksudian, who was supposedly the personal banker of the valide sultan, could exploit his connections in the government to create problems for Khrimian.[34] Boghos grasped at every available lever to disrupt Khrimian's rule.

Finally, on August 24, 1872, Srvantstiants wrote to confirm receipt of letters from the Porte and the Patriarchate that secured Melikian's exile. Upon becoming aware of the orders, Melikian attempted to flee, only to be captured later by the police.[35] By the following week, the governor of Van reported to Srvantstiants that he was forwarding a list of Melikian's crimes to the Sublime Porte.[36] Then, as Srvantstiants had hoped, Aghvanian was sent to Van as a patriarchal vicar, where he would continue the work of implementing the Constitution.

Khrimian and Srvantstiants won this stanza. Their victory came not as any "middle point" in a multilocal national awakening but instead as partisans on behalf of a centralizing state. With Melikian removed, Aghvanian successfully convened assemblies, held elections, and implemented the Constitution in Van and the surrounding areas. This meant a standardization of official relations between local governors and *millet* bodies, as well as between *millet* bodies and the Patriarchate. During the final months of his reign, Khrimian emphasized this point by issuing a set of orders entitled *Instructions to Provincial Prelates and Administrations for [Conducting] Relations with the Local Government* in 1873. These orders fully articulated the political and spiritual responsibilities of a prelate, the codification of these responsibilities in Ottoman law and its confirmation by the Sublime Porte, its role before local officials, and its responsibilities to the flock.[37] Khrimian and Srvantstiants were building the central state through the Armenian community by restructuring relations along the lines of a gridded polity in which Istanbul was the center. It is within those constraints and the assumptions they provided that political culture was being articulated. Subsequent conflict would bear this out.

A REACTIONARY RESTRAINED

Khrimian's decision to request an order for Melikian's exile from the Sublime Porte in 1872, which did not proceed properly through the councils of the National Administration, was regarded by some as an autocratic move and in violation of the Constitution. Those opposed to Khrimian of course cared little that he had violated a procedural technicality. Still, Khrimian had once more found himself ensnared by nuance and minor details that ultimately distracted him and his allies from larger issues. Members of the Religious Council took this opportunity to undermine the Patriarch.[38] Just as the notables of Van had hoped, Maksudian and his fellow conservative, Arakel Dadian, seized on the chance to revisit the circumstances surrounding Melikian's exile. Melikian was subsequently returned to Van in 1874 and sent to the Lim Monastery, located on an island in the northeast corner of Lake Van, with instructions not to interfere in community affairs. Given that the Constitution had stripped monasteries of most their political and economic power, this decision appeared to have left Melikian without any official capacity for influencing the new system governing the *millet*. Melikian would continue to pay these instructions little heed. Yet, as the decreasing number of tools available to him was to demonstrate, he would soon discover that the Van to which he returned differed greatly from the one that he had left. Ultimately, Melikian's revamped approach offers us a look into the paradox of Armenian engagement with the Tanzimat; successful reform yielded marginalization.

Before his resignation in 1873, Khrimian argued that the National Administration would have to bring Melikian to Istanbul for questioning if the councils overturned his decision. The Religious Council countered that any hearing instead take place in Van where Melikian would of course have a more sympathetic audience.[39] Most probably at the urging of conservatives in the community's leadership, Constantinople once again sent Harutiun Vehabedian to Van to investigate. Vehabedian, a member of the St. James Order at Jerusalem, had previously partnered with Melikian. Their collaboration had led, in part, to the exoneration of Khachadur Shiroian, the catholicos of Aghtamar, on charges of murdering his predecessor. When together in Van, Melikian is alleged to have told Vehabedian in his vulgar Armenian that Van was his "fief" (*em timaren*).[40]

Moreover, according to Tevkants, Vehabedian had been dispatched to Van to investigate Aghvanian, as the wealthy of Van had filed several complaints with the Patriarchate against the reigning prelate.[41] Vehabedian promptly dissolved the Constitutional assemblies established by Aghvanian and installed an ally of Melikian, Tateos Vartabed, as patriarchal vicar.[42]

Khrimian had entrusted Aghvanian and Srvantstiants with implementing the Constitution in Van, which they had accomplished in part through the institution of councils and elections. Yet within a year of Khrimian's resignation, Melikian, with the support of his old ally Vehabedian, had succeeded in having those victories reversed. The following year, he took aim at Eremia Tevkants, another of Khrimian's allies. Melikian reported to the Patriarchate that Tevkants had violated Church law by ordaining two priests without permission. Given the nature of the alleged crimes, this was an opportunity for the Catholicos of Etchmiadzin once more to interfere in Constantinople's affairs. Moreover, the priests he had ordained had already been deemed unworthy by a bishop in the Caucasus in the Russian Empire; the two allegedly had to bribe Tevkants to receive their ordination to the holy orders.[43] The charges seem to have inconvenienced only Tevkants, who was compelled to pen a voracious self-defense but realizing no lasting harm to him or his reputation. This particular accusation, however, reflected an important change in repertoire of actions available to Melikian.

As we have seen, only a few years earlier Melikian could rely on recourse to his Kurdish allies to intimidate his political rivals in the city or terrorize villagers living in the surrounding areas. This form of coercion, to which Melikian enjoyed access, existed outside of the official purview of the state or the *millet* authorities. Having returned from exile, however, Melikian and his allies were compelled to work within the system. The effort to involve the catholicos of Etchmiadzin, either through the solicitation of pontifical bulls or by leveling charges of impropriety against other priests, reveals Melikian's need to resort to ecclesiastical intervention to stop Khrimian. In so doing, Melikian hoped to exacerbate conflicts over jurisdiction, which had plagued the Constitutional order since its establishment in 1860. The appeal to the Mother See, in particular, was made with the aim of calling into question the legitimacy of the Patriarchate of Constantinople and its Constitution. Varjabedian, unlike Khrimian four years earlier, more adeptly handled the challenge.

Three observations explain why Melikian could no longer simply bully his way through problems. First, reform programs standardized the points of contact between Armenians and the government. The growing presence of the Patriarchate in day-to-day affairs of the Church in the provinces sealed off the structural holes that Melikian had previously exploited. Failure to comply could lead to exile, as Melikian now knew from experience. Second, structures had shifted during his absence and new relations had been forged without his knowledge or participation. For these two reasons, he was no longer the social broker he had been in years past. Finally, the government began engaging certain Kurdish tribes directly throughout the 1870s and 1880s. Melikian's role as an intermediary between the two groups no longer carried the same meaning or consequence as it had in years past. The following years point to some combination of these three explanations.

Tateos, an ally of Boghos, had served in the prelacy for a brief period at some point in the 1860s,. Because he was dependent on Melikian for support, he failed to win the favor of the flock. He assumed the position of prelate in 1874, a post he later resigned on July 4, 1876. The Patriarchate then sent Tevkants to Van as patriarchal vicar.[44] Tevkants initially wished to decline the appointment but ultimately accepted it. This would be the sixth time that Tevkants, who had briefly taken high-profile posts as a preacher at different churches in Istanbul, would hold a position in Anatolia. He had previously served as prelate in both Dikranagert (Diyarbakir) and Kharpert (Harput). It was hoped that the wealth of knowledge and experience he had acquired, coupled with his connections in his native Van, would help him put an end to the "thirty-year war."[45]

A NETWORKING PARADOX

As he approached Van, Tevkants made it a point to preach in churches located in outlying areas. Opposition to his presence, however, greeted him upon entrance into the city. Because of his proximity to Khrimian, Melikian's supporters wanted nothing to do with him. For reasons that remain unclear but Srvantstiants alludes to in letters to Khrimian, the anti-Melikian party was lukewarm about Tevkants's arrival. He likewise found problems with the local government, which initially refused to seat him on the local council, despite being a violation of the Düstur.[46] This friction with local government officials reflected transformations that were responsible for limiting the scope of Armenians' connections with unofficial sites of power in the former networked world of governance. Reform had politicized the community and its institutions and brought Armenians closer to one another. The appearance of closure from imperial society along ethno-religious lines was, in fact, the bridging and connecting of the Armenian community to the official Ottoman government.

Tevkants labored to make that system, of which he and the reformers viewed their own communal institutions a part, work. Beyond his struggles with local government officials, he tried to subordinate the rival factions within his own community to the office of Prelate and, consequently, the Patriarchate. He used institutions of the Armenian Church to compile information on oppression and corruption, which he then forwarded to the Patriarchate in the hope of winning the Porte's intervention. Petitions and reports requested the removal of local military leaders, including the *tabur ağası* and the *el ağası*. Most notably, there were numerous complaints against the Haydaranlı Kurds, who had begun attacking and stealing from monasteries with increasing regularity. In addition to attacking Khrimian's base at Varak, they also stole from the less important Skanchelagorts Monastery, which had traditionally been allied with Melikian. Generally, Tevkants described the movement of Kurds along the Iranian-Ottoman border as a principle source of danger for the Armenians of Van.[47]

The torching of Van's bazaar in December 1876 perhaps best illustrates the extent to which Armenians, including those allied to Melikian, had been marginalized in a world of unofficial governance that remained resilient. On the evening of December 6, a blaze spread among the shops of the bazaar. Commerce in Van, with the exception of butcher and grocery shops, was overwhelmingly in the hands of the Armenians. These Armenians, through Melikian and the Church, were generally allied with other power brokers in the region. Not only did the local government do little to prevent the spread of the fire, it appears to have actively encouraged the looting of Armenian-owned shops. In the middle of the fire, armed Kurds and regular soldiers appeared amidst the blaze and began pillaging the stores.[48] Tevkants entered the bazaar, shouting to anyone who would listen to stop and that "the wealth of [Armenian] society is the wealth of the government!" His failed intervention earned him a beating at the hands of five or six soldiers.[49]

Harutiun Jangiulian, a native of Van who published his memoirs after the Young Turk Revolution, argued that the fire was an act of arson planned in advance by the local military commander, Mehmet Bey, and in conjunction with the Timurzades.[50] Of the approximately one hundred Armenian-owned stores in the bazaar, only three were spared from looting. Grocery and butcher shops, owned by Muslims, were left untouched. The Armenians suffering the greatest losses were Sharan Bey and Kevork Bey Kaljian. Sharan Bey had begun making overtures to Khrimian in the early 1870s and would be an open ally of the reform program in 1880s. Kaljian, meanwhile, would later spend time in a local jail. According to Jangiulian, Mehmet Bey had obsessed over destroying the wealth of the notable Armenians Sharan Bey and Kaljian.[51]

The Timurzades, the Kurds (most probably Haydaranlı), and officials within the police and military had turned a blind eye to the probable arson and subsequent looting, but the governor of Van tried in vain to help.[52] The Armenians held both Governor Ziya Pasha and his son Cemil Bey in high regard. This should come as no surprise: Ziya Pasha and the Armenian community were both allied in the project of state centralization. Reform within the *millet* theoretically incorporated more provincial Armenians into the Ottoman body politic and subsequently projected the authority of the Patriarchate and the Sublime Porte into Van. Ziya Pasha's interests thus converged with those of the reforming Armenians. The Timurzades, who still held positions at multiple levels of the local government, the Kurdish Haydaranlıs, and some segments of the military, however, had moved on to other business.

FALLING OUT FROM WAR

The Russo-Turkish War ushered in many tangible changes to politics and society in the Ottoman Empire. Included among the concessions the defeated Ottomans were compelled to make were the annexation of Kars by the Russians and promises to carry out reforms on behalf of the embittered Armenians in the eastern provinces. The war witnessed not only the occupation of Anatolia as far west as Erzurum but also the visible presence of Armenians in the Russian officer corps. Some provincial Ottoman Armenians found these Armenians soldiers—who were no less than conquerors of Ottoman territory—inspiring. Yet the Ottomanism repertoire that had shaped their worldview would prove resilient.

Consonant with demands for reform of Anatolia, the Ottoman state dispatched Reform Commissioners to the provinces with executive authority to convene assemblies, remove officials, and conduct elections. These were not too dissimilar from Tanzimat clerks, who circulated throughout the empire in the nineteenth century, or even the Armenian "examiners" who entered towns and villages to implement the Armenian National Constitution. Likely, Armenians saw the parallels to what they had already experienced in their own community. British consular reports contain significant details on the Armenians' interactions with the Reform Commissioners. In their councils, which had been created by the Constitution, Armenians composed documents that enumerated the crimes perpetrated against them by their Muslim neighbors and, more importantly, articulated their own plans for reforming the empire. Three general demands emerge from these plans: proportional ethno-religious representation based on accurate census data, punishment for crimes, and protections against possible future assaults or retribution. Rather than forging closure around ethnic markers in the wake of the war, Armenians were renewing the efforts Khrimian had made only a few years prior in the *Report* as part of a bid to integrate themselves and their institutions more fully into the imperial body politic. They were still challenging the state to monopolize the legitimate use of violence (and punish those who claimed that right for themselves), extend the capacity of the central state to the provinces, and carve out a space for themselves in a reconfigured imperial society. The war, therefore, did not ignite nationalism or create a rupture between Armenians and Ottoman society. In a moment where uncertainty may have reigned, the Armenians relied on actions socially and culturally proscribed over the preceding years; they fell back on Ottomanism.

Ottomanism helped Armenians make sense of a changing world. Still, that world remained in motion. In addition to war, Van had been subject to drought and an ensuing famine. Out of the disorder created by these forces in an imperial borderland, where jurisdictional authority was contested and reproduced daily, a Kurdish leader named Shaykh Ubeydullah came to the fore.[53] A notable who had been feted upon his entrance to major Ottoman cities in prior decades, Ubeydullah filled a political vacuum the central state could not. In 1880, he tested the state's limits by way of rebellion. Ubeydullah's revolt ultimately failed to carve out a buffer state between the Qajars and the Ottomans. Although his forces were largely routed, he did demonstrate the limits of official Ottoman state power in a sensitive part of the empire. The engagement between Kurdish tribes and the official state, which had intensified during the 1870s, entered a new phase in the 1880s and 1890s. Preventing future Ubeydullahs required a different approach to statecraft. The Ottomans instead decided to coopt provincial magnates in the eastern provinces. It plied them with medals, official posts, and tax farms as part of an effort to project the image of state sovereignty in eastern Anatolia. The pinnacle of these practices was the establishment of the Hamidiye cavalry units in 1891, which in important ways formalized the relationship that the imperial government had been cultivating with the tribes throughout the 1880s. The meaning of the Tanzimat state, therefore, had changed; the Armenians carried on as though it had not. It was into these new political arrangements that Khrimian made his return to Van.

CONCLUDING KHRIMIAN'S OTTOMAN LIFE

Against the backdrop of war, famine, dispossession, and the embers of a nascent rebellion, Khrimian came home for the second time in an official capacity. On September 15, 1879, the assembly of the Van prelacy, still presided over by Tevkants, elected Khrimian as its new prelate. Within one week, the Patriarchate not only ratified the election but also charged Khrimian with distributing aid to those starving under the auspices of the Famine Relief Committee.[54] Khrimian set out for Van at the very end of October and arrived in the vicinity of Van in November. He met with old friends, such as Harutiun Aghvanian, a relative of Krikoris. Upon entering the city, he was greeted by more friends. One, fearing Khrimian might be exasperated from the trip, brought the city's doctor. Khrimian, who had other ideas, explained to the doctor, "There's nothing wrong with me. His Grace Eremia [Tevkants] is the sick one. He just keeps getting fatter. Can you give something so that he'll get skinny?"[55] People filled the streets with shouts of "Hayrik has come!" Just like his march to Istanbul almost one decade earlier, optimism abounded. And just like Khrimian's term as Patriarch of Constantinople, it would end in disappointment.

Khrimian assembled his committees and the rest of his administration. The Relief Committee included most of his old friends and students: Bishop Eremia Tevkants, Setrak Tevkants, Karekin *Vardapet* Srvantstiants, Mkrtich Portugalian, and Garabed Terlemezian. A new friend, Kevork Bey Kaljian, joined them. As a gesture of goodwill, Khrimian also included Melikian's old allies, Garabed Isajanian and Mkrtich Efendi Marutian. Khrimian then deputized Srvantstiants as his vice prelate, which charged him with conducting most of the prelacy's day-to-day business. It was under these conditions that Khrimian set about continuing the reform projects to which he had devoted most of his public life. Education remained, as it had been before, the primary project. At Varak, for example, Khrimian and his acolytes established an agricultural school to develop practices that would mitigate the consequences of future drought or famine. As Armenian *millet* institutions became loci of formal politics and contested sites of power, different empire-wide Armenian civic organizations came to the fore to try influencing policy decisions. Many of these eventually fell under the umbrella of the United Associations (*Miatseal enkerutiunk*), which coordinated efforts to build Armenian community schools throughout the empire. In Van, these schools fell under the directorship of the Istanbul-born Mkrtich Portugalian.

However, things had changed. The comparatively successful implementation of reform in the Armenian community had, on one hand, made Portugalian and Khrimian somewhat tone deaf to this new reality. Invoking the spirit of reform as he understood it, and as head of the Famine Relief Committee in Van, Khrimian reached across ethno-confessional lines and distributed some of the aid earmarked for Armenians to Kurds. He renewed his friendship with a grandson of Khan Mahmud, Mutullah Bey.[56] Portugalian and his students, meanwhile, hosted and organized public speeches, plays, and parades. Khrimian invited the British and Russian vice-consuls, whom he had befriended, to these events. With the social gulf widening between the Armenian community, on one hand, and the local government and Muslims, on the other, vibrant Armenian social institutions came to be seen in an increasingly seditious light. Absent the rigorous implementation of reform policies, local government officials would have no incentive to prioritize Armenian concerns. As noted earlier, what seemed to be closure around ethnic bonds—which was in fact the severing of the Armenian community's links to other groups in society—reinforced anti-Armenian prejudices that saw a revolutionary hiding behind the hood of every priest. In a post-Ubeydullah Anatolia during the reign of Abdülhamid II, Khrimian was no longer viewed as a servant of the sublime state, but rather its subversive.

Srvantstiants, for his part, had spent most of the previous decade on the ground in eastern Anatolia. Better attuned to the changing dynamics of politics and society in the region, Srvantstiants advocated a more measured approach to reform. Portugalian remained adamant that reforms continue unabated and that the community still host its public events. A schism subsequently appeared among the anti-Melikian party, with factions supporting either Khrimian or Srvantstiants. Eventually, in 1882, Srvantstiants tendered his resignation from his post as vice-prelate, which he submitted to Khrimian personally. As Srvantstiants approached to kiss Khrimian's hand, Khrimian stopped him and then "covered his forehead in kisses and drenched it in tears."[57] Srvantstiants's reading of the situation proved correct. Khrimian found himself unable to resolve his problems with the government. Even his friendship with the governor, Hasan Pasha, who had privately expressed the pressure Istanbul had placed on him to take action against the Armenians, would not be enough.

The growing integration of Kurdish tribes into the apparatus of the central state, without the mediating role of Armenian clergymen like Melikian or his allies, had contributed to the erosion of the Armenian community's role in networked governance. Moreover, at the imperial level in the capital, the responsibility for overseeing the administration of the *millets* had passed to the Ministry of Justice in 1881. In prior generations, Armenian reformers' connections to the Porte had placed them at the ground floor of reform projects: Reşit Pasha had relied on Hagop Grjigian, Servichen Efendi and Nahabed Rusinian had forged friendships with Ali and Fuat, and of course Krikor Odian had authored the Ottoman Constitution in collaboration with Midhat Pasha, whom he had also advised previously in other capacities. Abdülhamid II's Ministry of Justice, particularly under Cevdet Pasha, took an entirely different view of Armenians. The point was made even more clear by the execution of Midhat and Krikor Odian's decision to live out the remaining years of his life as an exile in Paris.

At both the imperial and local levels, therefore, the meaning of the Tanzimat had changed. As Bernard Lewis argued decades ago, the reign of Abdülhamid II was marked overwhelmingly by continuity with the Tanzimat period, particularly with regard to the ongoing effort to centralize the state.[58] The Hamidian Tanzimat (or Islamic Ottomanism, as Julia Phillips Cohen described it) did continue the project of building a bureaucratic state.[59] Unlike the Tanzimat as envisioned or understood by Reşid Pasha, Midhat Pasha, or Khrimian, however, it had no need for either the Armenians or their institutions. Varjabedian's deft maneuvering in the capital was all the political cover that reformers in the province would enjoy. Closure around community did occur; it was, however, Muslims who had forged closure, not the Armenians.

Varjabedian passed away on October 25, 1884. Khrimian learned of Varjabedian's passing while presiding over an assembly in the Van prelacy. Although he was mourning the loss of a friend, Khrimian likely understood the political ramifications of the Patriarch's death. Interrupting the meeting, he paced the hall in tears, repeating to himself, "Nerses has died. . . . Hayrik has died. . . . Khrimian has died. . . . Varjabedian has died."[60] And he was right: one month later, the Patriarchate of Constantinople and the Sublime Porte ordered Khrimian, now seen as a security risk, into internal exile in Jerusalem. After waiting for the winter to conclude, Khrimian left the place of his birth for the final time in April 1885. Seven years later, over the vocal protests of the Russian government, which the Ottomans had always suspected of supporting, Khrimian was elected Catholicos of All Armenians in Etchmiadzin. He traveled to the Caucasus through Europe.

By the time the government of Sultan Abdülhamid II had seen through his expulsion to Jerusalem in 1885, Khrimian had come to understand the lessons that his former student, Srvantstiants, had tried in vain to impart. These changes in governance required that Armenians plot a different chart for engaging imperial politics and society. For Khrimian, this meant a last-ditch effort at resurrecting the old order that he had worked so hard to defeat. He thus returned Melikian to community work at the prelacy as vice-prelate.[61] He hoped that Melikian would provide the Armenians of Van some connection to the new arrangements of social and political power that had been established over the preceding years.

Khrimian and Varjabedian had spent fifteen years implementing a constitutional order that placed the Patriarchate of Constantinople, and consequently the Sublime Porte, at the center of Ottoman Armenian politics. This was not, as argued throughout this chapter, any expression of nationalism, as Armenian political action continued seeking its legitimation in the imperial capital and the Tanzimat project. Nor did these programs or the actions of Armenians, therefore, constitute closure and a rejection of Ottomanism. Despite their intentions, successful execution of these reform programs increasingly isolated Armenians from local society and the imperial government. The Ottoman Empire, particularly in the provinces, was a series of delicately constructed interpersonal networks that simultaneously transcended and combined ethnicity and religion. Actors who could successfully navigate these relationships could position themselves as social bridges that bound this provincial society together. Armenian zest for the projects of the central state, however, unmixed the sites of power that were enmeshed in those networks. The Tanzimat had promised equality and security within the parameters of a gridded imperial polity; instead, Armenians, as an Ottoman confessional community, were left with far less collective social capital than they had previously possessed. Unmixed sites meant fewer bridges to other networks. The death of Varjabedian and exile of Khrimian appear to have signaled not just the unhappy end of the Tanzimat in the Armenian community or the victory of the conservatives. It also signaled, as demonstrated by Melikian's increasingly unimportant role in local society, the end of any meaningful place for the Armenian community in imperial governance. Without a consonant effort on the part of the government to reform local government and society, reform internal to the Armenian community would find itself without partners for making the Tanzimat, as they understood it, work. Yet the relatively successful implementation of reform within their own community meant that they no longer had informal connections to the networked world of governance that the Tanzimat had aimed to eliminate. The Armenians were, in the end, victimized by their own success.

CONCLUSION

THE TANZIMAT, AS THE MEANING OF THE WORD suggests, sought the reorganization and reordering of all facets of Ottoman imperial society and governance. In many respects, this reorganization of society sought to make imperial subjects legible to the central state in Istanbul. Doing so did not simply entail introducing a handful of new councils or courts, codifying non-Muslim prerogatives relating to the administration of their own communities, or brokering new relations with political power brokers. It instead required a wholesale transformation of the imperial state from a networked world that had stitched together a multitude of spaces to something that better resembled a center-periphery model with clear lines of authority marking the relationship between Istanbul and its subjects spread throughout the empire. In other words, the nineteenth-century Ottoman reformers labored to shred one vision of empire—an imperial tapestry into which various communities were woven as they shared sovereignty—with the intention of crafting something different. As the nineteenth century wound to a close, Armenians would find themselves disappointed by the shape this new iteration of Ottoman imperium was beginning to take.

To explore the ramifications these dynamics had for the Armenian community of the empire, the experiences of Boghos Natanian and Boghos Melikian are a useful point of departure. These two clergymen differed in significant ways. Although both were high-ranking Armenian priests from Van—the latter having been elevated to the rank of bishop—they found themselves on opposite sides of a political divide.[1] Melikian, as we have seen, was a bitter enemy of Mkrtich Khrimian and the reformers. He was an enforcer, a violent man who willingly employed the tools of coercion he wielded to preserve a social order that, in the course of being brought under siege by a centralizing state, had been made a deviant legal order that rested in contention with state law. Natanian, on the other hand, was a former student and close ally of Khrimian; he and his extended family had served on the front lines of the battles over reform all across eastern Anatolia.[2] The fates of these two clergymen, which played out over the last decade or so of the nineteenth century, would at first suggest the perpetuation of their differences. They were, however, manifestations of the same phenomenon: the unraveling of the imperial tapestry and the subsequent transformation of imperial governance to a center-periphery model brokered on the basis of newly established relationships and institutions. This new center-periphery model reified connections between communities. Armenians would be left with not only far fewer meaningful points of contact with either the government or other groups in imperial society but also the mutual obligations that invested them all in one another.

As the calendar turned from 1889 to 1890, Natanian languished away in Istanbul's central prison.[3] He would eventually die there. His imprisonment and the circumstances surrounding it represent an important shift in the Ottoman state's view of Armenian clergymen. In prior decades, they had operated as intermediaries to whom the business of state had been delegated. Moreover, this intermediary role had allowed them to act as a fulcrum around which other relationships were brokered. The decision to send Khrimian to Jerusalem as an internal exile in 1885, however, made clear that the state now viewed clergymen in a different light and was willing to use its tools of coercion against them. In Khrimian's case, the state at least extended a traditional courtesy reserved for clergymen. Although the government had wished to remove him from the public sphere, it contented itself with shuttering him in a monastery sufficiently distant from his power base. In fact, the order for Khrimian's exile was officially issued by the Patriarchate—though it could not have done so without the government's authorization. The government had taken a similar course of action on behalf of the reformers in previous decades: as we saw earlier, a Catholicos of Aghtamar was temporarily moved to a monastery near Şebinkarahisar at the request of the Patriarchate of Constantinople. The state also approved the removal of Melikian to a monastery near Erzurum when Khrimian had his rival banished from Van. And out of deference to the clergy and respect for the

Armenian population, the police at Van had decided against bringing Bishop Khachadur Shiroian to the city for interrogation—though they were convinced he had played a role in the murder of Catholicos Bedros—without first informing the Church authorities.

The police appear to have understood that, as representatives of the community, clergymen—particularly those who were either high ranking or publicly visible—required the respect of state officials. Such respect communicated to other sectors of society that the Armenians and their church were seminal to imperial governance and, in fact, partners of the Porte. Although they were marked by difference as Christians in a Muslim state, they were a protected and integral part of society. Natanian, by contrast, was not confined in a monastery; he was instead placed among the general prison population where, according to a visitor, he was malnourished and emaciated.[4] Nor was Natanian the only pro-reform clergyman to find himself the target of government violence.[5] In persecuting such figures, the government communicated the exact opposite of what the police had tried to convey in 1864 when, shortly after the reinstitution of the Armenian Constitution, the partnership between the Patriarchate and the Porte was strong: Armenians were not worthy of respect, and their institutions no longer played any role in imperial governance. Any action that Armenians might take to better their situation could now be read as a transgression against the status quo.

Even though he no longer enjoyed the influence he once did, Melikian, stalwart of the old order, continued to benefit from the connections he had forged over the course of the preceding decades. As his allies and partners, such as the Timurzade clan, tightened their grip on provincial offices in Van, Melikian found himself that much more insulated from the consequences of the transgressions he had committed to establish his influence in local society. The state, therefore, never designed to target him. Violence still managed to find him. On January 18, 1896, the governor at Van informed his superiors in the capital that Melikian had been murdered.[6] The British vice-consul at Van sent a similar message to his embassy in Istanbul.[7] Many people, as we have seen in Chapters 4 and 5, would have had incentive to kill Melikian. Only in a memoir published more than thirty years after the killing, however, do we learn that the triggerman was in fact a member of the revolutionary Social Democratic Hnchakian Party.[8]

Revolutionary violence rests beyond the scope of this study. The assassination of Melikian by a revolutionary is symbolic of the extent to which Ottoman politics and society had changed irreversibly in response to the Tanzimat reforms and the efforts to centralize the state's bureaucracy. For most of the nineteenth century, Ottoman Armenians had debated among themselves how their community would participate in imperial governance. Their communal politics—within which Natanian and Melikian represented opposing poles—was largely conversant with larger developments in imperial society. It remained so because the Church, shepherded by its clergy, was a conduit that facilitated the forging of connections between the community and those other sectors of Ottoman society, including official state bodies. State violence—unquestionably the most powerful force here—directed against the Armenian clergy made clear that these politics had irreversibly changed. The assassination of Melikian demonstrated the collapse of those politics entirely. Armenians had worked to help the government unravel one form of governance as part of an effort to weave something else: a centralized state from which they were now excluded.

As part of the Tanzimat reforms, the state's efforts at centralization had promised Armenians a new form of governance that would have rid society of the informal relationships and networks responsible for exacting such heavy tolls from the community. Network structures had woven the communal space into the imperial tapestry. Those same network structures therefore connected Armenians to both other communities and the institutions of the imperial state and therefore played a key role in perpetuating one iteration of imperial governance. Community institutions, which rested at the intersection of various network structures, were thus woven tightly into the imperial tapestry. The hard work of severing those threads—with the promise of stitching together something new and more equitable—fell to the reformers in the Armenian community. Ideally, they would have been presented opportunities for interlacing new connections that were to weave the community into formal state institutions. Instead, the restructuring that ultimately took place privileged other more powerful groups in imperial society. Exploring the circumstances under which we learn of Natanian's suffering and Melikian's death will provide insight on the dynamics that were at play.

MASSACRES AS CONTEXT

Word of Melikian's assassination reaches us from the two aforementioned sources—the British vice consul and the Ottoman governor at Van. Each was preoccupied at that time with collective violence that had been directed at Armenians throughout the empire over the preceding two years. Most historians describe that violence as the Hamidian massacres. Throughout the years 1894–96, entire Armenian communities fell victim to mass killings that culminated in refugees spilling into the Caucasus, an irreversible loss of communal wealth, and in some cases widespread conversions to Islam.[9] Numbers vary; all told, there may have been as many as 200,000 victims, if not more. For the Ottoman state and its apologists, this was an appropriate albeit harsh response to what it perceived as encroachments on its sovereignty by both European Great Power diplomacy and the seditious efforts of Armenian revolutionaries who sought—so the Ottomans claimed—to carve out a state for themselves in eastern Anatolia. This latter interpretation, which has come to be known as the provocation thesis, takes two tacks.[10] The first places blame on the victims for instigating the violence. The second holds Great Power politics responsible for the Ottoman state's decision to murder its own subjects, as the massacres precluded the introduction of provincial reforms mandated by European governments. Although the provocation thesis has rightly come under fire, the discussion needs to move away from revolutionaries, nationalism, or diplomats and back to questions of imperial governance and its transformations during the Tanzimat era.

A small-scale uprising on the part of Armenians near Sasun seems to have precipitated the killings. From there, massacres spread all across eastern Anatolia, leaving broken communities, forced conversions, abductions, refugees, and orphans in their wake. The archives of the Catholicosate of Etchmiadzin for this period are, for example, inundated with the pleas of refugees who had spilled into the Caucasus to flee the violence.[11] Although some Armenians did commit acts of violence, the phenomenon was hardly extensive or popular. The myth of widespread violence perpetrated by Armenians derives in large part from the presumption that the Tanzimat reforms had placed non-Muslim *millet*s on the pathway to nationalism. As this book has demonstrated, that argument is not tenable. Ottoman subjectivity was a given for Ottoman Armenians and structured both their worldview and the political or social action that they would take.

As I discuss below, the *millet*—rather than nation—merits reintroduction to this discussion. Once more, however, it must be analyzed in conjunction with the other primary facet of the Tanzimat reforms—namely, state centralization. Here it bears exploring why the Ottoman response to isolated episodes of Armenian violence was excessively harsh. In numerous respects it marked a departure from past practice. As historical sociologist Karen Barkey demonstrated, provincial rebellion was oftentimes a pathway to greater political power.[12] Rebels at the edges of the empire presented the state with a dilemma: Should Istanbul break those who raised the banner of revolt, or was it more prudent to coopt the insurrectionists? By and large, the Ottomans opted for the latter. A similar tradition of negotiation was reflected in the state's response to most of the major uprisings of the nineteenth century. In Egypt, Muhummad Ali and his sons converted insurrection into political power and recognition of a hereditary governorship. While Bedirkhan Bey, Khan Mahmud, and Shaykh Ubeydullah—the leaders of various Kurdish uprisings—would each live out the rest of their lives as internal exiles, the constituencies they represented were offered pathways back into the imperial fold. Similar opportunities awaited Türkmen leaders in Cilicia. The state did not simply deny Armenians that pathway; it instead punished them collectively.

While Abdülhamid II presided over Armenian deaths from the capital, it was Kurdish tribesmen who carried out the overwhelming majority of the violence. These tribesmen were, in turn, largely affiliated with the Hamidiye cavalry units that the Ottoman state had organized in 1891. Although Ottoman tribal policies such as the cavalry forces were not aimed solely at the Kurds—Arabs, Circassians, and others formed Hamidiye units and attended schools established for tribal use—they were the state's primary consideration as it bid to reorganize the empire's eastern periphery. As others have noted, this served at least two purposes.[13] One, it afforded Kurdish tribes—many of which were open to overtures from other states such as England, Russia, or Iran—a greater stake in the Ottoman enterprise. Two, in addition to securing the loyalty of those Kurdish tribes, it provided Istanbul another tool for hunting down Armenian revolutionaries.

These may have been the very concerns that occupied the minds of policymakers in the capital as they plotted an "eastern politics." Historians, however, should not succumb to the temptation to reduce those politics purely to a center-periphery story. Istanbul's turn to the Kurds, the murder of Melikian, and the massacres of the Armenians in 1894–96 were connected elements of a larger transformation of imperial governance born out of the changing interaction between the two principal markers of difference—periphery and confession—that legitimized the Ottoman enterprise in the nineteenth century.

SHREDDING THE EMPIRE

The Ottomans' decision to bring powerful Kurdish tribes into the state—to the detriment of the Armenian community given its culmination with the massacres—was not simply a response to an exaggerated Armenian threat or the state's desire to secure its eastern frontier. Reform within the Armenian community had taken aim at the informal relationships that stitched imperial spaces together; it had, in effect, ripped at the threads of the imperial tapestry by severing the links that had connected the Armenian community to those other spaces and placed Armenian clergymen at the intersection of those connections. But the Armenian reformers were soon to learn that Istanbul would select a different thread for reconstituting the imperial state. The Tanzimat did reorganize the empire, though not as the state had originally planned.

That Natanian, a respected clergyman from a prominent family, languished away in Istanbul's central prison demonstrates as much. The circumstances surrounding the transmission of his story to us drive the point home. We do not learn of Natanian's condition from Church documents or other contemporary sources but rather from a memoir written by Harutiun Jangiulian—an activist associated with a revolutionary party—and published only after the Young Turk revolution of 1908. During the 1880s and 1890s, we witness a shift in the manner that Armenian attempts to engage with and participate in imperial governance are archived. Instead of working through the Church, Armenian petitions increasingly find their way into consular archives.[14] This was, of course, an example of European infringement on Ottoman sovereignty. It was not, however, an example of Armenian insubordination or disloyalty. It instead demonstrates the failure of imperial and communal institutions that had partnered in imperial governance to implement Tanzimat policies. Armenians gradually lost venues for making political or social commentary—the press, the *millet*, or elsewhere—which they had learned to use throughout the Tanzimat period. These ceased to be options during Abdülhamid's reign and compelled Armenians to search for new outlets and methods. Censorship—which even extended to productions of the Holy Bible—policed Armenian voices as never before. As a further infringement on community prerogatives, state censorship replaced communal policing. Armenian protests from the provinces, the cause célèbre of reformers in the 1870s that had captured the attention of the government on multiple occasions, now made their way into either the aforementioned consular records or the organs of the Armenian revolutionary parties.[15]

Networked connections had not only provided the Armenian community a stake in imperial politics and society but also afforded them lines of communication with other groups in the empire. This was, after all, one of the reasons the *millet* was an attractive partner for centralizing the state and why

Armenians such as Khrimian, Srvantstiants, and others believed they were transforming the empire by reorganizing their own community. The state's silencing of Armenian voices was thus not simply about oppression; it was a consequence of shifting strategies made by the imperial government in the course of centralizing the state. Abdülhamid II had decided on a new partnership for reorganizing the empire.

Jangiulian once more sets the stage for us. For Jangiulian, Natanian's travails were only one manifestation of the Patriarchate's institutional flailing. The more consequential episode with which he found himself occupied in late 1889 was the story of the Kurdish notable Musa Bey and the Armenians of Mush.[16] Musa Bey had committed a litany of crimes against the Armenians on the Plain of Mush, the most brazen of which was the rape of a young woman named Giulizar and the murder of her husband. The Armenians of Mush, however, pressed for justice. Unable to find redress locally, they traveled to the imperial capital and presented their case at the Yıldız Palace to representatives of the Sultan. Because of this and foreign pressure, the government agreed to try the case in Istanbul and issued an order for Musa Bey to be brought to the capital.

Approximately sixty Armenian villagers had traveled from Mush to the capital for the trial. There, they received little support from the Church and instead had to rely on charity from individual members of the community for food and accommodation. Their condition in the capital contrasted sharply from that of Musa Bey himself, who, during his time in Istanbul, enjoyed the patronage of Bahri Pasha, a former governor in the Balkans who had been brought into Palace service.[17] This juxtaposition foreshadowed how the trial was to unfold. And in fact, the trial was a sham. Despite overwhelming evidence to the contrary, the court ruled Musa Bey innocent and ordered the Armenians to compensate him for the inconveniences he had endured in being brought to the capital. As a final insult, the government returned him to Mush with gifts and money.

Of course the verdict was preordained. One of Abdülhamid's closest advisers, Minister of Justice Cevdet Pasha, had been charged with orchestrating the trial. This was not the first time that Cevdet Pasha, in conjunction with his reactionary sultan, had signaled to the Armenians that their relationship to imperial governance had changed. In 1881, Cevdet and Abdülhamid transferred administration of the *millet*s to the Ministry of Justice; rather than partners of the empire, their government now viewed them and their institutions with suspicion. Those institutions had provided Armenians with the means by which they could communicate with the imperial government. In 1881, Cevdet Pasha and Abdülhamid told the Armenians they could no longer speak. In 1889, the Musa Bey verdict told those same Armenians that should they dare to ignore that dictate, not only would their pleas fall on deaf ears, they would be sanctioned for doing so in the first place.

Most important, the verdict communicated to both the Kurdish leadership and the Armenian community was that Kurdish assaults on Armenian lives, bodies, and property enjoyed the state's blessing. It is in this light that we must read the formation of the Hamidiye units and the decision to farm out sovereignty and the right to coerce other imperial subjects to select tribes. Abdülhamid and his government had put together a new and different imperial state. Imperial communities no longer operated in governance as communal spaces; this fresh iteration of Ottoman imperialism produced network structures that connected actors at the edges to the imperial center through newly established institutions and relationships. This imperial idiom, based on a politics of Muslim solidarity and legitimized by Abdülhamid's appropriation of Caliphate symbolism, was the thread that now wove the Ottoman state together in the last decades of the nineteenth century.[18] Although it was on an unequal basis, layered and shared sovereignty had threaded the Armenian community into structures of imperial power. Abdülhamid's empire denied them even that.

FROM THE POLITICS OF DIFFERENCE TO THE POLITICS OF EXCLUSION

This book has argued that markers of difference must be analyzed in conjunction with one another to properly understand the dynamics of Ottoman imperialism. Strategies of imperial rule oftentimes unfolded at the intersection of those markers. During the Tanzimat period, the state bid to reorganize its imperial domains along the lines of top-down relationships. Through the expansion of a professional bureaucracy, this entailed a shift from a nodal form of governance, predicated on networks that connected non-Muslim communities to other groups in imperial society, to a center-periphery model. Confessional difference had afforded those non-Muslim communities a share of imperial sovereignty that allowed them to integrate into networks of power. The unmaking of those networks—a seminal step for centralizing the state—divested non-Muslims' financial, political, and social capital from imperial governance.

This broader shift in strategies of imperial governance led to other shifts. The imperial government had, in its earlier efforts to centralize the state administration before and during the Tanzimat period, entered into a de facto partnership with the Armenian community to pursue such policies. As Armenians withdrew themselves and their institutions from the relationships that had made them such attractive partners of the state, the imperial center found itself positioned to broker new connections on more advantageous terms. Thus, it shifted its partnership to the Kurds. In this respect, Ottoman Armenians found themselves bearing consequences similar to those experienced by other non-Muslims in the course of Ottoman centralization. The Greek rebellion, stoked in large part by the central government's assaults on Balkan notables, precipitated the collapse of the Phanariots, the Orthodox Christian elite who had formed households that allowed them to control both governorships in the European provinces and high office in the government. The collapse of the Phanariots was instrumental to the breakdown of relationships between the Janissaries, notables, and the central government. This paved the way for the removal of the Janissaries, which Mahmud II completed by massacring the corps in 1826. Several major Jewish bankers, the exclusive financiers of the Janissary corps, were massacred along with them.

For Ottoman Armenians in the middle and late nineteenth century, the brokering agent was not a household or a class of bankers but the communal space that constituted their *millet*. Because their communal space was marked by religious confession, the entirety of the Armenian community was integrated into a politics of difference that propelled the clergy to the fore. These politics of difference placed Armenian clergymen at opposite poles in the context of the reform program. At first, those clergymen who advocated for policies of state centralization in the idiom of the Tanzimat found themselves the targets of violence by a mix of Muslim and non-Muslim guardians of the old order. As the imperial state reconciled with those Muslim groups initially targeted by the centralization efforts—such as the Türkmen in Cilicia, but especially the Kurds in the eastern provinces—the politics of difference transformed into a politics of exclusion. As Armenians were excluded from the new connections brokered in the context of this reconciliation, their community and their clergy now had no role to play in imperial governance. They had been cut from the tapestry.

Armenians, as we have seen, had cultivated and practiced an Ottomanist repertoire in the course of the battles over reform. This repertoire continued to structure the worldview of most Ottoman Armenians and their analyses of imperial politics. They thus continued to pursue reform. Now, however, these actions constituted a threat to the politics of exclusion that Abdülhamid's government had decided to pursue. The absence of conduits for communication, which the reformers had worked so hard to establish, exacerbated this. Any Armenian activity won the suspicion of the authorities. Clergymen remained at the front lines of these politics; only now it was the violence of the state that would target them. State violence against clergymen of all ranks, including bishops, constituted assaults on the community itself. The community no longer had a place in imperial governance or society and any claim to the contrary merited discipline—discipline that would be meted out collectively over the course of 1894–96.

NOTES

INTRODUCTION

1. Hakob Paronean, *Azgayin jojer. ute antip kensagrakannerov* (K. Polis: Tparan u gratun Nshan Papikean, 1912), 71–84.

2. For comparative examples, particularly those that emphasize a relationship between empire and religion, see among others, Robert Crews, "Empire and the Confessional State: Islam and Religious Politics in the Nineteenth Century Russia," *American Historical Review* 108, no. 1 (February 2003): 50–83; Pieter Judson, *The Habsburg Empire: A New History* (Cambridge, MA: Harvard University Press, 2015); Michael Miller, *Rabbis and Revolution: The Jews of Moravia in the Age of Emancipation* (Stanford, CA: Stanford University Press, 2010); and Paul Werth, *The Tsar's Foreign Faiths: Toleration and the Fate of Religious Freedom in Imperial Russia* (New York: Oxford University Press, 2014).

3. For examples, see Vartan Artinian, "The Armenian Constitutional System in the Ottoman Empire: A Study of its Historical Development" (PhD diss., Brandeis University, 1969); Victor Roudometof, "From *Rum Millet* to Greek Nation: Enlightenment, Secularization, and National Identity in Ottoman Balkan Society, 1453–1821" *Journal of Modern Greek Studies* 16, no. 1 (May 1998): 11–48; and Dimitri Stamatopoulos, "From *Millet*s to Minorities in the Nineteenth Century Ottoman Empire: Am Ambiguous Modernization," in *Citizenship in Historical Perspective*, eds. S. G. Ellis, G. Hálfadanarson, and A. K. Isaacs (Pisa, Italy: Edzioni Plus-Pisa University Press, 2006), 253–73.

4. Julia Phillips Cohen, *Becoming Ottomans: Sephardi Jews and Imperial Citizenship in the Modern Era* (New York: Oxford University Press, 2014); Hasan Kayalı, *Arabs and Young Turks: Ottomanism, Arabism, and Islamism in the Ottoman Empire, 1908–1918* (Berkeley: University of California Press, 1997); and Adam Mestyan, *Arab Patriotism: The Ideology and Culture of Power in Late Ottoman Egypt* (Princeton, NJ: Princeton University Press, 2017).

5. Matenadaran Katoghikosakan Divan, 205/1601, "Khoren *vardapet* Shahnazarian to Patriarchate of Constantinople" (November 30, 1874).

6. Karen Barkey, *Empire of Difference: The Ottomans in Comparative Perspective* (New York: Cambridge University Press, 2008).

7. Like Barkey, I benefit from Ronald Burt's theorization of social capital, brokerage, closure, and network structures. Ronald Burt, *Brokerage and Closure: An Introduction to Social Capital* (New York: Oxford University Press, 2005).

8. The introduction of this paradigm into Ottoman and Middle Eastern historiographies dates to the 1960s. See Albert Hourani, "Ottoman Reform and the Politics of Notables," in *Beginnings of Modernization in the Middle East*, eds. William R. Polk and Richard L. Chambers (Chicago: University of Chicago Press, 1968), 41–68; Şerif Mardin, "Center-Periphery Relations: A Key to Turkish Politics?" *Daedelus* 102, no. 1 (Winter 1973): 169–90. The paradigm has had tremendous influence on the scholarship on national identity formation in particular.

9. Ussama Makdisi, *Culture of Sectarianism: Community, History, and Violence in Nineteenth Century Ottoman Lebanon* (Berkeley: University of California Press, 2000). On the Balkans, see Isa Blumi, *Reinstating the Ottomans: Alternative Balkan Modernities, 1800–1912* (New York: Palgrave Macmillan, 2011).

10. Ronald Grigor Suny, "The Empire Strikes Out: Imperial Russia, 'National' Identity, and Theories of Empire," in *A State of Nations: Empire and Nation-Making in the Age of Stalin and Lenin*, eds. Ronald Grigor Suny and Terry Martin (New York: Oxford University Press, 2001), 23–66.

11. H. A. R. Gibb and Harold Bowen, *Islamic Society and the West, Volume 1: A Study of the Impact of Western Civilization on Moslem Culture in the Near East, Part II* (New York: Oxford University Press, 1957); Steven Runciman, *The Great Church in Captivity: A Study of the Patriarchate of Constantinople from the Eve of the Turkish Conquest to the Greek War of Independence* (London: Cambridge University Press, 1968).

12. Benjamin Braude, "Foundation Myths of the *Millet* System," in *Christians and Jews in the Ottoman Empire: The Functioning of a Plural Society. Volume I: The Central Lands*, eds. Benjamin Braude and Bernard Lewis (New York: Holmes and Meier, 1982), 69–88.

13. See, for example, Leslie Peirce, *Morality Tales: Law and Gender in the Ottoman Court of Aintab* (Berkeley: University of California Press, 2003).

14. Paraskevas Konortas, "From Tā'ife to Millet: Ottoman Terms for the Ottoman Greek Orthodox Community," in *Ottoman Greeks in the Age of Nationalism: Politics, Economy, and Society in the Nineteenth Century*, eds. Dimitri Gondicas and Charles Issawi (Princeton, NJ: Darwin Press, 1999), 169–79.

15. Carter Findley, "Tanzimat," in *The Cambridge History of Turkey, volume four*, ed. Reşat Kasaba (New York: Cambridge University Press, 2008), 29 (my italics). For an important revisionist account of nationalism in the Balkans, see İpek Yosamoğlu, *Blood Ties: Religion, violence, and Nationhood in Macedonia, 1878–1908* (Ithaca, NY: Cornell University Press, 2013).

16. Christine Philliou, "The Ottoman Empire's Absent Nineteenth Century: Autonomous Subjects." In *Untold Histories of the Middle East: Recovering Voices from the 19th and 20th Centuries*. Edited by Amy Singer, Christoph K. Neumann, and Selçuk Akşin Somel (London: Routledge, 2011), 141–58.

17. For example, see Masayuki Ueno, "Religious in Form, Political in Content? Privileges of Ottoman Non-Muslims in the Nineteenth Century." *Journal of the Economic and Social History of the Orient* 59, no. 3 (March 2016): 408–41.

18. Jane Burbank and Frederick Cooper, *Empires in World History: Power and the Politics of Difference* (Princeton, NJ: Princeton University Press, 2011), 17.

19. Christine Philliou, *Biography of an Empire: Governing Ottomans in an Age of Revolution* (Berkeley: University of California Press, 2010), xxiii.

20. Tom Papademetriou, *Render Unto the Sultan: Power, Authority, and the Greek Orthodox Church in the Early Ottoman Centuries* (New York: Oxford University Press, 2015). Macit Kenanoğlu makes a similar argument in *Osmanlı Millet Sistemi: Gerçek ve Mit* (İstanbul, Turkey: Klasik Yayınları, 2004).

21. On the expansion of the authority of the Greek Patriarchate of Constantinople, see Hasan Çolak, "Relations Between the Ottoman Central Administration and the Greek Orthodox Patriarchates of Antioch, Jerusalem and Alexandria: 16th–18th Centuries" (PhD diss., University of Birmingham, 2012).

22. "Communal space" builds upon "nation-space" as described in Sanna Turoma and Maxim Waldstein, "Introduction: Empire and Space: Russian and the Soviet Union in Focus," in *Empire De/Centered: New Spatial Histories of Russia and the Soviet Union*, ed. Sanna Turoma and Maxim Waldstein (Burlington, VT: Ashgate, 2013), 1–28.

23. Matenadaran Katoghikosakan Divan 205/1601 "Timoteos *vardapet* Saprichian to Patriarchate" (January 26, 1875).

24. James Reid, "Was There a Tanzimat Social Reform?" *Balkan Studies: Biannual Publication of the Institute for Balkan Studies* 40, no. 1 (May 1998): 11–48.

25. For examples, see James Etmekjian, *The French Influence on the Western Armenian Renaissance, 1843–1915* (New York: Twayne, 1964), Aylin Koçunyan, "Long Live Sultan Abdülaziz, Long Live the Nation, Long Live the Constitution..." in *Constitutionalism, Legitimacy, and Power*, Kelly Grotke and Markus Prutsch, eds. (New York: Oxford University Press, 2014), 189–210; Ueno, "Religious in Form, Political in Content?" For the Greek Orthodox community, see Jack Fairey, *The Great Powers and Orthodox Christendom: The Crisis over the Eastern Church in the Era of the Crimean War* (New York: Palgrave, 2015).

26. Avigdor Levy, "*Millet* Politics: The Appointment of a Chief Rabbi in 1835," in *The Jews of the Ottoman Empire*, ed. Avigdor Levy (Princeton, NJ: Darwin Press, 1994), 425–38.

CHAPTER 1

1. For a description of celebrations in Van, see Harutiun Chankiulean, *Hishatakner haykakan chknazhamen* (mas ayb) (K. Polis: Tparan "Kohak"i, 1913), 89–91. See also Matenadaran Ay lev ayl heghinakneri arkhiv 240a/44 (May 25, 1882) for celebrations hosted elsewhere.

2. See James Etmekjian, *The French Influence on the Western Armenian Renaissance* (New York: Twayne, 1964) and Aylin Koçunyan, "Long Live Sultan Abdülaziz, Long Live the Nation, Long Live the Constitution...." in *Constitutionalism, Legitimacy, and Power*, Kelly Grotke and Markus Prutsch, eds. (New York: Oxford University Press, 2014), 189–210.

3. For examples, see Etmekjian, *The French Influence* and Masayuki Ueno, "Religious in Form, Political in Content? Privileges of Ottoman Non-Muslims in the

Nineteenth Century." *Journal of the Economic and Social History of the Orient* 59, no. 3, 408–41.

4. For the "classics" on the reform period, see Bernard Lewis, *The Emergence of Modern Turkey*, 3rd ed. (New York: Oxford University Press, 2002); Albert Hourani, "Ottoman Reform and the Politics of Notables," in *Beginnings of Modernization in the Middle East, The Nineteenth Century*, ed. William R. Polk and Richard L. Chambers (Chicago: University of Chicago Press, 1968), 41–68; Stanford Shaw, *Between Old and New: The Ottoman Empire Under Sultan Selim III* (Cambridge, MA: Harvard University Press, 1973); and Stanford Shaw and Ezel Kural Shaw, *History of the Ottoman Empire and Modern Turkey*, vol. 2, *Reform, Revolution, and Republic* (New York: Cambridge University Press, 1977).

5. Şerif Mardin, *The Genesis of Young Ottoman Thought: A Study in the Modernization of Turkish Political Ideas* (Princeton, NJ: Princeton University Press, 1962).

6. Dimitri Stamatopolous, "From *Millet*s to Minorities in the Nineteenth Century Ottoman Empire: An Ambiguous Modernization," in *Citizenship in Historical Perspective*, ed. S. G. Ellis, G. Hálfadanarson, and A. K. Isaacs (Pisa, Italy: Edizioni Plus-Pisa University Press, 2006), 253–73.

7. The framing of a social or cultural "mosaic" has exacerbated the impact of this approach, particularly for the Levantine provinces. For a critical assessment of this approach, particularly its interaction with modernization theory, see James Gelvin, "The 'Politics of Notables' Forty Years After." *Middle East Studies Association Bulletin* 40, no. 1 (June 2006): 19–29.

8. Butrus Abu-Manneh, "The Islamic Roots of the Gülhane Rescript." *Die Welt des Islams* 34, no. 2 (November 1994): 173–203

9. Douglas McAdam, Sidney Tarrow, and Charles Tilly, *Dynamics of Contention* (New York: Cambridge University Press, 2001): "By contentious politics we mean: episodic, public, collective interaction among makers of claims and their objects when (a) at least one government is a claimant, an object of claims, or a party to the claims and (b) the claims would, if realized, affect the interests of at least one of the claimants" (5).

10. For the Greek Orthodox case, see Dimitris Stamatopoulos, "Holy Canons or General Regulations? The Ecumenical Patriarchate *vis-à-vis* the Challenge of Secularization in the Nineteenth Century," in *Innovation in the Orthodox Christian Tradition? The Question of Change in Greek Orthodox Thought and Practice*, ed. Trine Stauning Willert and Lina Molokotos-Liederman (Burlington, VT: Asghate, 2012), 143–62.

11. Molly Greene, *The Edinburgh History of the Greeks, 1453–1768* (Edinburgh: Edinburgh University Press, 2015), 163–91.

12. Halil İnalcık, "Status of the Greek Orthodox Patriarch Under the Ottomans," *Turcica* 21–23 (1991): 407–36; Constantin A. Panchenko, *Arab Orthodox Christians Under the Ottomans: 1516–1831* (Jordanville, NY: Holy Trinity Seminary Press, 2016).

13. This discussion of the Armenian Patriarchate of Constantinople borrows heavily from Kevork Bardakjian, "The Rise of the Armenian Patriarchate of Constantinople," in *Christians and Jews in the Ottoman Empire: The Functioning of a Plural Society*, vol. 1, *The Central Lands*, ed. Benjamin Braude and Bernard Lewis (New York: Holmes and Meier, 1982): 89–100.

14. Robert Crews, "Empire and the Confessional State: Islam and Religious Politics in Nineteenth Century Russia," *American Historical Review* 108, no. 1 (February 2003): 50–83; William O. McCagg Jr., *A History of Habsburg Jews (1670-1918)* (Bloomington: Indiana University Press, 1992), esp. 123–40. See also Andreas Kappeler, *The Russian Empire: A Multi-Ethnic History* (London: Routledge, 2001); Dominic Lieven, *Empire: The Russian Empire and Its Rivals* (New Haven, CT: Yale University Press, 2002).

15. In particular, see Vartan Artinian, *The Armenian Constitutional System in the Ottoman Empire, 1839-1863: A Study of Its Historical Development.* (Istanbul, 1988); "The Armenian Amira Class of Istanbul." PhD diss., Columbia University, 1980; Hayk Ghazaryan, *Arevmtahayeri sotsial-tntesakan ev kaghakakan katsutyun, 1800-1970 tt* (Erevan: Haykakan SSH Gitutyunneri Akademiayi Hratarakchutyun, 1967); and Arakel Sarukhan, *Haykakan khndrin ev azgayin sahmanadrutiune Turkiayum* (Tiflis, 1912).

16. Kevork Bardakjian recently argued that Armenian usage of the term *amira* derives from the term *âmire*, a homonym that the Turkish borrowed from Arabic. See Kevork Bardakjian, "Ottoman Servants, Armenian Lords: The Rise of the *Amiras*," *Journal of the Society for Armenian Studies* 26 (2017): 17–38, esp. 34–38.

17. During his travels in Anatolia, Henry Barkley recorded descriptions of both a typical *amira*'s career arc and the mansions that their entrepreneurship provided for their families in Akn. See Henry Barkley, *A Ride Through Asia Minor and Armenia: Giving a Sketch of the Character, Manners, and Customs of Both the Mussulman and Christian Inhabitants* (London: John Murray, 1891), 321–23.

18. On Basmajian's struggles with *amira* interference in his patriarchate, see *Hishatakaran Pasmachean Grigor Patriarki. Hratarakets Papgen Dz. V. Giuleserean* (Paris: Panaser, 1908).

19. See Chapter 2 in this book for a discussion on *mütevelli*s in an Ottoman Armenian context.

20. Barsoumian, "The Armenian Amira Class of Istanbul." PhD diss., Columbia University, 1980., 174–75; Ormanean, *Azgapatum: Hay Ughghapar Ekeghetsvoy antskere skizben minchev mer orere,* (volume 3) (Erusaghem: Tparan Srbots Hakobeants, 1927), col. 2592

21. Edhem Eldem, *A History of the Ottoman Bank* (Istanbul: Ottoman Bank Historical Research Center, 1999), 21; Ormanean, col. 2592.

22. Ormanean, 2587.

23. The Armenian liturgy is loaded with political meaning. This was especially true for the Ottoman period. Following the Epiclesis, when the bread and wine are seen definitively as the body and blood of Jesus Christ, remembrances are made for prelates, a patriarch, and the Catholicos of Etchmiadzin, thereby communicating ecclesiastical authority and legitimacy to the community. Later, prayers are also made for political leaders, such as governors and, of course, the sultan.

24. Matenadaran Zanazan Heghinakneri Arkhiv 50/10 (September 23, 1844).

25. Ormanean, col. 2595. For the text of the imperial orders, see BOA İ. MSM 33/939, 33/940.

26. Ormanean, col. 2590-2591.

27. As discussed below, Armenians were financiers of the state and its centralization policies. While the Ottoman Greek elites, such as the Phanariots, may not have enthusiastically embraced centralization policies, they were still allied (particularly in the Balkans) with Muslim notables disinclined to challenge the central state. Jewish bankers, meanwhile, provided credit to the Janissaries, who were generally allied with antireform notables.

28. Ormanean, col. 2592.

29. Ormanean, col. 2692.

30. In addition to the works already discussed, see James Etmekjian, *The French Influence on the Western Armenian Renaissance* (New York: Twayne, 1964); Louise Nalbandian, *The Armenian Revolutionary Movement* (Los Angeles: University of California Press, 1963); and Razmik Panossian, *The Armenians: From Kings and Priests to Merchants and Commissars* (New York: Columbia University Press, 2006).

31. For a descriptive overview of Grjigian's life, see Masayuki Ueno, "Empire as a Career: Hagop Grjigian or an Armenian in the Ottoman Bureaucracy." *Memoirs of the Research Department of the Tokyo Bunko* 76 (2019): 57–80.

32. Barsoumian, "Amira Class," 139.

33. Sanna Turoma and Maxim Waldstein, "Introduction: Empire and Space: Russian and the Soviet Union in Focus," in *Empire De/Centered: New Spatial Histories of Russia and the Soviet Union*, ed. Sanna Turoma and Maxim Waldstein (Burlington, VT: Ashgate, 2013), 1–28.

34. Baki Tezcan, *The Second Ottoman Empire: Political and Social Transformation in the Early Modern World* (New York: Cambridge University Press, 2010).

35. Greene's description of the ecumenical patriarchate as a "partner" builds on Ali Yaycıoğlu's dissertation, later published as *Partners of the Empire: The Crisis of the Ottoman Order in the Age of Revolutions* (Stanford, CA: Stanford University Press, 2016).

36. Richard Antaramian, "*Amira* Money and Alemdar Mustafa: Armenians and Ottoman Reform Before the Tanzimat" (paper presentation, New Directions in Armenian Ottoman Studies, University of California, Berkeley, April 8, 2017).

37. Antaramian, "*Amira* Money."

38. Of these, the 1826 and 1830 versions are available for consultation at the National Library of Armenia. *Sahman Azgayin Zhoghovoyn: Vor eghev yami tearn 1826 i marti 4, i Patriargarans amenayn hayots vor i Kostandnupolis. Hramanav amenapativ ev vehapar Patriargi aynm kaghaki Tearn Karapeti srbazan ark Episkoposi kostandnupolsetsvoy. Yaghags barekargutean ark Episkoposakan ev Episkoposakan atorots, ev hamoren zharangavorats ekeghetsvoy* (Kostandnupolis, 1826) and *Sahman Azgayin Zhoghovoy: Yaghags barekargutean surb ukhti ekeghetsvoy, ev varzhapetats, ev hamoren zhoghovrdots. Hramanav amenapativ ev vehapar Patriargi Tearn Karapeti Srbazan Ark Episkoposi* (Kostandnupolis: Tparani Poghos Arapean Apuchekhtsvoy, 1830). A manuscript copy of the 1830 document is located in the Matenadaran (Matenadaran Zanazan Heghinakneri Arkhiv 48/45).

39. Artinian was the first to make this correlation. Saro Dadyan echoes the claim uncritically; Saro Dadyan, *Osmanlı'da Ermeni Aristokrasisi* (İstanbul, Turkey: Everest

Yayınları, 2011). The Young Ottomans wished to retain the imperial character of Islam in Ottoman society, and the Armenian reformers saw the Tanzimat as a path to full inclusion in the formal politics of state.

40. Ormanean, col. 2706.

41. Ormanean, col. 2707.

42. Consider the examples of Mkrtich Dikranian, Mkrtich Khrimian, Eremia Tevkants, Karekin Srvantstiants, and Hagop Topuzian, among many others, discussed throughout this book.

43. My references here are to the original 1860 version. See *Azgayin Sahmanadrutiun Hayots* (1860), 10–16.

44. *Sahamanadrutiun*, 25–37.

45. *Sahamanadrutiun*, 25–37.

46. *Atenagrutiunk azgayin zhoghovoy, 1860–1870* (Session III, November 4, 1860). The debt was mostly taxes in arrears, the nonpayment of which compounded debt accrued by Constantinople; Ormanean, col. 2702.

47. Ormanean, col. 2701.

48. *Boghok erkrord ar azgayin endhanur zhoghovn, zvor khonarhabar matutsane amboghj miabanutiun Surb Erusaghemi* (Jerusalem: Tparan srpots, 1861), 4.

49. Ormanean, col. 2718.

50. *Atenagrutiunk* (Session IX, August 5, 1861).

51. Ormanean, col. 2719.

52. "Bardzragoyn dran ev azgayin handznazhoghovnerun ar kayserakan karavarutiun matutsats haytagrin orinakn," in *Azgayin sahmanadrutiun hayots* (1863), see esp. 7 for the signatures.

53. "Nezareti jelilei kharijiye, aded 191. Badrik ka'immakame dirayetlu efendiye" (Official Turkish in Armenian script), published in both *Sahmanadrutiun* and *Atenagrutiunk* (Session X, February 20, 1862).

54. "Bardzragoyn dran," 2.

55. "Bardzragoyn dran," 3–6.

CHAPTER 2

1. Eremia Tevkants, *Chanaparhordutyun bardzr Hayk ev Vaspurakan, 1872–73 tt. Dzeragire patrastel ev tsanotagrel e H.M. Poghosyan* (Erevan: Hayastani GA Hratarakutyun, 1991), 302–6.

2. The Armenian *amira*s were the near-exclusive financiers of the Porte and the Palace. See Onnik Jamgocyan, *Les banquiers des sultans: Juifs, Francs, Grecs et Arméniens de la haute finance: Constantinople, 1650–1850* (Paris: Les Editions du Bosphore, 2013), 284–87.

3. On the *amira*s and their ascendance in Ottoman imperial society, see Hagop Barsoumian, "The Armenian *Amira* Class of Istanbul" (PhD diss., Columbia University, 1981); Arakel Kechean, *Akn ev Akntsik* (Paris: Amerikayi Aknay Hayrenaktsakan Miutean, 1952).

4. On religious endowments, their use, and abuse, see John Robert Barnes, *An Introduction to Religious Foundations in the Ottoman Empire* (Leiden, the Netherlands:

Brill, 1986). Barsoumian offers an abbreviated discussion of Armenian *mütevelli*s in the fourth chapter of his dissertation.

5. The imperial government in fact created a special ministry for vakıfs to police abuses of the system in 1840.

6. BNU CP 23/1 "Lim Monastery to *Mütevelli* Kaspar Agha" (December 21, 1851), "Topuzian to *Mütevelli* Kaspar Agha" (August 8, 1852), "Topuzian to *Mütevelli* Kaspar Agha" (October 1, 1852), "Topuzian to *Mütevelli* Kaspar Agha" (January 21, 1853).

7. BNU 125/P.I.3.2.

8. Hrant Asatur, *Kostandnubolsoy hayere ev irents patriarknere* (Stanpul: Patriarkutiun Hayots, 2011), 189. Harutiun Bezjian, who had replaced the Diuzians as the head of the imperial mint, went into exile for three years. Garabed Amira Aznavurian fled to Chios.

9. Most of these are outlined in Article 48.

10. *Atenagrutiunk azgayin zhoghovoy* 1860–1870 (Session XXII, July 22, 1866).

11. *Atenagrutiunk* (Elections, October 15, 1863).

12. *Atenagrutiunk* (Session VIII, February 25, 1865).

13. *Atenagrutiunk* (Session X, March 5, 1865).

14. Family History Library (Salt Lake City, Utah), Microfilms #1037130, 1213466, 1213467.

15. *Atenagrutiunk* (Session X, March 5, 1865), 183.

16. Unless otherwise noted, my presentation of Vehabedian's life borrows heavily from *Azgapatum*, cols. 2651–2652.

17. Tevkants, *Chanaparhordutyun*, 36.

18. BNA FO 195/889 No. 44 (December 24, 1868).

19. On at least two of those occasions, the great provincial proponent of reform, Bishop Mkrtich Khrimian, likely played a prominent role in convincing the Patriarchate of Constantinople to have Vehabedian removed. Khrimian stayed in Erzurum for a time following his consecration as bishop in 1868. See Tevkants, *Chanaparhordutyun*, 37, and GAT Khrimyani Fond 875/1 (September 23, 1868). For a discussion of Vehabedian's removals, see Y. Tolga Çora, "Transforming Erzurum/Karin: The Social and Economic History of a Multi-Ethnic Ottoman City in the Nineteenth Century" (PhD diss., University of Chicago, 2016).

20. FO 195/889 No. 44 (December 24, 1868).

21. *Khrimean ev gortsk iur. Herkumn ambastanagri Poghos Vardapeti* (1874), 18.

22. Ormanean, 1818.

23. *Atenagrutiunk* (Session IX, February 25, 1865), 167–68.

24. *Atenagrutiunk* (Session XI, March 12, 1865), 198.

CHAPTER 3

1. *Atenagrutiunk azgayin zhoghovoy*, 1860–1870 (Session XI, March 12, 1865), 199.

2. For examples from the Ottoman case, see Ussama Makdisi, "Ottoman Orientalism," *The American Historical Review*, 107, no. 3 (June 2002), 768–96, and Selim Deringil, "'They Live in a State of Nomadism and Savagery: The Late Ottoman Empire and

the Post-Colonial Debate." *Comparative Studies in Society and History*, 45, no. 2 (April 2003), 311–42.

3. James Scott, *Seeing Like a State: How Certain Schemes to Improve the Human Condition Have Failed* (New Haven: Yale University Press, 1998), 2.

4. John Griffiths, "What is Legal Pluralism?" *The Journal of Legal Pluralism and Unofficial Law* 18, no. 24 (1986).

5. Bernard Lewis's *Emergence of Modern Turkey*, which treats the Hamidian period as an extension of the Tanzimat, is a notable exception to this consensus. Erik Jan Zürcher famously extended the Young Turk period to 1950.

6. Yusuf Akçura, *Üç Tarz-ı Siyaset* (Ankara, Turkey: Türk Tarih Kurum Basımevi, 1976).

7. John Griffiths, "What Is Legal Pluralism?" *The Journal of Legal Pluralism and Unofficial Law* 18, no. 24 (1986): 3.

8. Benedict Anderson, *Imagined Communities: Reflections on the Origin and Spread of Nationalism* (London: Verso, 2006), 7.

9. Akçura dwells on this point at some length in *Üç Tarz-ı Siyaset*. See also Carter Findley, "The Advent of Ideology in the Islamic Middle East (Part I)." *Studia Islamica* 55 (1982): 143–69; Carter Findley, "The Advent of Ideology in the Islamic Middle East (Part II)." *Studia Islamica* 56 (1982): 147–80. Soviet scholarship also insisted on this point. See, for example, Ruben A. Safrastyan, *Doktrina Osmanizma v Politicheskoi Zhizni Osmanskoi Imperii (50–70 gg. XIX v.)* (Erevan: Izdatel'stvo AN Armianskoi SSR, 1985), 33–47. For a critique of Akçura's influence on the historiography, see Howard Eissenstat, "Modernization, Imperial Nationalism, and the Ethnicization of Confessional Identity in the Late Ottoman Empire," in *Nationalizing Empires*, ed. Stefan Berger and Alexei Miller, (Budapest: Central European University Press, 2015), 429–59.

10. James Reid, "Was There a Tanzimat Social Reform?" *Balkan Studies: Biannual Publication of the Institute for Balkan Studies* 40, no. 1 (1999): 173–208.

11. Karen Barkey, "Aspects of Legal Pluralism in the Ottoman Empire," in *Legal Pluralism and Empires, 1500–1850*, ed. Lauren Benton and Richard J. Ross (New York: New York University Press, 2013), 83–107; Timur Kuran, "The Economic Ascent of the Middle East's Religious Minorities: The Role of Islamic Legal Pluralism." *Journal of Legal Studies* 33, no. 2 (June 2004): 475–515.

12. Consular courts were another forum available to privileged non-Muslims. See for example, Cihan Artunç, "The Price of Legal Institutions: The *Beratlı* Merchants in the Eighteenth-Century Ottoman Empire." *The Journal of Economic History*, 75, no. 3 (September 2015), 720–48 and Frank Castiglione, "'Levantine' Dragomans in Nineteenth Century Istanbul: The Pisanis, the British, and Issues of Subjecthood." *Osmanlı Araştırmaları/The Journal of Ottoman Studies*, XLIV (2014), 169–95.

13. BNU DC 2/3. It remains unclear whether another cache of Armenian court documents exists elsewhere.

14. Barkey, "Aspects of Legal Pluralism."

15. For examples, see Yuvan Ben-Bassat, *Petitioning the Sultan: Protests and Justice in Late Ottoman Palestine, 1865–1908* (New York: I.B. Tauris, 2013); Köksal, "Local

Intermediaries and Ottoman State Centralization: A Comparison of the Tanzimat Reforms in the Provinces of Ankara and Edirne, 1839–1878" (PhD diss., Columbia University, 2002); Dzovinar Derderian, "Nation-Making and the Language of Colonialism: Voices from Ottoman Van in Armenian Print Media and Handwritten Petitions (1820s to 1870s)" (PhD diss., University of Michigan, 2019); Nilay Özök-Gündoğan, "A 'Peripheral' Approach to the 1908 Revolution in the Ottoman Empire: Land Disputes in Peasant Petitions in Post-Revolutionary Diyarbekir," in *Social Relations in Ottoman Diyarbekir, 1870–1915*, ed. Joost Jongerden and Jelle Verheij (Leiden, the Netherlands: Brill, 2012), 179–215; Evthymios Papataxiarchis, "Reconfiguring the Ottoman Political Imagination: Petitioning and Print Culture in the Early Tanzimat," in *Political Initiatives 'From the Bottom Up' in the Ottoman Empire*, ed. Antonis Anastasopoulos (Rethymno, Greece: Crete University Press, 2012), 191–227; Michael Ursinus, "Local Patmians in Their Quest for Justice: Eighteenth Century Examples of Petitions Submitted to the *Kapûdân Paşa*." *Documents de travail du CETOBAC* 1 (January 2010): 20–23; and Michael Ursinus, "Petitions from Orthodox Church Officials to the Imperial Diwan, 1675." *Byzantine and Modern Greek Studies* 18 (1994): 236–47.

16. M.B. Hooker, *Legal Pluralism: An Introduction to Colonial and Neo-Colonial Laws* (Oxford, UK: Clarendon, 1975).

17. For empire as a composite polity, see J. H. Elliott, "A Europe of Composite Monarchies." *Past & Present*, No. 137 (November 1992), 48–71. For the Ottoman case, see Daniel Goffman and Christopher Stroop, "Empire as Composite: The Ottoman Polity and the Typology of Dominion," in *Imperialisms: Historical and Literary Investigations, 1500–1900*. Balachandra Rajan and Elizabeth Sauer, eds. (New York: Palgrave, 2004), 129–45.

18. Griffiths, "What Is Legal Pluralism?" 38.

19. James Scott, *Domination and the Arts of Resistance: Hidden Transcripts* (New Haven: Yale University Press, 1990).

20. BNU CGPR XIX 81 "Kakmajian to Vehabedian" (October 2, 1864).

21. BNU CGPR XIX 81 "Kakmajian to Constantinople" (November 14, 1865).

22. BNU CGPR XIX 81 "Kakmajian to Constantinople" (January 15, 1865).

23. *Teghekagir kharn hantznazhoghovoy Aghtamaray atoroy katoghikosakan khndroyn* (K. Polis: i tparan Hovhannu Miuhentisean, 1872).

24. Eremia Tevkants, *Chanaparhordutyun i Bardzr Hayk ev Vaspurakan (1872-1873 tt) Dzeragire patrastel ev tsanotagrel e H.M. Poghosyane* (Erevan: Hayastani GA Hratarakchutyun, 1991). Tevkants reproduced many of his findings on Aghtamar in another report, *Krkin teghekagir aghetali antsits ev ankargutean tan Aghtamaray* (K. Polis: Tpagrutiun Mikaeyeli Eksercheean, 1874). Another report, which was written by an Aghtamar clergyman and originally submitted to the Catholicos of All Armenians in Etchmiadzin in 1866 (and published in Istanbul seven years later), also lays blame at the feet of Shiroian. Hovsep Vardapet, *Teghekagir aghetali antsits ev ankarguteants tan Aghtamaray* (K. Polis: i tparan R.Y. Kiurkchean, 1873).

25. The episode was memorialized in Srvantsiants's *Hamov Hotov*. See Garegin Srvandztyants, *Erker (Hator 1)* (Erevan: Haykakan SSH GA Hratarakchutyun, 1978), 380.

26. See KD 209/141, "Vehabedian to Catholicos of Etchmiadzin" (June 22, 1872), for an example. See also Dzovinar Derderian, "Shaping Subjectivities and Contesting Power Through Images of Kurds, 1860s," in *The Ottoman East in the Nineteenth Century*, ed. Yaşar Tolga Cora, Dzovinar Derderian, and Ali Sipahi (New York: I.B. Tauris, 2016): 91–108.

27. Tevkants, *Chanaparhordutyun*, 200.

28. Matteos Izmirlean, *Hayrapetutiun Hayastaneats Arakelakan Ekeghetsvoy ev Aghtamar u Sis* (K. Polis: Tpagr. Zardarean, 1881), 297–309.

29. Michael Eppel, "The Demise of the Kurdish Emirates: The Impact of Ottoman Reforms and International Relations on Kurdistan During the First Half of the Nineteenth Century." *Middle Eastern Studies* 44, no. 2 (March 2008): 237–58.

30. Izmirlean, *Hayrapetutiun*, 400.

31. *Ajapahean tohme dareru entatskin* (Los Angeles: Araks Tparan, 2008), 17.

32. On the murders, see the individual biographies in *Ajapahean*, 54–66; Maghakia Ormanean, *Azgapatum: Hay ughghapar ekeghetsvoy antskere skizben minchev mer orere yarakits azgayin paraganerov patmuats (h. 2)* (Kostandnupolis: Hratarakutiun V. ev H. Ter-Nersisean, 1914), cols. 2050, 2104, 2172, 2173; and Babgen Kiuleserean, *Patmutiun Katoghikosats Kilikioy: 1441-en minchev mer orere* (Antilias, Libanan: Tparan Dprevanuts Katoghikosutean Kilikioy, 1939), 501–5, 528–32, 560.

33. According to one story, the Grand Vizier knew Der Husik (patriarch of the dynasty), who traveled to Istanbul to procure a berat for his son, Ghugas I, thus beginning the Ajapahian dynasty. Per Giuleserean, Catholicos Mikael I was twice granted an audience with the Porte and the Patriarchate in Istanbul. Fraternal relations were oftentimes maintained between individual catholicoi and patriarchs until the reform period commenced.

34. Andrew Gould, "Lords or Bandits? The *Derebeys* of Cilicia" *International Journal of Middle East Studies* 7, no. 4 (October 1976): 494–95.

35. Cevdet Paşa, *Tezâkir 21-39* (Ankara: Türk Tarih Kurumu Basımevi, 1963), 113–14.

36. Meltem Toksöz, *Nomads and Migrants and Cotton in the Eastern Mediterranean: The Making of the Adana-Mersin Region, 1850–1908* (Leiden, the Netherlands: Brill, 2010), 66.

37. Gould, "Lords or Bandits," 494–95.

38. Ali Yaycioğlu, *Partners of the Empire: The Crisis of the Ottoman Order in the Age of Revolutions* (Stanford, CA: Stanford University Press, 2016).

39. For the text of the encyclical, see Kiuleserean, *Patmutiun Katoghikosats Kilikioy*, 1441.

40. Victor Langlois, *Voyage dans la Cilicie et dan les montagnes du Taurus. Exécuté pendant les années 1852-1853* (Paris: Chez Benjamin Duprat, 1861), 126. The interaction between a French traveler and Mikael II Ajapahian tells us as much. The traveler made note, for example, of Mikael's poor clothing—something very unusual for a clergyman of his standing. In the course of their conversation, Mikael both bemoaned Kozanoğlu oppression and denounced the Catholicos of All Armenians in Etchmiadzin as a usurper and a schismatic.

41. Izmirlean, *Hayrapetutiun*, 481–85.

42. Khrimian's report is partially reproduced in Izmirlean, *Hayrapetutiun*, 486–96. For a discussion of Khrimian's mission to Cilicia, see K. Tiurean, "Khrimean Hayrik." *Handes Amsoreay* (1892), 247–49.

43. The Sublime Porte officially recognized the Protestant community as a *millet* in 1847.

44. Gould, "Lords or Bandits," 495.

45. Izmirlean, *Hayrapetutiun*, 500.

46. *Atenagrutiunk azgayin zhoghovoy*, 1860–1870 (Session XXII, July 22, 1866).

47. Consider the following connections: The Patriarchate's rebuke of Mikael Ajapahian in 1839 was for his decision to consecrate the prelate of Egypt a bishop. That same bishop, Kapriel, had helped oversee Egypt's secession from the ecclesiastical jurisdiction of the Patriarchate of Jerusalem; he also sponsored Kefsizian after Kefsizian had fled to Egypt to avoid bearing any responsibility for his transgressions while Prelate of Ankara. Kefsizian, in turn, was one of four Anatolian prelates consecrated bishop in 1860 by the catholicos of Etchmiadzin. Another of the four—and therefore Kefsizian's spiritual brother in the culture of the clergy—was Harutiun Vehabedian, who, as described, had used his time in both Jerusalem and Erzurum to defeat reform efforts. He was also instrumental in securing Khachadur Shiroian's exoneration.

48. Izmirlean, *Hayrapetutiun*, 860–73.

49. Upon conversion to Islam, Bishop Harutiun took both a wife and the name Emin Efendi. Selim Deringil has traced out Harutiun's postconversion life in Deringil in *Conversion and Apostasy in the Late Ottoman Empire* (New York: Cambridge University Press, 2012), 145–51.

50. *Kilikya'nın Esrarı ve Sefaleti* (1872). The 52-page booklet, which divulges no information on its publisher, was penned as an open letter dated January 23, 1872.

51. Reverend E. J. Davis, *Life in Asiatic Turkey. A Journal of Travel in Cilicia (Pedias and Trach(ea), Isauria, and Parts of Lycanoia and Cappadocia* (London: Edward Stratford, 1879), 87–90. Davis's Armenian host proudly displayed a rifle he had taken from another Armenian during the assault on Zeytun.

52. For the notables of Hajin, see H. P. Poghosean, *Hacheni endhanur patmutiune ev shrjakay Gozan-Taghi hay giughere* (Antilias: Metsi Tann Kilikioy Katoghikosutiun, 2014), 141–44. Adana's geographic location generally placed it beyond the reach of the Kozanoğlus. The notable who hosted Davis lived near Marash.

53. Stephan Astourian, "Testing World-System Theory, Cilicia (1830s–1890s): Armenian-Turkish Polarization and the Ideology of Modern Ottoman Historiography" (PhD diss., University of California, Los Angeles, 1996).

54. These arguments were advanced in Sessions V and VI of the National Assembly in September 1870. A special report drafted by a committee of clergymen was in general agreement with their lay counterparts. See Izmirlean, *Hayrapetutiun*, 639–49.

55. Izmirlean, *Hayrapetutiun*, 738–40, 895–98.

56. *Hrahang Kilikioy vichakats hamar* (Kostandnupolis: Tpagrutiun H. Miuhentisean, 1874).

57. Izmirlean, *Hayrapetutiun*, 1255–60.

58. Izmirlean, 1030–33, 1067.
59. Izmirlean, 413–21.
60. For text of the conditions, see Izmirlean, *Hayrapetutiun*, 383–412.
61. Izmirlean, *Hayrapetutiun*, 404.
62. Tevkants, 172.
63. Izmirlean, *Hayrapetutiun*, 1067.
64. H. F. B. Lynch, *Armenia, Travels and Studies. Volume II: The Turkish Provinces* (London: Longman, Green, 1901), 127–36.
65. Griffiths, "What Is Legal Pluralism?" 38.
66. Hendrik Hartog, "Pigs and Positivism." *Wisconsin Law Review* 899 (1985): 899–935.

CHAPTER 4

1. Hasan Kayalı, *Arabs and Young Turks: Ottomanism, Arabism, and Islamism in the Ottoman Empire, 1908–1918* (Berkeley: University of California Press, 1997); Julia Phillips Cohen, *Becoming Ottomans: Sephardi Jews and Imperial Citizenship in the Modern Era* (New York: Oxford University Press, 2014); and Adam Mestyan, *Arab Patriotism: The Ideology and Culture of Power in Late Ottoman Egypt* (Princeton, NJ: Princeton University Press, 2017).
2. The cultural toolkit (or repertoire) concept was first advanced by Ann Swidler. See Ann Swidler, "Culture in Action: Symbols and Strategies," *American Sociological Review* 51, no. 2 (1986): 273–86. While the concept has attained significance in the study of social movements, scholars of empire have appropriated it to explain strategies of imperial rule. See Jane Burbank and Frederick Cooper, *Empires in World History: Power and the Politics of Difference* (Princeton: Princeton University Press, 2010).
3. Ussama Makdisi, "Ottoman Orientalism." *The American Historical Review* 107, no. 3 (June 2002); also Bruce Masters stuff on Arabs, arguably Philliou, probably also others Jens Hanssen or whatever, provincial cities book, etc.
4. Ignatios Kakmachean, *Batsatrutiun i veray s. haghordutean ev pataragi* (Kostandnupolis: i tparani H. Miuhendisean, 1862).
5. BNU CGPR XIX 81 "Kakmajian to Patriarchate" (April 14, 1864).
6. BNU CGPR XIX 81 "Kakmajian to Patriarchate" (August 9, 1866).
7. For a particularly detailed description of Kurds rebelling against the state, see BNU CGPR XIX 81 "Kakmajian to Patriarchate" (September 23, 1864).
8. Appropriately enough, an early complaint made against Kakmajian bemoaned his ignorance of the Kurdish language. BN CP 23/1 "The Community of Van to its Brothers in Constantinople" (March 12, 1863). As we see, Kakmajian's opponents soon learned how to use his limitations against him.
9. See Hakob Shahpazean, *Kiurdo-Hay patmutiun* (K. Polis: Tparan Araks, 1911), 70–72.
10. Ter Mkrtchean, 530.
11. BNU CP 23/1 (May 24, 1851). Prominent signatures include those of Mahdesi Alkhas Agha Terlemezian, Avedis Agha Ayazian, Apraham Boghosian, and Mahdesi

Kevork Agha Kaljian. The honorific "*mahdesi*," an Armenian corruption of the Arabic term *muqqadasi*, suggests that its bearer had made the pilgrimage to Jerusalem.

12. BNU CP 23/1 "The Brotherhoods of the Monasteries of Lim and Gduts to Hamamjian" (December 21, 1851); "Topuzian to Hamamjian" (August 8, 1852); "Topuzian to Hamamjian" (October 1, 1852); and "Topuzian to Hamamjian" (January 21, 1853).

13. Kakmajian, for example, sent word to the patriarchate that two Muslims had fled to Egypt without repaying a loan made by Boghos Adomian of Van. BNU CGPR XIX 81 "Kakmajian to Patriarchate" (October 21, 1865).

14. *"Armenia"i Husharar, arajin tari* (Marseyl: Hayeren tparan M. Portukaleani, 1890), 89–93. The sermon is dated March 31, 1885.

15. FO 78/4432 No. 9 Confidential, Van (April 13, 1889).

16. Mat. MS 4180, 99–100; BOA A. DVN MHM 27.100 (1275 AH/1858-1859).

17. BNU DC 2/3.

18. *Ambastanutiun Vanay Poghos Vardapetin vray* (K. Polis: Tpagrutiun Partizpanean ev Enk., 1874), 4.

19. BNU CP 23/1 "The Brotherhood of the Gduts Monastery to the Patriarch of Constantinople" (September 25, 1860).

20. *Khrimean ev gortsk iur: Herkumn ambastanagri Poghos Vardapeti. Hator arajin, i Van 1874 april 9* (Kostandnupolis, 1874).

21. *Ambastanutiun*, 5.

22. *Ambastanutiun*, 31–50.

23. *Ambastanutiun*, 49–50.

24. BNU CGPR XIX 81 "Kakmajian to Patriarchate" (February 2, 1865).

25. Sinan Hakan, *Osmanlı Belgelerinde Kürtler ve Kürt Direnişleri, 1817–1867* (Istanbul: Döz Yayıncılık, 2007), 204–15.

26. Richard Antaramian, "Armenians and Sufis." Paper presented at the Middle East Studies Association Annual Meeting (2019).

27. Shahpazean, *Kiurdo-Hay patmutiun*, 70–74.

28. For a rich accounting of Kurdish tribes in the Ottoman Empire, see Mark Sykes, "The Kurdish Tribes of the Ottoman Empire," *Journal of the Royal Anthropological Institute of Great Britain and Ireland* 38 (July–December 1908): 451–86.

29. *Ambastanutiun*, 24.

30. The two made it a point to be seen together in public. Hambardzum Erameam, *Van-Vaspurakan* (Agheksandria: Tpagr. Aram Geghamean, 1929), 64.

31. KD 205/1601 "Timoteos *Vardapet* Saprichian to Patriarchate" (January 26, 1875).

32. On fixers, see Craig Jeffrey, Christine Philliou, Douglas Rogers, and Andrew Shryock. "Fixers in Motion. A Conversation." *Comparative Studies in Society and History* 53, no. 3 (July 2011), 692–707.

33. GAT Srvantstyani Fond 27/II (Srvantstiants to Khrimian, June 5, 1872).

34. Mat. MS 4180, 43–44.

35. Mat. MS 4180, 45.

36. See *Amenayn Hayots Hayrik* (New York: Hratarakutiun hamavaspurakani hayrenaktsakan miutean, 1957).

37. Louise Nalbandian cudgels Khrimian into the pantheon of proto-revolutionaries. Louise Nalbandian, *The Armenian Revolutionary Movement: The Development of Armenian Political Parties Through the Nineteenth Century* (Los Angeles: University of California Press, 1963); Richard Hovannisian locates Khrimian's activism in the context of national identity formation and demands for autonomy in "The Armenian Question in the Ottoman Empire, 1876 to 1914," in *Armenian People from Ancient to Modern Times, Volume II: Foreign Dominion to Statehood: The Fifteenth to the Twentieth Century*, edited by Richard Hovannisian.(New York: St. Martin's Press, 1997); see also Emma Kostandyan, *Mkrtich Khrimyan: hasarakakan-kaghakakan gortsuneutyune* (Erevan: "Zangak-97" hrataraktyun, 2000). Despite an absences of evidence, academic proponents of Turkish nationalism connect the efforts in which Khrimian was engaged with nationalist agitation and demands for independence. See Stanford Shaw and Ezel Kural Shaw, *History of the Ottoman Empire and Modern Turkey, Volume II: Reform, Revolution, and Republic: The Rise of Modern Turkey* (New York: Cambridge University Press, 1977), 188–189.

38. Unless otherwise cited, biographical information on Khrimian presented next is drawn from Hayk Achemean, *Hayots Hayrik: nuagogh vshtits hayreneats Hayots* (Tavrz: Atrpatakani Hayots temakan tparan, 1929).

39. Mkrtich Khrimean Vanetsi, "Metsimast ev bazmahmut Hord, duyzn govestits ban shnorhapart yashakerte dzoneal" *Bazmavep* 11/20 (October 15, 1849), 308–10.

40. Anne Swidler, "Culture in Action: Symbols and Strategies," *American Sociological Review* 51, no. 2 (April 1986): 273–86.

41. Mat. MS 4180, 90–94.

42. Mat. MS 4180, 95.

43. BNU CGPR 100 "St. Garabed Monastery to Patriarchate" (September 6, 1864).

CHAPTER 5

1. Hayk Achemean, *Hayots Hayrik: nuagogh vshtits hayreneats Hayots* (Tavriz: Atrpatakani hayots temakan tparan, 1929), 511–14.

2. Older scholarship, for example, organized these themes under the umbrella of a so-called "Eastern Question." See, for example, M.S. Anderson, *The Eastern Question, 1774–1923: A Study in International Relations* (London: Macmillan, 1966).

3. Among Khrimian's works of fiction, see *Hravirak Araratean* (1850), *Hravirak erkrin aveteats* (1851), or *Babik u tornik* (1894).

4. Achemean, *Hayots Hayrik*, 384–93.

5. *Atenagrutiunk azgayin zhoghovoy* 1860–1870 (Session 32, November 12, 1869), 413.

6. Achemean, *Hayots Hayrik*, 395. The *Atenagrutiunk* only states that the patriarch swore an oath.

7. Ashot Hovhannisyan, *Nalbandyane ev nra zhamanake*, 2 vols. (Erevan: Haypethrat, 1955–1956); Ghazaryan, *Arevmtahayeri* (1967).

8. Razmik Panossian, *The Armenians: From Kings and Priests to Merchants and Commissars* (New York: Columbia University Press, 2006).

9. Karen Barkey, *Empire of Difference: The Ottomans in Comparative Perspective* (New York: Cambridge University Press, 2008), 279, emphasis mine.

10. *Teghekagir gavarakan harstharuteants* (K. Polis, 1876).
11. *Teghekagir*, 6.
12. *Teghekagir*, 7.
13. *Teghekagir*, 1.
14. *Teghekagir*, 2–3.
15. *Teghekagir*, 5.
16. *Teghekagir*, 43.
17. Lynch compared Varak favorably with other Armenian monasteries that he visited.
18. Two of the speeches were later published as Arsen Tokhmakhean, *Hayreniki pahanjere ev hay giughatsin: hraparakakhosutiun katarvats mayisi 21-in ev krknats hunisi 12-in Artsrunu Tatronum* (Tiflis, 1881), and Tokhmakhean, *Masisi lerneri haravayin storotner: hraparakakhosutiun katarvats april 21-in Artsrunu Tatronum* (Tiflis, 1882).
19. "Srvantstiants to Khrimian" (July 1868), in *Divan Hayots Patmutean. Girk ZhG: Harstharutiunner Tachkahayastanum (vaveragrer 1801-1888)*, ed. Giut Aghaneants (Tiflis: Tparan N. Aghaneantsi, 1915), cols. 106–108.
20. According to Eremia Tevkants, Khachadur Khan Der-Nersisian, an Armenian notable from Erzurum who supported Khrimian, hesitated to embrace the reform program completely because Melikian was positioned to threaten his economic interests.
21. BNU DC 2/3 (April 26, 1865) for a report on abuses committed by Melikian and the Armenian notables of Van.
22. GAT Srvantstyani Fond 12/II (Srvantstiants to Khrimian, December 28, 1871) Srvantstiants reveals in a letter dated March 29, 1872, that he had arrived in Van on December 3, 1871, under orders from Khrimian to implement the Constitution (GAT Srvantstyani Fond 23/II).
23. GAT Srvantstyani Fond 17/II (Srvantstiants to Khrimian, February 16, 1872).
24. GAT Srvantstyani Fond 18/II (Sravantstiants to Khrimian, February 29, 1872).
25. GAT Srvantstyani Fond 18/II.
26. GAT Srvantstyani Fond 18/II.
27. GAT Srvantstyani Fond 23/II (Srvantstiants to Khrimian, March 29, 1872).
28. GAT Srvantstyani Fond 25/II (Srvantstiants to Khrimian, May 2, 1872).
29. GAT Srvantstyani Fond 26/II (Srvantstiants to Khrimian, May 24, 1872).
30. GAT Srvantstyani Fond 27/II (Srvantstiants to Khrimian, June 5, 1872).
31. GAT Srvantstyani Fond 30/II (Srvantstiants to Khrimian, June 29, 1872).
32. GAT Srvantstyani Fond 32/II (Srvantstiants to Khrimian, July 13, 1872).
33. GAT Srvantstyani Fond 33/II (Srvantstiants to Khrimian, July 27, 1872).
34. GAT Srvantstyani Fond 34/II (Srvantstiants to Khrimian, August 3, 1872).
35. GAT Srvantstyani Fond 35/II (Srvantstiants to Khrimian, August 24, 1872).
36. GAT Srvantstyani Fond 36/II (Srvantstiants to Khrimian, August 31, 1872).
37. *Hrahang haraberutean arajnordats ev gavarakan varchuteants end teghakan karavarutean* (K. Polis: Miuhentisean, 1873).

38. *Hamaratuutiun kronakan zhoghovoy ketronakan varchutean 1872–74 ami ar Azgayin Zhoghovn* (K. Polis, 1874), 9–11.
39. *Hamaratuutiun*, 9–11.
40. *Ambastanutiun Vanay Poghos Vardapetin Vray* (K. Polis, 1874), 15.
41. Mesrop Mashtotsi Anvan Matenadaran Dzeragir 4182, 3.
42. Mat. MS 4182, 4.
43. Mesrop Mashtotsi Anvan Matenadaran, Katoghikosakan Divan 205/1601 (1874–1875).
44. Mat. MS. 4182, 4–5. Important to note, the Patriarchate's orders included the provision that the churches of Van recite Tevkants's name during the liturgy. Srvantstiants had complained in 1872 that preachers loyal to (or intimidated by) Boghos refused to recognize his authority during the liturgy. The order for Tevkants's appointment is dated July 20, 1876.
45. Terzipashean, *Artsiv ir boynin mej* (Paris: Der Agopian, 1938), 119.
46. Mat. MS 4182, 12.
47. Mat. MS 4182, 19–22.
48. Harutiun Chankiulean, *Hishatakner Hay Chgnazhamen* (K. Polis: Kohak, 1913), 17.
49. Mat. MS. 4182, 24–30.
50. Chankiulean, *Hishatakner*, 13–14.
51. Chankiulean, 19.
52. Chankiulean, 18. Tevkants also writes positively of Ziya Paşa (Mat. Ms. 4182, 22). He noted that the inability to remove lower-level officials merely emboldened their actions against implementing proper governing institutions.
53. On Ubeydullah, see Sabri Ateş, *Ottoman-Iranian Borderlands: Making a Boundary, 1843–1914* (New York: Cambridge University Press, 2013).
54. The Famine Relief Committee had been established by the patriarchate and worked independently of international and Ottoman imperial relief programs.
55. Terzipashean, *Artsivn*, 14–15.
56. Terzipashean, *Artsivn*, 14–15.
57. Terzipashean, *Artsivn*, 69.
58. Bernard Lewis, *The Emergence of Modern Turkey*, 3rd ed. (New York: Oxford University Press, 2002), 178–79.
59. Julia Phillips Cohen, "Between Civic and Islamic Ottomanism: Jewish Imperial Citizenship in the Hamidian Era." *International Journal of Middle East Studies* 44, no. 2 (2012): 237–55.
60. Achemean, *Hayots Hayrik*, 571.
61. Terzipashean, *Artsivn*, 111–19.

CONCLUSION

1. Melikian's elevation to bishop was made at the request of Patriarch Varjabedian and over the objections of Khrimian, who, when asked his opinion on the matter,

mused, "Perhaps this Boghos is unknown to you?" Matenadaran Izmirlyani Fond 12/22 "Khrimian to Patriarchate" (September 15, 1880). As might be expected, Melikian appears to have violated the ecclesiastical hierarchy by communicating with the Catholicosate of Etchmiadzin directly (and without the mediation of the Patriarchate of Constantinople) on the matter. See BNL CGPR XIX 128 "Melikian to Archbishop Vahram (at Etchmiadzin)" (May 6, 1881).

2. Boghos Natanian's cousins, Kapriel and Garabed, were the best known of these. On the Natanian clan, see Ervand Ter-Mkrtchean, *Gandzer Vaspurakani* (Boston: Tparan Paykar, 1966), 435–50. The family claimed nobility that extended back to Safavid rule in Van.

3. Ter-Mkrtchean's book, which is otherwise the authoritative reference work on Van, incorrectly suggests that Natanian had passed away in 1856 (p. 441). Jangiulian did not note dates in his memoir, leaving it to the reader to deduce that he had visited Natanian in late 1889. From Ottoman state documents, we know that an Armenian priest named Boghos Natanian, the author of *Artosr Hayastani*, had been taken into custody by the police in Van and transferred to Istanbul in September 1888. DH MKT 1545/11 (15 Muharrem 1306, September 21, 1888).

4. Harutiun Chankiulean, *Hishatakner Hay Chgnazhamen (mas ayb ev ben)* (K. Polis: Tparan "Kohak"i, 1913), 152–54.

5. The list is long and includes Khrimian, Natanian, Arsen Tokhmakhian (who was tortured), and a prelate of Mush.

6. BOA Y. PRK. ZB 17/21 (2 Şaban 1313, January 18, 1896), BOA Y. MTV 135/24 (5 Şaban 1313, January 21, 1896).

7. FO 195/1944 No. 5 (Van, January 26, 1896), FO 195/1944 (Decypher 30, January 31, 1896).

8. Hambartsum Eramean, *Hushardzan: Van-Vaspurakani* (Agheksantria: Tpagr. Aram Gasapean, 1929), 292.

9. On conversions, see Selim Deringil, *Conversion and Apostasy in the Ottoman Empire* (New York: Cambridge University Press, 2012), 197–238.

10. The "provocation thesis" animates much of Turkish nationalist historiography and its practitioners abroad. For a recent example, see Justin McCarthy, Ömer Turan, and Cemalettin Taşkıran, *Sasun: The History of an 1890s Armenian Revolt* (Salt Lake City: University of Utah Press, 2014). Scholars of collective violence have dismissed the provocation thesis. Sociologist Robert Melson was among the first to do so in his article "A Theoretical Inquiry into the Armenian Massacres of 1894–96," *Comparative Studies in Society and History* 24, no. 3 (July 1982): 481–509. See also Margaret Lavinia Anderson, "A Responsibility to Protest? The Public, the Powers, and the Armenians in the Era of Abdülhamit II," *Journal of Genocide Research* 17, no. 3 (2015): 259–83.

11. Requests for aid from Armenians seeking refuge in the Russian-controlled Caucasus fill the archives of the Catholicosate of Etchmiadzin. See Matenadaran Mkrtich Khrimyan Katoghikosi Arkhiv 46a/101-103 for hundreds of such documents.

12. Karen Barkey, *Bandits and Bureaucrats: The Ottoman Route to State Centralization* (Ithaca, NY: Cornell University Press, 1994).

13. Janet Klein, *The Margins of Empire: Kurdish Militias in the Ottoman Tribal Zone* (Stanford, CA: Stanford University Press, 2011), 5; Bayram Kodaman, *Sultan II. Abdulhamid Devri Doğu Anadolu Politikası* (Ankara: Ankara Üniversitesi Basımevi, 1987), 11. To be clear, Klein's analysis is more sensitive to the structural discrepancies that marked the relationship between sedentary Armenians and Kurdish cavalrymen. Kodaman's work, on the other hand, belongs to Turkish nationalist historiography.

14. Consonant with terms set out in the Treaty of Berlin, the number of consuls in the eastern provinces grew during the 1880s. Armenians began to turn to them as their appeals to local Ottoman officials became increasingly less effective.

15. Both the *Hnchak*, the Hnchakian Party's organ, and *Droshak*, the Armenian Revolutionary Federation's newspaper, published accounts of crimes committed by either the state or Muslim neighbors against Armenians in the eastern provinces.

16. For Jangiulian's coverage of Musa Bey and Giulizar, see Chankiulean, *Hishatakner*, 156–72. Armenuhi Garabedian, Giulizar's daughter, tells her mother's story in *Giulizar* (Paris: A Der Agopian, 1946).

17. Bahri Pasha would be appointed governor of Van, where he gave tacit approval to Kurdish appropriation of Armenian property. For an example of his interaction with Kurdish shaykhs, see William Willard Howard, *Horrors of Armenia: The Story of an Eye-Witness* (New York: Armenian Relief Association, 1896), 40.

18. On these processes, see Selim Deringil, *The Well-Protected Domains: Ideology and the Legitimation of Power in the Ottoman Empire, 1876–1909* (London: I.B. Tauris, 1999) and Kemal Karpat, *The Politicization of Islam: Reconstructing Identity, State, Faith, and Community in the Late Ottoman State* (New York: Oxford University Press, 2001).

BIBLIOGRAPHY

ARCHIVAL MATERIALS

Republic of Armenia
Eghishe Charentsi anvan grakanutyan ev arvesti tangaran (GAT)
Mesrop Mashtotsi anvan hin dzeragreri institut (Matenadaran)

France
La Bibliothèque Nubarian (BNU)

Republic of Turkey
Başbakanlık Osmanlı Arşivleri (BOA)

United Kingdom
British National Archives (BNA)

United States of America
Family History Library, Salt Lake City

NEWSPAPERS
Arevelean Mamul
Armenia
Artsvi Vaspurakan
Masis
Meghu
Sion

PRINTED OR PUBLISHED MATERIALS

Abu-Manneh, Butrus. 1994. "The Islamic Roots of the Gülhane Rescript." *Die Welt des Islams* 34, no. 2 (November): 173–203.

Achemean, Hayk. 1929. *Hayots hayrik: Nuagogh vshtits hayreneats hayots*. Tavriz: Atrpatakani Hayots Temakan Tparan.

Agapi: Ormeanean Entaniken. Mihran Ef. Ter-Nersiseani Amusin Tikin Agapi. Anmoray Hishatakin Hushartzan. 1906. K. Polis: Tpagrutiun V. ev. H. Ter-Nersesean.

Aghaneants, Giut Kahanay. 1915. *Divan hayots patmutean, girk ZhG: Harstharutiunner tachkahayastanum (vaveragrer 1801–1888). Havelvatsnerov, tsanotutiunnerov, ev pargrkov*. Tiflis, Georgia: Tparan N. Aghaneantsi.

Akçura, Yusuf. 1976. *Üç Tarz-ı Siyaset*. Ankara: Türk Tarih Basımevi.
Akinean, Nerses. 1920. *Gavazanagirk katoghikosats Aghtamaray. Patmakan usumnasirutiun*. Vienna: Mkhitarean Tparan.
Alpoyachean, Arshak. 1910. "Azgayin sahmanadrutiune, ir tsagume ev kirarutiune." In *Endardzak oratsuyts s. Prkchean hivandanotsi hayots*. K. Polis, 76–528.
Ambastanutiun vanay poghos vardapetin vray. 1874. K. Polis: Tpagrutiun Partizpanean ev Enk.
Amenayn hayots hayrik. 1957. New York: Hratarakutiun hamavaspurakani hayrenaktsakan miutean.
Anderson, Benedict. 2006. *Imagined Communities: Reflections on the Origin and Spread of Nationalism*. London: Verso.
Anscombe, Frederick. 2014. *State, Faith, and Nation in Ottoman and Post-Ottoman Lands*. New York: Cambridge University Press.
Antaramian, Richard. "Armenians and Sufis." Paper presented at the Middle East Studies Association Annual Meeting, 2019.
———. "*Amira* Money and Alemdar Mustafa: Armenians and Ottoman Reform Before the Tanzimat." Paper presented at New Directions in Armenian Ottoman Studies, University of California, Berkeley, April 8, 2017.
———. "In Subversive Service of the Sublime State: Armenians and Ottoman State Power, 1844–1896." PhD diss., University of Michigan, 2014.
Arpee, Leon. 1909. *The Armenian Awakening*. Chicago: University of Chicago Press.
Artinian, Vartan. 1988. *The Armenian Constitutional System in the Ottoman Empire, 1839–1863: A Study of Its Historical Development*. Istanbul.
Artunç, Cihan. 2015. "The Price of Legal Institutions: The *Beratlı* Merchants in the Eighteenth Century Ottoman Empire." *The Journal of Economic History* 75, no. 3, 720–48.
Asatur, Hrant. 2011. *Kostandnupolsoy hayere ev irents patriarknere*. Stanpul: Patriarkutiun Hayots.
Astourian, Stephan. "Testing World-System Theory, Cilicia (1830s–1890s): Armenian-Turkish Polarization and the Ideology of Modern Ottoman Historiography." PhD diss., University of California, Los Angeles, 1996.
Atenagrutiunk Azgayin Endhanur Zhoghovoy. 1860–1896.
Ateş, Sabri. 2013. *The Ottoman-Iranian Borderlands: Making a Boundary, 1843–1914*. New York: Cambridge University Press.
———. "Empires at the Margins: Towards a History of the Ottoman-Iranian Borderland and the Borderland Peoples." PhD diss., New York University, 2006.
Aydıngün, İsmail, and Esra Dardağan. "Rethinking the Jewish Communal Apartment in the Ottoman Communal Building." *Middle Eastern Studies* 42, no. 2, 319–34.
Azatean, Toros. 1953. *Tatean kerdastane*. Istanbul.
Azgayin Sahmanadrutiun Hayots. 1860. K. Polis: Tpagrutiun F. Y. Kiurkchean.
Bardakjian, Kevork. 2017. "Ottoman Servants, Armenian Lords: The Rise of the *Amiras*." *Journal of the Society for Armenian Studies* 26: 17–38.
———. 1982. "The Rise of the Armenian Patriarchate of Constantinople." In *Christians and Jews in the Ottoman Empire: The Functioning of a Plural Society*. Vol. 1 The

Central Lands, edited by Benjamin Braude and Bernard Lewis, 89–100. New York: Holmes and Meier.

Barker, William Burckhardt. 1853. *Lares and Penates: or, Cilicia and Its Governors*. London: Ingram, Cookie.

Barkey, Karen. 2013. "Aspects of Legal Pluralism in the Ottoman Empire." In *Legal Pluralism and Empires, 1500–1850*, edited by Lauren Benton and Richard J. Ross, 83–107. New York: New York University Press.

———. 2008. *Empire of Difference: The Ottomans in Comparative Perspective*. New York: Cambridge University Press.

———. 1994. *Bandits and Bureaucrats: The Ottoman Route to State Centralization*. Ithaca, NY: Cornell University Press.

Barkley, Henry. 1891. *A Ride Through Asia Minor and Armenia: Giving a Sketch of the Character, Manners, and Customs of Both the Mussulman and Christian Inhabitants*. London: John Murray.

Barnes, John Robert. 1986. *An Introduction to Religious Foundations in the Ottoman Empire*. Leiden, the Netherlands: Brill.

Barsoumian, Hagop. 1982. "The Dual Role of the Armenian *Amira* Class Within the Ottoman Governman and the Armenian *Millet* (1750–1850)." In *Christians and Jews in the Ottoman Empire: The Functioning of a Plural Society*. Vol. 1 *The Central Lands*, edited by Benjamin Braude and Bernard Lewis, 171–84. New York: Holmes and Meier.

———. "The Armenian Amira Class of Istanbul." PhD diss., Columbia University, 1980.

Behbudean, Sandro. 2002. *Vaveragrer Hay ekeghetsu patmutean, girk zh (1ord). Nerses Arkepiskopos Varzhapetean Kostandnupolsi Hayots Patriark (1837–1884). Pastatghteri ev niuter zhoghovatsu*. Erevan: Zangak-97.

Ben-Bassat, Yuvan. 2013. *Petitioning the Sultan: Protests and Justice in Late Ottoman Palestine, 1865–1908*. New York: I.B. Tauris.

Benton, Lauren. 2008. "From International Law to Imperial Constitutions: The Problem of Quasi-Sovereignty, 1870–1900." *Law and History Review* 26 (3): 595–619.

Berkes, Niyazi. 1964. *The Development of Secularism in Turkey*. Montreal, QC: McGill-Queen's University Press.

Bir Adana'lı Hay Eridasart [Mkrtich Kefsizian]. 1872. *Kilikianın Esrarı ve Sefaleti*.

Blumi, Isa. 2011. *Reinstating the Ottomans: Alternative Balkan Modernities, 1800–1912*. New York: Palgrave McMillan.

Boghok Erkrord ar Azgayin Endhanur Zhoghovn, zvor khonarhabar matutsane amboghj Miabanutiun Surb Erusaghemi. 1861. Erusaghem: Tparan Srbots.

Braude, Benjamin. 1982. "Foundation Myths of the *Millet* System." In *Christians and Jews in the Ottoman Empire: The Functioning of a Plural Society*. Vol. 1, *The Central Lands*, edited by Benjamin Braude and Bernard Lewis, 69–88. New York: Holmes and Meier.

Braude, Benjamin, and Bernard Lewis, eds. 1982. *Christians and Jews in the Ottoman Empire: The Functioning of a Plural Society*. Vol. 1, *The Central Lands*. New York: Holmes and Meier.

Burbank, Jane, and Frederick Cooper. 2010. *Empires in World History: Power and the Politics of Difference*. Princeton, NJ: Princeton University Press.

Burt, Ronald. 2010. *Neighbor Networks: Competitive Advantage, Local and Personal*. New York: Oxford University Press.

——. 2007. *Brokerage and Closure: An Introduction to Social Capital*. New York: Oxford University Press.

Carmont, Pascal. 1999. *Les Amiras: Seigneurs de l'Arménie ottomane*. Paris: Salvator.

Castiglione, Frank. 2014. "'Levantine' Dragomans in Nineteenth Century Istanbul: The Pisanis, the British, and Issues of Subjecthood." *Osmanlı Araştırmaları/The Journal of Ottoman Studies*, XLIV, 169-195.

Cevdet Paşa. 1963. *Tezâkir 21-39. Yayınlayan Ord. Prof. Cavid Baysun*. Ankara: Türk Tarih Kurumu Basımevi.

Chankiulean, Harutiun. 1913. *Hishatakner haykakan chknazhamen*. K. Polis: Tparan "Kohak"i.

Chilinkirean, Hakobos. 1866. *Patmutiun erkameay antsits*. K. Polis: Tpagrutiun Aramean.

Chituni, Tigran. 1910. *Varagay hobelean: hishatakaran u koch Varagay krtakan hastutean hisnameay hobeleani (1857-1907)*. K. Polis: Osmanean Gortsaktsakan Enkerutean.

Clogg, Richard. 2013. *A Concise History of Greece. Third Edition*. New York: Cambridge University Press.

Cohen, Julia Phillips. 2014. *Becoming Ottomans: Sephardi Jews and Imperial Citizenship in the Modern Era*. New York: Oxford University Press.

——. 2012. "Between Civic and Islamic Ottomanism: Jewish Imperial Citizenship in the Hamidian Era." *International Journal of Middle East Studies*, 44, no. 2, 237-55.

Crews, Robert. 2003. "Empire and the Confessional State: Islam and Religious Politics in Nineteenth Century Russia." *American Historical Review* 108, no. 1 (February): 50-83.

Çadırcı, Musa. 2007. *Tanzimat Sürecinde Türkiye Ülke Yönetimi*. Ankara: İmge Kitabevi.

——. 1991. *Tanzimat Döneminde Anadolu Kentlerin Soyal ve Ekonomik Yapıları*. Ankara: Türk Tarih Kurumu Basımevi.

Çark, Y. G. 1953. *Türk Devleti Hizmetinde Ermeniler*. İstanbul: Yeni Matbaa.

Çolak, Hasan. "Relations Between the Ottoman Central Administration and the Greek Orthodox Patriarchates of Antioch, Jerusalem and Alexandria: 16th-18th Centuries." PhD diss., University of Birmingham, 2012.

Çora, Y. Tolga. "Transforming Erzurum/Karin: The Social and Economic History of a Multi-Ethnic Ottoman City in the Nineteenth Century." PhD diss., University of Chicago, 2016.

Dadyan, Saro. 2011. *Osmanlı'da Ermeni Aristokrasisi*. İstanbul: Everest Yayınları.

Davis, E. J. 1879. *Life in Asiatic Turkey. A Journal of Travel in Cilicia (Pedias and Trach(ea), Isauria, and Parts of Lycanonia and Cappadocia*. London: Edward Stratford.

Davison, Roderic. 1963. *Reform in the Ottoman Empire*. Princeton, NJ: Princeton University Press.

Derderian, Dzovinar. "Nation-Making and the Language of Colonialism: Voices from Van in Armenian Print Media and Handwritten Petitions (1820s to 1870s)." PhD diss., University of Michigan, 2019.

———. 2016. "Shaping Subjectivities and Contesting Power Through Images of Kurds, 1860s." In *The Ottoman East in the Nineteenth Century*, edited by D. Derderian and Y. Tolga Çora, 91–108. New York: I.B. Tauris.

Deringil, Selim. 2012. *Conversion and Apostasy in the Late Ottoman Empire*. New York: Cambridge University Press.

———. 1998. *The Well-Protected Domains: Ideology and the Legitimation of Power in the Ottoman Empire, 1876–1909*. London: I.B. Tauris.

Dwight, Harrison Gray Otis. 1854. *Christianity in Turkey: A Narrative of the Protestant Reformation in the Armenian Church*. London: James Nisbet Co.

Eissenstat, Howard. 2015. "Modernization, Imperial Nationalism, and the Ethnicization of Confessional Identity in the Late Ottoman Empire." In *Nationalizing Empire*, edited by Stefan Berger and Alexei Miller, 429–59. Budapest: Central European University Press.

Eldem, Edhem. 1999. *A History of the Ottoman Bank*. Istanbul: Ottoman Bank Historical Research Center.

Elliott, J. H. "A Europe of Composite Monarchies." *Past & Present*, No. 137 (November 1992), 48–71.

Engelhardt, Edouard. 1882. *La Turquie et Le Tanzimat ou Histoire des Réformes dans L'Empire Ottoman*. Paris: A. Cotillon.

Eppel, Michael. 2008. "The Demise of the Kurdish Emirates: The Impact of Ottoman Reforms and International Relations on Kurdistan During the First Half of the Nineteenth Century." *Middle Eastern Studies* 44, no. 2 (March): 237–58.

Eramean, Hambartsum. 1929. *Hushardzan: Van-Vaspurakani*. Agheksantria: Tpagr. Aram Gasapean.

Etmekjian, James. 1964. *The French Influence on the Western Armenian Renaissance*. New York: Twayne.

Fairey, Jack. 2015. *The Great Powers and Orthodox Christendom: The Crisis over the Eastern Church in the Era of the Crimean War*. New York: Palgrave Macmillan.

Faroqhi, Suraiya. 1999. *Approaching Ottoman History: An Introduction to the Sources*. New York: Cambridge University Press.

Findley, Carter. 2010. *Turkey, Islam, Nationalism, and Modernity*. New Haven, CT: Yale University Press.

———. 2008. "Tanzimat." In *The Cambridge History of Turkey*, Vol. 4, edited by Reşat Kasaba, 11–37. New York: Cambridge University Press.

———. 1982. "The Acid Test of Ottomanism: The Acceptance of Non-Muslims in the Late Ottoman Bureaucracy." In *Christians and Jews in the Ottoman Empire: The Functioning of a Plural Society*. Vol. 1, *The Central Lands*, edited by Benjamin Braude and Bernard Lewis, 339–68. New York: Holmes and Meier.

———. 1982. "The Advent of Ideology in the Islamic Middle East (Part I)." *Studia Islamica*, no. 55, 143–69.

———. 1982. "The Advent of Ideology in the Islamic Middle East (Part II)." *Studia Islamica*, no. 56, 147–80.

Gazi, Erdem. "Osmanlı İmparatorluğ'unda Hıristiyanların Sosyal ve Dini Hayatları (1856–1876)." PhD diss., Ankara Üniversitesi, 2005.

Gelvin, James. 2006. "The 'Politics of Notables' Forty Years After." *Middle East Studies Association Bulletin* 40, no. 1 (June): 19–29.

Georgeon, François. 1980. *Aux Origines du Nationalisme Turc: Yusuf Akçura (1876–1935)*. Paris: Éditions ADPF.

Ghazaryan, Hayk. 1967. *Arevmtahayeri Sotsial-Tntesakan ev Kaghakakan Katsutyun, 1800–1870 tt.* Erevan: Haykakan SSH Gitutyunneri Akademiayi Hratarakchutyun.

Gibb, H. A. R., and Harold Bowen. 1957. *Islamic Society and the West*, Vol. 1. *A Study of the Impact of Western Civilization on Moslem Culture in the Near East, Part II.* New York: Oxford University Press.

Goffman, Daniel, and Christopher Stroop, "Empire as Composite: The Ottoman Polity and the Typology of Dominion." In *Imperialisms: Historical and Literary Investigations, 1500-1900*, edited by Balachandra Rajan and Elizabeth Sauer, 129–45. New York: Palgrave.

Gould, Andrew. 1976. "Lords or Bandits? The Derebeys of Cilicia." *International Journal of Middle Eastern Studies* 7, no. 4, 485–506.

Gratien, Christopher. "The Mountains Are Ours: Ecology and Settlement in Late Ottoman and Early Republic Cilicia, 1856–1956." PhD diss., Georgetown University, 2015.

Greene, Molly. 2015. *The Edinburgh History of the Greeks, 1453–1768: The Ottoman Empire*. Edinburgh, Scotland: Edinburgh University Press.

Greene, Molly, ed. 2005. *Minorities in the Ottoman Empire*. Princeton, NJ: Markus Wiener.

Griffiths, John. 1986. "What Is Legal Pluralism?" *The Journal of Legal Pluralism and Unofficial Law* 18, no. 24, 1–55.

Hakan, Sinan. 2007. *Osmanlı Arşiv Belgelerinde Kürtler ve Kürt Direnişleri (1817–1867)*. İstanbul: Döz Yayıncılık.

Hamaratuutiun kronakan zhoghovoy ketronakan varchutean 1872–74 ami ar Azgayin Zhoghovn. 1874. K. Polis.

Hanioğlu, M. Şükrü. 2008. *A Brief History of the Late Ottoman Empire*. Princeton, NJ: Princeton University Press.

Hanssen, Jens. 2002. "Models of Integration: Centre-Periphery Relations in the Ottoman Empire." In *Empire in the City: Arab Provincial Capitals in the Late Ottoman Empire*, edited by Jens Hansse, Thomas Philipp, and Stefan Weber, 49–74. Beirut, Lebanon: Orient Institute.

Hartog, Hendrik. 1985. "Pigs and Positivism." *Wisconsin Law Review* 899.

Hishatakaran Pasmachean Grigor Patriarki. Hrataraketś Papgen Dz. V. Giuleserean. 1908. Paris: Panaser.

Hooker, M. B. 1975. *Legal Pluralism: An Introduction to Colonial and Neo-Colonial Laws*. Oxford: Clarendon.

Hourani, Albert. 1968. "Ottoman Reform and the Politics of Notables." In *Beginnings of Modernization in the Middle East*, edited by William R. Polk and Richard L. Chambers, 41–68. Chicago: University of Chicago Press.

Hovannisian, Richard (ed.). 1997. *Armenian People From Ancient to Modern Times, Volume II: Foreign Dominion to Statehood: The Fifteenth Century to the Twentieth Century*. New York: Palgrave Macmillan.

Hovhannisyan, Ashot. 1957–59. *Drvagner hay azatagrakan mtki patmutyan*, 2 vols. Erevan: Haykakan SSR GA Hratarakchutyun.

———. 1955–1956. *Nalbandyane ev nra zhamanake*, 2 vols. Erevan: Haypethrat.

Hovsep Vardapet. 1873. *Teghekagir aghetali antsits ev ankarguteants tan Aghtamaray*. K. Polis: i tparani R.H. Kiurkchean.

Howard, William Willard. 1896. *Horrors of Armenia: The Story of an Eye-Witness*. New York: Armenian Relief Association.

Hrahang haraberutean arajnordats ev gavarakan varchuteants end teghakan karavarutean. 1873. K. Polis: Miuhentisean.

Hrahang Kilikioy vichakats hamar. 1874. Kostandnupolis: Tpagrutiun H. Miuhentisean.

İnalcık, Halil. 1991. "Status of the Greek Orthodox Patriarch Under the Ottomans," *Turcica* 21–23, 407–36.

İnalcık, Halil, and Donald Quataert, eds. 1994. *An Economic and Social History of the Ottoman Empire*, 2 vols. New York: Cambridge University Press.

Izmirlean, Matteos. 1881. *Hayrapetutiun Hayastaneats Arakelakan Egeghetsvoy ev Aghtamar u Sis*. K. Polis: Tpagr. Zardarean.

Jamgocyan, Onnik. 2017. *Les Francs-Maçons Arméniens: La "Constitution" de l'Arménie ottomane, Constantinople—1863*. Paris: Les Editions du Bosphore.

———. 2015. *Le Temps des Réformes: "L'Arménie ottomane," Mahmoud II, le Tanzimat, Constantinople 1800–1860*. Paris: Les Editions du Bosphore.

———. 2013. *Les banquiers des sultans: Juifs, Francs, Grecs et Arméniens de la haute finance: Constantinople, 1650–1850*. Paris: Les Editions du Bosphore.

Jeffrey, Craig, Christine Philliou, Douglas Rogers, and Andrew Shryock. 2011. "Fixers in Motion: A Conversation." *Comparative Studies in Society and History* 51, no. 3, 692–707.

Kabadayı, Mustafa Erdem. 2008. "Mkrdich Cezayirlian, or the Sharp Rise and Sudden Fall of an Ottoman Entrepreneur." In *Merchants in the Ottoman Empire*, edited by Suraiya Faroqhi and Gilles Veinstein, 281–99. Paris: Peeters.

Kappeler, Andreas. 2001. *The Russian Empire: A Multi-Ethnic History*. London: Routledge.

Karpat, Kemal. 2001. *The Politicization of Islam: Reconstructing Identity, State, Faith, and Community in the Late Ottoman State*. New York: Oxford University Press.

———. 1982. "*Millets* and Nationality. The Roots of the Incongruity of Nation and State in the Post Ottoman Era." In *Christians and Jews in the Ottoman Empire: The Functioning of a Plural Society*. Vol. 1, *The Central Lands*, edited by Benjamin Braude and Bernard Lewis, 141–70. New York: Holmes and Meier.

Kasaba, Reşat, ed. 2008. *The Cambridge History of Turkey*, vol. 4. New York: Cambridge University Press.

Kayalı, Hasan. 1997. *Arabs and Young Turks: Ottomanism, Arabism, and Islamism in the Ottoman Empire, 1908-1918*. Berkeley: University of California Press.

Kenanoğlu, Macit. 2004. *Osmanlı Millet Sistemi: Gerçek ve Mit*. İstanbul: Klasik Yayınları.

Keyder, Çağlar, and Huri İslamoğlu. 1977. "Agenda For Ottoman History." *Review* 1.1, 31–55.

Khrimean ev gortsk iur. Herkumn ambastanagri Poghos Vardapeti. 1874. Konstandnupolis.

Kharadyan, Albert. 2008. "Dardzyal arevmtahayeri azgayin sahmanadrutyan masin." *Patma-banasirakan handes* no. 2, 81–93.

Khrimean Vanetsioy, Mkrtich. 1850. *Hravirak Araratean*. Kostandnupolis: Tparan Miuhentisean.

Kiuleserean, Babgen. 1939. *Patmutiun Katoghikosats Kilikioy: 1441-en minchev mer orere*. Antilias, Libanan: Tparan Dprevanuts Katoghikosutean Kilikioy.

Klein, Janet. 2011. *The Margins of Empire: Kurdish Militias in the Ottoman Tribal Zone*. Stanford: Stanford University Press.

Koçunyan, Aylin. 2017. "The *Millet* System and the Challenge of Other Confessional Models." *Ab Imperio* 1, 59–85.

———. 2014. "'Long Live Sultan Abdülaziz, Long Live the Nation, Long Live the Constitution . . .'" in *Constitutionalism, Legitimacy, and Power*, edited by Kelly Grotke and Markus Prutsch, 189–210. New York: Oxford University Press.

Kodaman, Bayram. 1987. *Kodaman, Sultan II. Abdulhamid Devri Doğu Anadolu Politikası*. Ankara, Turkey: Ankara Üniversitesi Basımevi.

Konortas, Paraskevas. 1999. "From Tā'ife to Millet: Ottoman Terms for the Ottoman Greek Orthodox Community." In *Ottoman Greeks in the Age of Nationalism: Politics, Economy, and Society in the Nineteenth Century*, edited by Dimitri Gondicas and Charles Issawi, 169–79. Princeton, NJ: Darwin Press.

Kosdantyan, Emma. 2000. *Mkrtich Khrimyan: hasarakakan-kaghakakan gortsuneutyune*. Erevan: "Zangak-97" hratarakutyun.

Köksal, Yonca. "Local Intermediaries and Ottoman State Centralization: A Comparison of the Tanzimat Reforms in the Provinces of Ankara and Edirne, 1839-1878." PhD diss., Columbia University, 2002.

Krikorian, Mesrob K. 1977. *Armenians In the Service of the Ottoman Empire, 1860-1908*. London: Routledge & Kegan Paul.

Kuran, Timur. 2004. "The Economic Ascent of the Middle East's Religious Minorities: The Role of Islamic Legal Pluralism." *The Journal of Legal Studies* 33, no. 2, 475–515.

Langlois, Victor. 1861. *Voyage dans la Cilicie et dan les montagnes du Taurus. Exécuté pendant les années 1852-1853*. Paris: Chez Benjamin Duprat.

Levy, Avigdor. 1994. "*Millet* Politics: The Appointment of a Chief Rabbi in 1835." In *The Jews of the Ottoman Empire*, edited by Avigdor Levy, 425–38. Princeton, NJ: Darwin Press.

Lewis, Bernard. 2002. *The Emergence of Modern Turkey*, 3rd ed. New York: Oxford University Press.
Libaridian, Gerard J. 2004. *Modern Armenia: People, Nation, State*. New Brunswick, NJ: Transaction.
———. "The Ideology of Armenian Liberation: The Development of Armenian Political Thought Before the Revolutionary Movement (1639–1885)." PhD diss., University of California, Los Angeles, 1987.
Lieven, Dominic. 2001. *Empire: The Russian Empire and its Rivals*. New Haven, CT: Yale University Press.
Lynch, Harry Finnis Blosse. 1901. *Armenia, Travels and Studies*. Vol. 2. *The Turkish Provinces*. London: Longmans, Green.
Makdisi, Ussama. 2002. "After 1860: Debating Religion, Reform, and Nationalism in the Ottoman Empire." *International Journal of Middle Eastern Studies* 34, no. 4, 601–17.
———. 2002. "Ottoman Orientalism." *American Historical Review* 107, no. 3, 768–98.
Mardin, Şerif. 1973. "Center-Periphery Relations: A Key to Turkish Politics?" *Daedelus* vol. 102, no. 1 (Winter), 169–90.
———. 1962. *The Genesis of Young Ottoman Thought: A Study in the Modernization of Turkish Political Ideas*. Princeton, NJ: Princeton University Press.
Masters, Bruce. 2001. *Christians and Jews in the Ottoman Arab World: The Roots of Sectarianism*. New York: Cambridge University Press.
McAdam, Douglas, Sidney Tarrow, and Charles Tilly. 2001. *Dynamics of Contention*. New York: Cambridge University Press.
McCagg, William O. 1992. *A History of Habsburg Jews (1670–1918)*. Bloomington: Indiana University Press.
McCarthy, Justin, Ömer Turan, and Cemalettin Taşkıran. 2014. *Sasun: The History of an 1890s Armenian Revolt*. Salt Lake City: University of Utah Press.
Melson, Robert. 1982. "A Theoretical Inquiry into the Armenian Massacres of 1894–96." *Comparative Studies in Society and History* 24, no. 3 (July): 481–509.
Mestyan, Adam. 2017. *Arab Patriotism: The Ideology and Culture of Power in Late Ottoman Egypt*. Princeton, NJ: Princeton University Press.
Nalbandian, Louise. 1963. *The Armenian Revolutionary Movement: The Development of Armenian Political Parties Through the Nineteenth Century*. Los Angeles: University of California Press.
Natanean, Poghos. *Artosr Hayastani kam teghekagir Paluay, Karberdu, Charsanchagi, Chapagh Juri, ev Erznkayu. Hauvelvats est khndranats azgasirats Khizan gavari. Gorts hingerord*. Kostandnupolis.
Ormanean, Maghakia. 1912–1927. *Azgapatum: Hay Ughghapar Ekeghetsvoy Antskere Skizben Minchev Mer Orere*, 3 vols. Kostandnupolis: Hrataraktiun V. ev H. Ter-Nersesean.
———. 1912. *Hayots ekeghetsin ev ir patmutiune, vardapetutiune, varchutiune, barekargutiune, araroghutiune, grakanutiune, ev nerkay katsutiune*. Kostandnupolis: V. ev H. Ter-Nersesean.

———. 1910. *Hishatakagirk Erkotasnameay Patriarkutean.* K. Polis: Tpagrutiun V. ev H. Ter-Nersesean.

Ortaylı, İlber. 2015. *İmparatorluğun En Uzun Yüzyılı.* Istanbul: Timaş Yayınları

Osmanlı Belgelerinde Ermeni İsyanları (bölüm 1-2). 2008. Ankara: T. C. Başbakanlık Arşivleri Genel Müdürlüğü.

Otean, Grigor. 1910. *Sahmanadrakan khosker u charer. Dambanakanner maheru artiv gruatsner. Hratarakich Mikael Kazmararean.* K. Polis: Tpagrutiun Gater.

Özoğlu, Hakan. 2004. *Kurdish Notables and the Ottoman State: Evolving Identities, Competing Loyalties, and Shifting Boundaries.* Albany: State University of New York Press.

Özok-Gündoğan, Nilay. 2012. "A 'Peripheral' Approach to the 1908 Revolution in the Ottoman Empire: Land Disputes in Peasant Petitions in Post-Revolutionary Diyarbekir. In *Social Relations in Ottoman Diyarbekir, 1870–1915,* edited by Joost Jongerden and Jelle Verheij, 179–215. Leiden, the Netherlands: Brill.

Panchenko, Constantin. 2016. *Arab Orthodox Christians Under the Ottomans: 1516–1831.* Jordanville, NY: Holy Trinity Seminary Press.

Panossian, Razmik. 2006. *The Armenians: From Kings and Priests to Merchants and Commissars.* New York: Columbia University Press.

Papademetriou, Tom. 2015. *Render Unto the Sultan: Power, Authority, and the Greek Orthodox Church in the Early Ottoman Centuries.* New York: Oxford University Press.

Papataxiarchis, Evthymios. 2012. "Reconfiguring the Ottoman Political Imagination: Petitioning and Print Culture in the Early Tanzimat." In *Political Initiatives 'From the Bottom Up' in the Ottoman Empire,* edited by Antonis Anastasopoulos, 191–227. Rethymno, Greece: Crete University Press.

Paronean, Hakob. 1912. *Azgayin jojer. ute antip kensagrakannerov.* K. Polis: Tparan u gratun Nshan Papikean.

Peirce, Leslie. 2003. *Morality Tales: Law and Gender in the Ottoman Court of Aintab.* Berkeley: University of California Press.

Perperean, Avetis. 1871. *Patmutiun hayots skseal i 1772 ame minchev tsamn 1860. Handerdz karevor teghekuteamb ev zhamanakagruteamb ereveli irats.* Kostandnupolis, 1871.

Philliou, Christine. 2011. "The Ottoman Empire's Absent Nineteenth Century." In *Untold Histories of the Middle East: Recovering Voices from the 19th and 20th Centuries.* Edited by Amy Singer, Christoph K. Neumann, and Selçuk Akşin Somel, 143–58. London: Routledge.

———. 2010. *Biography of an Empire: Governing Ottomans in an Age of Revolution.* Los Angeles: University of California Press.

Poghosean, H. P. 2014. *Hacheni endhanur patmutiune ev shrjakay Gozan-Taghi hay giughere.* Antilias: Metsi Tann Kilikioy Katoghikosutiun.

Quataert, Donald. 2005. *The Ottoman Empire, 1700–1922,* 2nd ed. New York: Cambridge University Press.

Rahme, Joseph G. 1999. "Namık Kemal's Constitutional Ottomanism and Non-Muslims." *Islam and Christian-Muslim Relations* 10, no. 1, 23–39.

Reid, James. 1999. "Was There a Tanzimat Social Reform?" *Balkan Studies: Biannual Publication of the Institute for Balkan Studies* 40, no. 1, 173–208.

Roudometof, Victor. 1998. "From *Rum Millet* to Greek Nation: Enlightenment, Secularization, and National Identity in Ottoman Balkan Society, 1453–1821." *Journal of Modern Greek Studies* 16, no. 1 (May): 11–48.

Runciman, Steven. 1968. *The Great Church in Captivity: A Study of the Patriarchate of Constantinople from the Eve of the Turkish Conquest to the Greek War of Independence.* London: Cambridge University Press.

Safrastyan, Ruben A. 1985. *Doktrina Osmanizma v Politicheskoi Zhizni Osmanskoi Imperii (50-70 gg. XIX v.)* Erevan: Izdatel'stvo AN Armianskoi SSR.

Sahman Azgayin Zhoghovoyn: Vor eghev yami tearn 1826 i marti 4, i Patriargarans amenayn hayots vor i Kostandnupolis. Hramanav amenapativ ev vehapar Patriargi aynm kaghaki Tearn Karapeti srbazan ark Episkoposi kostandnupolsetsvoy. Yaghags barekargutean ark Episkoposakan ev Episkoposakan atorots, ev hamoren zharangavorats ekeghetsvoy. 1826. Kostandnupolis.

Sahman Azgayin Zhoghovoy: Yaghags barekargutean surb ukhti ekeghetsvoy, ev varzhapetats, ev hamoren zhoghovrdots. Hramanav amenapativ ev vehapar Patriargi Tearn Karapeti Srbazan Ark Episkoposi. 1830. Kostandnupolis: Tparani Poghos Arapean Apuchekhtsvoy.

Sanjian, Avedis K. 1965. *The Armenian Communities in Syria Under Ottoman Dominion.* Cambridge, MA: Harvard University Press.

Saprichean, Timoteos. 1871. *Erkameay pandkhtutiun i Hapeshstan kam baroyakan, kaghakakan ev kronakan vark Hapeshits.* Erusaghem: i tparani arakelakan atoroy s. Hakovbeants.

Sarukhan, Arakel. 1912. *Haykakan khndirn ev azgayin sahmanadrutiune Turkiyayum.* Tiflis.

Scott, James. 1999. *Seeing Like a State: How Certain Schemes to Improve the Human Condition Have Failed.* New Haven, CT: Yale University Press.

———. 1990. *Domination and the Arts of Resistance: Hidden Transcripts.* New Haven, CT: Yale University Press.

Shahpazean, Hakob. 1911. *Kiurto-Hay patmutiun.* K. Polis: Tparan "Araks."

Sharkey, Heather. 2017. *A History of Muslims, Christians, and Jews in the Middle East.* New York: Cambridge University Press.

Shaw, Stanford. 1973. *Between Old and New: The Ottoman Empire Under Sultan Selim III.* Cambridge, MA: Harvard University Press.

Shaw, Stanford, and Ezel Kural Shaw. 1977. *History of the Ottoman Empire and Modern Turkey, Volume 2: Reform, Revolution, and Republic: The Rise of Modern Turkey, 1808-1975.* New York: Cambridge University Press.

Shils, Edward. 1961. "Centre and Periphery." In *The Logic of Personal Knowledge: Essays Presented to Michael Polanyi on His Seventieth Birthday*, 117–30. London: Routledge and Kegan Paul.

Siruni, H. J. 1967. *Polis ev ir dere (errord hator).* Antilias, Libanan: Tparan Katoghikosutean Hayots Metsi Tann Kilikioy.

Sruandzteants, Garegin. 1978. *Erker. Hator 1.* Erevan: Haykakan SSH GA Hratarakchutyun.

———. 1879. *Toros aghbar: Hayastani chambort.* K. Polis: Tpagrutiun E. M. Tntesean.

———. 1876. *Mananay.* K. Polis: Tpagrutiun E. M. Tntesean.

Stamatopoulos, Dimitri. 2012. "Holy Canons or General Regulations? The Ecumenical Patriarchate *vis-à-vis* the Challenge of Secularization in the Nineteenth Century," in *The Question of Change in Greek Orthodox Thought and Practice.* Edited by Trine Stauning Willert and Lina Molokotos-Liederman. Burlington, VT: Ashgate.

———. 2006. "From *Millet*s to Minorities in the Nineteenth Century Ottoman Empire: An Ambiguous Modernization." In *Citizenship in Historical Perspective*, edited by S. G. Ellis, G. Hálfadanarson, and A. K. Isaacs, 253–73. Pisa, Italy: Edizioni Plus-Pisa University Press.

Swidler, Ann. 1986. "Culture in Action: Symbols and Strategies." *American Sociological Review* 51, no. 2, 273–86.

Sykes, Mark. "The Kurdish Tribes of the Ottoman Empire." *Journal of the Royal Anthropological Institute of Great Britain and Ireland* 38 (July–December 1908), 451–86.

Şaşmaz, Musa. 2004. *Kürt Musa Bey Olayı.* İstanbul: Kitabevi.

Teghekagir gavarakan harstharuteants. 1876. K. Polis: Tpagir Aramean.

Teghekagir kaghakakan zhoghovoy ketronakan varchutean 1870–1871 ami ar Azgayin Endhanur Zhoghov. 1871. K. Polis: Tpagrutiun Miuhentisean.

Teghekagir kharn hantznazhoghovoy Aghtamaray atoroy katoghikosakan khndroyn. 1872. K. Polis: I Tparan Hovhannu Miuhentisean.

Ter-Karapetean, Armenuhi. 1946. *Kiulizar.* Paris: Der Agopian.

Ter-Mkrtchean, Ervand. 1966. *Gandzer Vaspurakani.* Boston: Tparan "Paykar."

Terzipashean, A. 1938. *Artsiv ir buynin mej.* Paris: Der Agopian.

Tevkants, Eremia. 1991. *Chanaparhordutyun Bardzr Hayk ev Vaspurakan, 1872–73 tt. Dzeragire patrastel ev tsanotagrel e H. M. Poghosyan.* Erevan, Armenia: Hayastani GA Hratarakchutyun.

———. 1874. *Krkin teghekagir aghetali antsits ev ankarguteants tann Aghtamaray.* K. Polis-Ghalatia: Tpagrutiun Mikaeli Ekserchean.

Tezcan, Baki. 2010. *The Second Ottoman Empire: Political and Social Transformation in the Early Modern World.* New York: Cambridge University Press.

Tigranean, Mkrtich. 1870. *Dzayn Kilikioy.* K. Polis: Tpagreal i gortsaran Zardarean.

———. 1864. *Hayeli gortsots.* Constantinople: i tparani Tivitchean Tadeosi.

Tiurean, K. 1892. "Khrimean Hayrik." *Handes Amsoreay.*

Tokhmakhean, Arsen. 1882. *Masisi lerneri haravayin storotner: hraparakakhosutiun katarvats april 21-in Artsrunu Tatronum.* Tiflis.

———. 1881. *Hayreniki pahanjere ev hay giughatsin: hraparakakhosutiun katarvats mayisi 21-in ev krknats hunisi 12-in Artsrunu Tatronum.* Tiflis.

Toksöz, Meltem. 2010. *Nomads, Migrants and Cotton in the Eastern Mediterranean: The Making of the Adana-Mersin Region, 1850–1908.* Leiden, the Netherlands: Brill.

Torgomean, Tokt. 1892. Vahram. *Bzhishk Tokt Servichen Efendi.* Vienna: Mkhitarean Tparan.

T.T.V. 1902. "Bzhishk Tokt. Nahapet Rusinean." *Handes Amsoreay.*

Tuğlacı, Pars. 1990. *The Role of the Balian Family in Ottoman Architecture.* Istanbul: Yeni Çığır Bookstore.

Turoma, Sanna, and Maxim Waldstein. 2013. "Introduction: Empire and Space: Russian and the Soviet Union in Focus." In *Empire De/Centered: New Spatial Histories of Russia and the Soviet Union,* edited by Sanna Turoma and Maxim Waldstein. Burlington, VT: Ashgate., 1–28.

Ubicini, M. A. 1856. *Letters on Turkey: An Account of the Religious, Political, Social, and Commercial Condition of the Ottoman Empire; the Reformed Institutions, Army, Navy, etc., etc. Translated from the French of M.A. Ubicini by Lady Easthope.* London: John Murray.

Ueno, Masayuki. 2019. "Empire as a Career: Hagop Grjigian or an Armenian in the Ottoman Bureaucracy." *Memoirs of the Research Department of the Tokyo Bunko,* 57–80.

———. 2016. "Religious in Form, Political in Content? Privileges of Ottoman Non-Muslims in the Nineteenth Century." *Journal of the Economic and Social History of the Orient* 59, no. 3, 408–41.

———. 2013. "'For the Fatherland and the State': Armenians Negotiate the Tanzimat Reforms." *International Journal of Middle East Studies* 45, no. 1, 93–109.

Ursinus, Michael. 2018. "Millet." In *Encyclopedia of Islam, Second Edition,* November 3, 2018, http://dx.doi.org/10.1163/1573-3912_islam_COM_0741.

———. 2010. "Local Patmians in their Quest for Justice: Eighteenth Century Examples of Petitions Submitted to the *Kapûdân Paşa.*" *Documents de travail du CETOBAC* 1 (January): 20–23.

———. 1994. "Petitions from Orthodox Church Officials to the Imperial Diwan, 1675." *Byzantine and Modern Greek Studies* 18, 236–47.

van Bruinessen, Martin. 1992. *Agha, Sheikh, State: The Social and Political Structures of Kurdistan.* London: Zed Books.

Vezenkov, Alexander. 2013. "Formulating and Reformulating Ottomanism." In *Entangled Histories of the Balkans: National Ideologies and Language Policies.* Edited by Roumen Dontchev Daskalov and Tchavdar Marinov, 241–71. Leiden, the Netherlands: Brill.

———. 2009. "Reconciliation of the Spirits and Fusion of the Interests: 'Ottomanism' as an Identity Politics." In *We, the People: Politics of National Peculiarity in Southeastern Europe,* edited by Diana Mishkova, 47–77. Budapest, Hungary: Central European University Press.

Yavuz, Hakan. 1993. "Nationalism and Islam: Yusuf Akçura and "Üç Tarz-ı Siyaset." *Journal of Islamic Studies* 4, no. 2 (July): 175–207.

Yaycıoğlu, Ali. 2016. *Partners of the Empire: The Crisis of the Ottoman Order in the Age of Revolutions.* Stanford, CA: Stanford University Press.

Yosmaoğlu, İpek. 2013. *Blood Ties: Religion, Violence, and the Politics of Nationhood in Ottoman Macedonia, 1878-1908.* Ithaca, NY: Cornell University Press.

Young, Pamela. "Knowledge, Nation, and the Curriculum: Ottoman Armenian Education, 1853-1913." PhD diss., University of Michigan, 2001.

Zürcher, Erik Jan. 2005. *Turkey: A Modern History,* 3rd ed. London: I.B. Tauris.

INDEX

Abdülaziz (Sultan), 132
Abdülhamid II (Sultan), 71, 114, 134, 140, 155–57, 164, 166–68
Abdülmecid I (Sultan), 2, 24–25
Abro, Sahag, 66
accommodation *(istimalet)*, 8
Accusations Against Boghos Vartabed of Van, The, 110–12, 116
Aghvanian, Harutiun, 154
Aghvanian, Krikoris, 141, 145–47, 149
Ajapahian, Giragos I, 61–62, 64, 85
Ajapahian, Giragos II, 87
Ajapahian, Kapriel I, 84, 182n47
Ajapahian, Mikael I, 84, 182n47
Ajapahian, Nigoghos, 87–89
Ajapahian, Teotoros III, 84–85
Ajapahian, Yeprem II, 118
Ajapahian Dynasty, 40, 84–91, 122–23, 181nn33; Harutiun, 90; Kapriel I (Ajapahian), 84–85; Mikael I (Ajapahian), 84, 182n47; Mikael II (Ajapahian), 86–87, 181n40; Nigoghos, 87–89; Teotoros III, 84–85
Akçura, Yusuf, 71, 100, 179n9
Ali Agha, 114, 116, 146
amira(s), Armenian, 12; and Akn, 29, 134, 175n17; and Armenian school controversy, 30; as bridge to state, patriarchate, 12, 14, 28; and Catholicism, 55; Dadian family, 128; financial capital of, 50–51, 53; financial control by, 30; guildsmen's denunciation of, 31; Hagop Barsoumian scholarship on, 37; Hagop Grjigian, 34; impact of on constitution, 27, 40–42, 48; influence of, 29, 52, 119;; Khrimian's connections to, 121–22, 125; lifestyle of, 35, 175n17; and Matteos Chukhajian, 31–34; and notables, 105, 119, 126; origin of term, 29, 175n16; politics of, 3; rise of, 30; supporting centralization, 29; and tax farming, 30, 51; as trustees, 53; use of financial capital, 12, 14
Anderson, Benedict, 71
Apoghoseank, 143
Armenian Constitution, 63, 82, 161; 1860 versus 1863 versions, 46–47, 49, 91; *amiras* and, 27, 40–42, 48; Apostolic Church preparing way for, 31; Article 46 on monastery finances, 55; Article 95 in, 47–48; catholicosates under, 91–94; ceding power to Ottoman rule, 27–28; and class tensions, 29, 33–35; creating Ottoman Armenian diocese, 55; governmental structure under, 55, 56–57; Imperial Reform Edict, 21–22; monasteries and, 96; and Tanzimat reform program, 96, 98, 144–45
Armenian Patriarchate of Constantinople, 22, 27, 38, 59, 66, 128
Armenian Patriarchate of Jerusalem, 13, 59, 61
Artsvik Taronoy newspaper, 141

Artsvi Vaspurakan (The Eagle of Vaspurakan), 121–22
Aznavurian, Garabed Amira, 178n8

Bahri Pasha, 166, 189n17
Balian, Garabed Amira, 30, 33
Balian, Nigoghos, 34–35, 121
Balkans, 5, 10, 15, 39, 128–29, 135, 168
Barkey, Karen, 4, 163
Barkley, Henry, 175n17
Barsoumian, Hagop, 37, 39, 178n4
Basmajian, Krikor, 29
Battle of Nezib, 14, 80
Bayraktar Mustafa Pasha, 25, 39, 117
Bedirkhan Bey, 78, 80–81, 83, 103, 113–14, 164
Bedros Bülbül: assassination of, 63, 77–79, 104; caught between sides, 95; consecrating bishops, 94; election, consecration of, 115; motives for assassination, 79–82; ratification of election, 95; sponsoring Topuzian, 118; suspects in assassination, 94, 96, 114, 141, 161
Bezjian, Harutiun, 178n8
Braude, Benjamin, 9
Brotherhood of St. James, 43, 130
Byzantine Empire, 8, 12, 83

Catholicosate of Aghtamar, 14, 68, 79, 82, 140; dispute, murder over catholicos, 58, 63, 78–79; Khachadur Shiroian as Catholicos, 63, 78–81, 88, 94, 96, 104, 115, 119, 122, 160
Catholicosate of (All Armenians in) Etchmiadzin, 32, 67, 80, 91, 101–2; Catholicos of, 58, 67, 80, 83, 89–91, 94, 180; Catholicos of (Khrimian as), 101–2, 156–57, 181n40. *See also* Etchmiadzin
Catholicosate of Cilicia (Sis), 14, 32, 58, 68–69, 82–84, 140; centralization efforts in, 168; collective punishment of, 164; Ghukas I Ajapahian as Catholicos, 84, 122–23; Izmirlian and, 140; Khrimian investigating, 122–23, 135, 147; Mkrtich Kefsizian as Catholicos, 64–65, 70, 82, 88, 89–94, 98, 117; Nigoghos Ajapahian as Catholicos, 87–88; Topuzian teaching in, 118
center-periphery, 164, 167; Ajapahian rule of Cilician Armenians, 86; effect of on Armenians, 88, 160, 167; legal pluralism, 75–76; Melikan resistance to, 110–13, 115; *millet* system and, 69, 165; modernization theory and, 26; positivist sociology and, 6; tapestry model alternative to, 6–7, 51, 159–60, 162, 165, 168
Cevdet Pasha, 156, 166
charters, 22–23, 27
"child ecclesiastics," 60
Chukhajian, Matteos, 31–34

Dadian, Arakel, 148
Dadian family, 40, 128
Davis, E. J., 90, 182n51
Davit of Erzurum, 64
Deed of Agreement *(Sened-i İttıfak)*, 25
Derviş Bey, 78–79, 114
Dikranian, Mkrtich, 1, 3–7, 13, 16, 19, 104
Düstur (Code of Laws), 139, 150

Edesian, Hagop (Bishop Hagop), 78, 79, 94–96, 125
Edict of Gülhane, 2, 24
educational reforms, 25; *amiras* opposing, 30; *amiras* supporting, 34, 41; Armenian, 34–35; Dikranian and, 1; Khrimian and, 102, 122, 135, 140–41, 154; Topuzian and, 119; and Young Ottomans, 25
Eghiazar (priest), 146
Egypt, 14, 58, 80, 164, 182n47
Esayi Talastsi (Patriarch of Jerusalem), 49, 58–59, 66–67

INDEX

Etchmiadzin, 28, 80; Catholicosate of, 47, 50, 163, 187n1; Catholicos of, 50, 95, 118, 149, 180n24; as highest seat, 50; and Khrimian, 131, 147; legitimizing Constitution, 58; relations with Constantinople, 27–28, 32, 42, 47, 50, 66, 95. *See also* Catholicosate of (All Armenians in) Etchmiadzin

Famine Relief Committee, 154–55, 187n54
financial capital, Armenian, 12, 14, 23, 50–51, 67
Findley, Carter, 10, 19
Fuad Pasha, 40

Gennadios, 9
Gevorg II, Catholicos of Armenia, 147
Giragosian, Hovsep, 61
Giulizar, rape of, 166
Gould, Andrew, 87
Grand Vizier, 48, 122; Bayraktar Mustafa Pasha, 25; Mahmud Nedim Pasha, 136; Mustafa Reşid Pasha, 25
Greek Orthodox Church: expansion of authority of, 10, 12, 28; Gennadios as bishop, 9; in *millet* system, 10; Phanariots, 12; tax collection by, 12
Greek Revolution (1821), 15
Greene, Molly, 27, 38
Griffiths, John, 71, 76, 97
Grjigian, Hagop, 34, 118
guilds, 16, 29–31, 33–35, 40, 63, 109
Gülhane Edict, 2, 24
Gülihan (son of Derviş Bey), 78

hahambaşı (Ottoman Jewish community leader), 17
Hamamjian, Kaspar Agha, 53–54, 107
Hamidian period, 70, 156, 163, 167
Harutiun (bishop). *See* Vehabedian, Harutiun
Hasan Pasha, 155
Haydaranlı Kurds, 82, 114, 116, 146, 151–52

hayrenasirutiun, 124
Hovakim (bishop of Bursa), 9, 27
Hravirak Araratean (Khrimian), 121
Hurşit Efendi, 90

Ibrahim Pasha, 44, 80, 83, 86
Imperial Reform Edict, 1856 *(Islâhat Fermânı)*, 21, 24–25, 27, 40
"Iron Ladle" sermon, 120, 129, 135
Isajanian, Garabed, 145–46, 154
Izmirlian, Matteos, 140

Jangiulian, Harutiun, 151–52, 165–66, 188n3
Janissaries, 12, 15, 24–25, 39, 168, 176n27
Jewish community, 2, 9–10, 17, 28, 134, 168, 176n27
Jezayirlian, Mkrtich, 122

Kakmajian, Iknadios, 184n13; ignorance of Kurdish language, 183n7; and Melikian, 115–16; misreading local society, 112; misreading politics, 124; as Patriarch of Constantinople, 131; as prelate of Van, 102–8; pro-reform, 110, 126, 143; regarding Bedros Bülbül murder, 77–79, 104; requesting military presence, 113
Kaljian, Kevork Bey, 106, 152, 154
Kefsizian, Mkrtich, 64–65, 70, 72, 82, 88–94, 98, 109, 117, 182n47
Kerestejian, Kevork, 41, 45–46, 62, 65, 92
Khanjalis, 49–50, 91
Khan Mahmud of Müküs, 78, 81–82, 95, 113, 115, 155
Khrimeanakanner, 143
Khrimian, Mkrtich, 77, 86, 140; birth and early life, 121; publication of *Hravirak Araratean*, 121; pilgrimage to Jerusalem, 122; ordainment, 122; *Artsvi Vaspurakan* journal, 122; investigating Ajapahians, 123; to Mush as prelate, abbot, 127, 142; and Shiroian, 125–26; as

Khrimian, Mkrtich (*continued*)
Patriarch of Constantinople, 127, 128, 130–35, 142, 157, 178n19; "Iron Ladle Sermon," 120, 129, 135; *Report on Provincial Oppression*, 135–40; supporting Armenians bearing arms, 137; teaching at Varak monastery, 140–41; return to Van, 102, 127, 154; internal exile in Jerusalem, 156–57, 160; as Catholicos of All Armenians in Etchmiadzin, 157; advocating open government, 139–40; body of work, 103; and Boghos Melikian, 101, 121, 143–50, 160; and Boghos Natanian, 160; called *hayrik* (papa), 127, 131–32, 142, 154, 156; *hayrenasirutiun*, 124; as reformer, 102, 117, 120–22, 135–36, 140–41, 145, 154–55; reports of on Cilicia, 86–87; scholarship on, 133–34; and Sharan Bey, 144; and Srvantstiants, 101, 121, 125, 142–49, 155, 160; and Vehabedian, 178n19; worldview of, 124
kışlak, 113
Klein, Janet, 188n13
Kodaman, Bayram, 188n13
Kör Mustafa, 114
Köse Mihal, 8
Kozanoğlu clan, 84–87, 90, 123, 181n40
Kurds: Haydaranlı tribe, 82, 114, 116, 146, 151–52; massacres against Armenians, 164–65
Kuyumjian, Sarkis, 41, 45–46

lay elites, 2, 54, 108
Lewis, Bernard, 156, 179n5

Mahmud II, 25, 72, 164, 168
Maksudian, Simon Bey, 147–48
Marutian, Mkrtich Efendi, 145–46, 154
Mehmed II (Sultan), 8–9
Mehmet Bey, 151–52
Mehmet II (Sultan), 27

Melikian, Boghos, 109, 187n1; *Accusations* booklet against, 110–12; and Aghtamar consecration, 94; anti-reform, 63, 109; assassination of, 161–62, 164; brokering tribal relations, 114–15, 161; campaigns against, 110; Kakmajian and, 116; versus Khrimian and Srvantstiants, 121, 125, 143–49, 160; Kurdish allies of, 115–16, 149–50, 156; and networked world, 117, 119–20, 150–51; providing barracks, bridge construction, 112–13; rebelling against Tanzimat, 145; temporary exiles, 116, 148, 160; versus Varjabedian, 149; as vice prelate, 82, 187n1; violence and abuse by, 101, 160
Melikset, 116
Mgrian, Hovhannes, 140
Midhat Pasha, 35, 122, 156
Mikael II (Ajapahian), 86–87, 181n40. See also Ajapahian Dynasty
millet system, 4–5, 8; Armenian community and, 23, 50, 68–70, 168; Article 95 effect on, 48; leading to greater control, centralization, 17, 70, 86, 147, 163, 165; as legal pluralism, 72–74, 75; Ministry of Justice control of, 156, 166; as networked communal space, 4, 7, 22, 35, 37, 48, 76, 119, 122; scholarship on, 8–10; segregating religion, 17; Tanzimat reforms as, 69; use of term, 10
Mirzaian, Manuk Bey, 38–39
modernization theory, 10, 26, 102, 174n7
Mokatsi, Khachadur (Bishop), 81
Movsesian, Hovhannes, 44
Muhummad Ali, 109, 164
Musa Bey, 166–67
Mustafa IV (sultan), 25
Mustafa Reşid Pasha, 25, 34, 118, 122, 156
mütevellis (monastery trustees), 30, 53, 107–8, 178n4
Mutullah Bey, 155

Nalian, Hagop, 29
Natanian, Boghos, 141, 159–62, 165–66, 188n3
Nationality Law (1869), 15, 25
nationalization and secularization, 7, 10, 22
"nation-space," 173n22
network analysis, 4, 67, 93
networked communal space, 7, 22, 35, 37, 48, 76
New Order troops *(Nizâm-ı Cedîd)*, 24
nodal governance: abolishing child ecclesiastics, 60; hurting Armenian elite, 55, 58; networked, 49–51; Ottoman ecclesiastics and, 58–59, 62, 64, 167; system of monasteries, 51–54; Topuzian not challenging, 119; in Van, 126
non-Muslim communities, 12; eliminating markers of difference, 16; Gülhane edict on, 2; Ottoman reform programs and, 22; religious rights of, 11; rights, responsibilities of, 9; role in tax collection, 12. *See also* Armenian Apostolic community; Greek Orthodox community; Jewish community

Odian, Boghos, 121, 125
Odian, Krikor Efendi, 35, 41, 121, 127, 131–32, 140, 143, 156
Orenburg Muslim Spiritual Assembly, 28
Orthodox Christians, 2, 10, 38, 168
Ottoman Constitution (1876), 25, 35, 122, 156
Ottomanism, defined, 71, 100
Ottoman Land Code (1858), 15, 49
Ottoman Nationality Law (1869), 15

Panosian, Garabed Efendi, 133
Panossian, Razmik, 134
Papademetriou, Tom, 12
Partughimeos, 112, 147

Patriarchate of Constantinople: Armenian, 22, 26, 27, 38, 66, 118, 128; compiling information on Armenians, 50; election of, 42; expansion of, 13–14, 28, 50–52, 54–55, 58–59, 62, 64; Grjigian persuading Reşid Pasha to accept, 34; sources of legitimacy, 31–33. *See also* Kerestejian, Kevork
Patriarchate of Jerusalem: Armenian, 13–14, 30, 43–44, 46–47, 58–63, 94, 131, 182n47; St. James Order/Monastery, 13, 43–45, 58–59, 61–65, 119, 130, 148
Patrona Halil uprising, 12
peripheralization, 88–97
Phanariots, 12, 15, 168, 176n27
Philliou, Christine, 11
Poghoseank, 143
Portugalian, Mkrtich, 154–55
Provincial Law (1864), 25
"provocation thesis," 163, 188n10

Reform Edict (1856), 21, 24–25, 27, 40
Reid, James, 72
Report on Provincial Oppression, 135–36
Rusinian, Nahabed, 156
Russo-Turkish War (1787–92), 25
Russo-Turkish War (1828–29), 32
Russo-Turkish War (1877–78), 21, 87, 92–93, 120, 128–29, 152

Sahatjian, Harutiun, 61
Saprichian, Timoteos, 13
sarrafs (non-Muslim bankers), 24, 29, 85
Sasuntsi Davit epic, 142
Scott, James C., 39, 69
Selim III (Sultan), 17, 24–25
Sened-i İttıfak (Deed of Agreement), 25
Seropian, Hagopos, 62
Serverian, Hovhannes Amira, 30
Shahbazian, Hagop, 114
Shahen Agha, 87, 90
Sharan Bey, 106, 126, 144, 152

shared sovereignty, 16, 159, 167
Shiroian, Kapriel, 109, 115, 119–20, 122–23, 125–26
Shiroian, Khachadur: and Boghos Melikian, 115–16; as catholicos, 81; death of, 97; and Harutiun Vehabedian, 182n47; and Kurdish elites, 82, 113; and murder of Bedros Bülbül, 63, 77–79, 94–96, 104, 141, 148, 161; network strategy of, 88, 89, 96, 98, 109; to Istanbul, 96; use of legal pluralism, 70, 72
Sis (Cilicia), Catholicosate of. *See* Catholicosate of Cilicia (Sis)
social capital, 4, 17, 51, 65–67, 88, 93–96, 98, 119, 140, 157
Social Democratic Hnchakian Party, 161
Srvantstiants, Karekin, 116, 141–49, 154–55, 157, 166, 187n44
St. Garabed Monastery, 118, 127, 132, 141
St. James. *See* Patriarchate of Jerusalem

Taktakian, Boghos, 131
Tanzimat reform program, 2, 4, 159; and *amiras*, 29–33; as an open text, 23–24; Armenian church and, 48, 168; and Armenian Constitution, 96, 98; and Armenian exclusion, 168; Armenian participation in, 20, 31, 67, 115, 126, 130, 141, 148; Armenians' strategy toward, 26, 35, 110, 112, 157–58, 165, 177n39; attempts to impede, 13, 18, 98; attempts to shape, 16, 19; as authoritative text, 25; Bedros and, 79; and Catholicosate of Cilicia, 84; causing peripheralization, 88; changes in meaning of, 154, 156; exacerbating inequalities, 13; forms of taxation under, 138; government strategy shifts, 162, 167–68; *Hatt-ı Şerif* of Gülhane (1839), 24; Ibrahim Pasha and, 86; *Islâhat Fermânı* (Reform Edict, 1856), 24; and Jerusalem, 66; Khrimian and, 120, 122–24, 126, 129–30, 135–41, 145–47, 152, 157; legal order of, 69, 71, 76, 98–99; limits of, 117; Melikan and, 144–45, 149–50; and millets, 42, 163; not in Jerusalem, 45; not secularization, 43; as only source of redress, 82; and Ottomanism, 26, 71–72, 100; and Patriarchate of Constantinople, 86, 95; as politicizing religion, 7; proclamation of, 24–25, 80; reorganizing empire, 165; resistance against, 61–63, 110; as restorationist, 15; scholarship on, 10, 15, 25–26, 100; state centralization under, 14, 163–64
tapestry model, 6–7, 51, 159–60, 162, 165, 168
Tateos Vartabed, 149–50
tax farming, 12, 24, 29–30, 51, 54–55, 81, 85, 87, 153
Terlemezian, Garabed, 154
Terlemezian, Mkrtich Agha, 122
Ter-Mkrtchean, Ervand, 188
Terzibashians, 106
Tevkants, Eremia: accusations against, 13, 116; and Bishops Hagop, Khachadur, 79, 96; compiling report on Armenians, 50, 141; embracing reform, 16, 186n20; inspection tour, 78–79; and Khrimian, 154; as patriarchal vicar of Van, 150–51, 154, 187n44; people "startled" by, 145; report on Aghtamar, 180n20; as "son" of Shiroian, 126; unable to remove lower-level officials, 187n52; and Vehabedian, 62, 148–49
Tevkants, Setrak, 154
Timurzades (Temuroğlus), 49–50, 104, 144–45, 151–52, 161
Tokhmakhian, Arsen, 141
Topuzian, Hagop, 53, 107–9, 117–21, 123–26, 144

Ubeydullah, Shaykh, 153, 164
United Associations (*Miatseal enkerutiunk*), 155

Varjabedian, Nerses, 66, 68–69, 131, 139–40, 149, 156–57, 187n1

Vehabedian, Harutiun: early life and education, 61; as Hovsep Giragosian, 61; as aide to Bishop Giragos, 61; ordained, 62; as Prelate of Karin (Erzurum), 62–65, 182n49; reporting on Bedros' murder, 78, 104; supporting Melikian, 109–10, 116–17, 119, 148–49; investigation of Aghvanian, 148–49; as prelate of Erzurum, 148; removed from office, 178n19; antireform efforts of, 62–63, 77, 109–10, 119, 182n47; as Emin Efendi, 182n49

Vichenian, Serovpe (Servichen), 34, 40, 45–46, 66, 156

Vilayet Law (1864), 138

Yeranos (village headman), 111–12

Young Ottomans, 25, 40, 177n39

Young Turk period, 70, 151, 165

Zakarian, Stepanos Aghavni, 30

Zakaria Vartabed, 118

Ziya Pasha, 152, 187n52